4-49

CRIME IN THE CITY

Readers in Social Problems

DONALD R. CRESSEY, CONSULTING EDITOR
UNIVERSITY OF CALIFORNIA, SANTA BARBARA

CRIME
IN THE
CITY

EDITED BY
DANIEL GLASER
UNIVERSITY OF SOUTHERN CALIFORNIA

HARPER & ROW
Publishers
NEW YORK, EVANSTON, AND LONDON

Library of Congress Catalog Card Number: 78-86990

Contents

v

PART III / CRIMINOGENIC
SOCIAL PROCESS IN CITY LIFE

PART IV / URBAN SOCIAL CONTROL

PART V / THE CITY OF THE FUTURE: PREDICTIONS AND PRESCRIPTIONS

Preface

S I N C E ancient times cities have been called "wicked" and "sinful." These labels probably are warranted, for as far as we can tell from our highly imperfect crime statistics, crimes of almost every type have been disproportionately frequent in cities.

The crime problem, or what politicians prefer to call the problem of "law and order" or of "safe streets," is one of growing concern in the United States. This may well be because the urban condition is increasingly the American way of life. But the relationship between crime and city life is complex and variegated. To understand it we must learn much about both crime and the city.

This reader provides an introduction to these dual and interlocking phenomena. Part I tells something of the growth and nature of city life. Part II relates crime and urbanism by what sociologists call a "structural" analysis, an interpretation in terms of social group differences, geography, and statistical trends. Part III presents a "social process" analysis; it is concerned with the emergence of crime from the content, sequences, settings, and styles of interpersonal communication. Part IV considers briefly the distinctive problems of crime control confronting urban police, courts, and jails. Part V concludes this reader with some speculations and recommendations on the crime reduction programs which the city of the future should develop.

The articles in this book employ highly diverse methods and styles of social science analysis. They not only provide insight into crime and the city, but also show the student the range and variety of means by which knowledge about man and society may be expanded.

DANIEL GLASER

Part I

City Growth and Social Problems

Introduction

TO UNDERSTAND the relationship of urban life to crime requires a knowledge of relevant aspects and dimensions of city life. In 1790 the United States had only 24 towns of 2500 or more population—the census definition of an urban area —and only one-twentieth of the nation's population lived in them. It was not until 1920 that more than half of our country's population was nonrural, but since then—and especially since mid-century—the rural to urban transition has been extreme. Its dimensions and some of its implications are described by Bebout and Popenoe.

That city growth heightens social problems is set forth vividly by the leaders of most of America's organized labor, the Executive Council of the AFL-CIO: "The Urban Crisis" is an apt title for their review of trends in American cities in the 1960s. Clinard provides a fuller historical and comparative analysis of urban social problems, indicating that throughout the world they are centered in slums. He also points out the functions of slums in societies, and consequently, the probable reasons for their origin and persistence. Such a broad perspective in urban sociology is prerequisite to understanding the relationship of city life to crime.

All footnotes appear in the Notes section, grouped by article, at the end of this book.

AMERICA AS AN URBAN SOCIETY

John E. Bebout and David Popenoe

T H E R E have been cities of sorts within the present domain of the United States since colonial days but until quite recently, the United States has been primarily a rural nation and until even more recently, most Americans have maintained an essentially rustic frame of mind. A very few of the leaders of the country at the time of the Revolution, Hamilton and Samuel Adams, for example, might have been qualified as urban men; but most of them, like Washington and Jefferson, were essentially rural people. We have no statistics on the point, but casual observation leads us to the conclusion that a majority of the people making the most important decisions, public and private, in the United States today have rural backgrounds and once thought of themselves as country boys and girls.

.   .   .

THE URBAN-RURAL DICHOTOMY

Considering the fact that the transition from rural to urban has occurred during the lifetime of most of the adults now living, and considering its galloping pace, it is no wonder that there has been a decided lag in intellectual, emotional and institutional adjustment to the altered nature of the American scene. It may be hard for young people to realize

Reprinted with permission of the authors and publisher from "America as an Urban Society" in Ralph Blasingame and Leonard Grunt (eds.), *Research on Library Services in Metropolitan Areas*, New Brunswick, N.J.: Rutgers University Press, 1967, pp. 1–9.

that in the early years of the century there were more horse-drawn than motor-driven vehicles on the streets of every American community. By the same token, it is hard for older people fully to keep up with the implications of the coming of the automobile, to say nothing of the jet airplane. In any case, it is important for everyone, young and old, to understand that the urbanization of the United States, a phenomenon that is more and more being matched throughout the world, is essentially machine made, the product of applied science. The one machine more than any other that has brought this about is the internal combustion engine, especially as it has powered automobiles and farm machinery. This engine not only made a massive urban development possible, it has, to a large extent, determined the nature and many of the details of that development, especially its almost formless lateral spread.

The pace and magnitude of the urban trend would not have been nearly so great if we had not learned to produce more food for more people on less land with less and less man power down on the farm. The result is that, although we tend to think of farming and "the country" as going together, only about one-quarter of the people now living in so-called rural areas live on farms, and the number and percentage of farmers is declining rapidly. Between 1960 and 1964 it is estimated that the rural farm population declined from about 15.6 million to 12.9 million, a decrease of about twenty percent. Along with the increase in productivity of farm labor has come an increase in corporate, as against family, farming and a narrowing of the social, cultural and economic distance between the agricultural and other segments of the society. Revolutions in transportation, communication and "home-making" have brought everyone closer to the city and have brought many urban amenities to people wherever they live. As factories move into the field and fields come more and more to be managed like factories, traditional ideas about the distinction between urban and rural become less and less relevant to reality. In short, while American society is becoming quantitatively more and more urban, it is everywhere becoming qualitatively more and more *urbane,* if we may use the word urbane to denote qualities hitherto pertaining mainly to the urban condition.

A result of all of these trends is that the old urban-rural dichotomy is becoming less and less important. The way in which urban settlements are distributed around the country and the differentiations and relationships within and among those settlements are much more significant for the future than the age old and somewhat synthetic distinction between the country bumpkin and city slicker.

CENTRAL CITIES AND SUBURBS

Aside from social and economic distinctions which exist in greater or less degree everywhere, one of the oldest divisions in urban society is between city and suburb, between the older, generally more thickly settled central areas, and the newer more sparsely settled but nevertheless urban outer or fringe areas. Until fairly recent times, the city was the area of prestige, the home and the chosen instrument of the rich, the powerful and the more highly cultured. Contrast this with the current stereotype of the old, decaying central city and the new, shiny suburbs, the preferred abiding places of those who can afford the choice. Whereas people used to be proud to claim to be city dwellers, many persons rightly listed by the Census as urban, who happen to live in suburbs, will hotly deny that they are urban.

. . .

While urban America has been growing at an explosive rate since the Second World War, the old central cities have in most cases grown very little, except where they were able to annex fringe territories; and, in many cases, have actually declined in population. Between 1950 and 1960 the population within Standard Metropolitan Statistical Areas grew at about twice the rate of the rest of the country. Within those areas, the population *outside the central cities,* increased forty-seven percent, while that *in* those cities increased only eleven percent. The same growth pattern continues with the result that the urbanization of the country means, in terms of traditional thinking, its suburbanization. In short, the suburban or fringe areas are growing rapidly while central cities and many rural and small town communities are hardly growing at all and some are undergoing an absolute, as well as a relative, decline in population.

THE DISTRIBUTION OF URBAN AREAS

. . . When one thinks of the phenomenal concentrations in the Northeast, around the Great Lakes and the Gulf of Mexico and in the Southwest, in contrast to the great open spaces over which one flies across the continent, one tends to think of urbanization as a highly regionalized phenomenon. . . . The fact is that urbanization has, in one way or another, reached into all sections of the country. The Census now lists only one region, the eastern south central, containing Kentucky, Tennessee, Alabama and Mississippi, as being predominantly rural; and it finds only eleven states with rural majorities: Vermont, North Dakota, South Dakota, West Virginia, North Carolina, South Carolina, Kentucky, Mississippi, Arkansas, Idaho and Alaska. Anyone familiar with the concerns of state and local policy makers and educators in a number of these states, Kentucky and North Carolina, for example, knows that they are heavily preoccupied with urban problems and with the accommodation of the increasing urbanization that they anticipate. The wide distribution of the urban condition is more impressively indicated by the fact that there are only three states that do not contain all or part of a Standard Metropolitan Statistical Area. These states are Alaska, Vermont, and Wyoming. . . .

Another significant fact about the national pattern of urban settlement is the way in which it has developed in ribbons or strips, sometimes extending hundreds of miles across several states. The best advertised of these strips, often spoken of as megalopolis, a name attached to it by Jean Gottman, can be traced on the map from Portsmouth, New Hampshire or Portland, Maine as far south as Norfolk, Virginia. There are a number of such developments along the

Great Lakes, and it takes little imagination to see these running into each other from New York State to Wisconsin, across northwestern Pennsylvania, northern Ohio, southern Michigan and northern Indiana and Illinois. One can see a spur of this region running along the Western side of Pennsylvania and into West Virginia. . . . Urban development along the Gulf Coast from Florida to Texas, though not yet continuous, gives every indication that it may become so. The other most massive urban developments are, of course, in California, in the Los Angeles and San Francisco areas. Still others may be discerned in a number of other regions. . . .

THE URBAN CRISIS

Executive Council, American Federation of Labor and Congress of Industrial Organizations

THE GROWTH of the American population has increased sharply—from several hundred thousand a year in the 1930s to an average yearly rise of 2.7 million since World War II. Moreover, the number of people in rural areas has been declining, while metropolitan area growth has been booming. Each year, the population of America's metropolitan areas grows by over 3 million, the size of a very large city.

Under the impact of the technological revolution in agriculture, employment in farming has dropped—it fell 3.2 million between 1950 and 1966. Hundreds of thousands of farmers, farm workers and their families—several million people—have been leaving the rural areas in search of jobs and homes in the cities.

Reprinted with permission from *The American Federationist*, October, 1967, pp. 1–3. This is a preface to a policy statement adopted by the Executive Council of the American Federation of Labor and Congress of Industrial Organizations in its September, 1967 meeting.

Many of those who seek their future in the cities are Negroes. Between 1940 and 1967, probably about 4 million Negroes moved from the South—primarily rural areas—to the cities of the North and West. In 1960, according to the Department of Labor, about 40 percent to nearly 50 percent of the Negro population of 10 major northern and western cities was born in the South.

The Department of Labor estimates that almost 1.5 million Negroes left the South in 1950–1960, following a similar migration of 1.6 million Negroes in the wartime decade, 1940–1950. This historic migration is continuing at about that rate in the 1960s.

For the country as a whole, the proportion of Negroes in city populations rose from less than 10 percent in 1940 to over 20 percent in 1965. In most of the large northern and western cities the rise was greater.

All of the new migrants to America's cities of the past quarter of a century—whites and Negroes, Puerto Ricans and Mexican Americans—have faced the difficulties of adjusting to a new and strange environment. But these difficulties have been especially harsh for Negroes.

The Negro migrants to the cities of the past quarter of a century have brought with them a history of slavery, segregation, lack of education and, frequently, poor health, as well as suspicion of government authorities. On coming to the cities of the North and the West, the new migrants have faced the discriminatory practices of those areas, lack of adequate housing and the impact of automation on job opportunities for uneducated, unskilled workers.

The northern and western cities are suffering, in part, from the social ills and delinquencies of the South—including color bars in private, state and local government employment; backward standards of education, vocational training and public welfare generally, with particularly low standards for Negroes and Mexican Americans; social patterns to enforce the dependency of both poor whites and Negroes.

Since World War II and particularly since the early 1950s, the spread of automation has been reducing the number of unskilled and semi-skilled jobs that require little or no education or training. The types of jobs that helped to adjust previous generations of foreign immigrants and rural American migrants to America's urban areas have not been expanding.

In ghetto areas in the cities, about 10 percent to 15 percent of the adult men and about 40 percent to 50 percent of out-of-school teenagers (including an estimate of those usually not counted by the Labor Department) are unemployed. In addition, a Labor Department survey of slum areas in November 1966 found that nearly 7 percent of those with jobs were employed only part-time, although they wanted full-time work, and 20 percent of those working full-time earned less than $60 a week. This same Labor Department survey found that nearly 40 percent of the families and unrelated individuals in big city slum areas earn less than $3,000 a year.

However, it costs about $7,000, at present prices, to maintain a modest standard of living, including a few amenities but no luxuries, for a family of four in America's metropolitan areas—more for a larger family and less for a smaller family. Elimination of the amenities would result in a cost of about $5,000 to maintain a minimum decent standard of living for a family of four in our urban areas—scaled up and down for different family sizes.

Yet government reports indicate that probably about 20 percent of the population, within city limits, earn less than the amount necessary for a minimum decent standard of living. Within ghetto areas, perhaps 60 percent to 70 percent or more of the families are in that category. The result is badly overcrowded housing, inadequate diet, poor medical care, few books and magazines for about 20 percent of city families and about 60 to 70 percent of those who live in ghetto slums.

The hardcore slum areas continue to deteriorate. People with jobs, some skills and some regular incomes have been moving out. They are replaced with new migrants from the rural South—adding to the remaining lowest-income families, the jobless, the aged and fatherless families.

A large proportion of these slum residents depend on welfare payments, often to mothers with dependent children and no father present. The Labor Department survey of November 1966 found that 30 percent of the population of East Harlem, 30 percent of the Watts population, 40 percent of the Bedford-Stuyvesant children and 25 percent of the adults receive welfare payments. Moreover, the lack of adequate child-care facilities in slum areas is a barrier to employment for women with children.

Trapped by a history of degradation and the recent impact of automation, these new migrants to the city are also trapped by the unavailability of low-and-moderate cost housing, as well as by discrimination against colored peoples.

The peak home construction year before World War II was 1925. From 1926 to 1945, a period of 20 years, home-building was in a slump. It wasn't until 1946 that the 1925-level of housing starts was reached.

Since 1945, the ups and downs of residential construction have followed conditions in the money market—interest rates and availability of money. Normal business operations and government programs have provided housing for families in the middle-income range and above (at present, about $7,000–$8,000 annual income and more).

The residential construction of the postwar period, however, has essentially ignored housing for the entire bottom half of our income distribution—for the lower middle-income group as well as the poor.

For lower middle-income families, with current incomes of about $5,000 to $8,000, the postwar years have seen only little new housing construction, with present rentals or carrying charges and taxes of about $85–$135 per month. This is particularly true for large families, with three or more children, in this income-range.

For the urban poor—families with current incomes of about $5,000 a year and less—there has been hardly any new housing construction during the 22 years since World War II and there was very little of such construction in the preceding 20 years from 1926 through 1945. Almost a half-century of rapid change in our cities—including the great Negro migration—has passed with hardly any housing construction for low-income families.

Realistic rentals for poor families would have to be concentrated around $40 to $70 a month. Since the private market cannot provide such housing, public housing and public rehabilitation are essential. But, in recent years, the total number of new public dwelling units has been only about 30,000–40,000 per year.

Moreover, the urban renewal program, which has bulldozed Negro slum areas, has concentrated on the construction of commercial buildings and luxury high-rise apartments. Relocation of families displaced from the slums has been neglected or ignored and there has been hardly any replacement of low-rental housing.

In addition, during the 1950s and early 1960s, the traditional conservative opposition to low-cost publicly subsidized housing for the poor was joined by many so-called liberals— the same coalition that debunked the impact of automation on unskilled and semi-skilled factory workers and on industrial location as a trade union myth.

At the same time, middle and upper-income families have been moving to the suburbs. This movement has opened up older housing in the cities. But, combined with the movement of industry to the suburbs and countryside, it has reduced the tax-base of the cities, when the demands on their financial resources for housing, welfare, education and public facilities are mounting. Moreover, the change of industrial location has compounded the problems of inadequate mass transportation facilities for low-income city-dwellers to get to the new areas of employment growth. And most suburban communities have rather rigid color-bar restrictions, as well as an absence of low-cost housing.

The New Deal's beginnings to provide low-cost public housing nearly perished between 1952 and 1966. And much of the long-delayed legislation of the 1960s to achieve partial adjustments to the radical changes in American life were first steps, without previous experience, precedents and trained personnel. Moreover, federal appropriations for even these purposes were kept down by public apathy. Yet, they were greatly oversold and their adoption aroused expectations of overnight solutions that were impossible to achieve.

America's urban crisis is a national complex of social problems—rather than simple problems of individual communities. No city or state government can solve them in isolation. Neither can private enterprise, even with the promise of tax subsidies. Their solution requires nationwide social measures, with adequate federal funds and standards.

· · ·

THE NATURE OF THE SLUM

Marshall B. Clinard

S L U M S constitute the most important and persistent problem of urban life; they are the chief sources of crime and delinquency, of illness and death from disease. Slums are of all types, shapes, and forms. Bombay has its packed multistoried chawls, New York its Harlem and its Lower East Side, Chicago its Black Belt, and London its well-known East End. Families in Bangkok crowd together in "pile villages," composed of poorly constructed wooden shacks raised on wooden stilts along the waterfronts. There are the tin shacks, bamboo huts, and straw hovels along the small lanes of Calcutta, Dacca, and Lagos, which steam with the high humidity and stink from the open drains. Improvised shanty towns or squatter shacks constructed from junk cover the hillsides of Rio de Janeiro, Lima, Hong Kong, and other Asiatic, African, and South American cities. No slums are more crowded than those of Hong Kong and Singapore, where a single room houses from ten to forty families, each with only "bed space" and no element of personal privacy. In areas of Canton,

Reprinted with permission of the author and The Macmillan Company from *Slums and Community Development: Experiments in Self-Help.* Copyright © 1966 by The Free Press of Glencoe, a Division of The Macmillan Company. Pp. 3–23.

Shanghai, and Hong Kong hundreds of thousands of families live in waterfront sampan or "floating" slums.

CHARACTERISTICS OF THE SLUM

Slums vary from one type to another, but certain general patterns of slum life are universal. Although the slum is generally characterized by inadequate housing, deficient facilities, overcrowding, and congestion, it involves much more than these elements. Sociologically it is a way of life, a subculture with a set of norms and values, which is reflected in poor sanitation and health practices, deviant behavior, and characteristic attributes of apathy and social isolation. People who live in slum areas are isolated from the general power structures and are regarded as inferior, and slum dwellers, in turn, harbor suspicions of the outside world.

The word "slum" has long had a negative connotation, has been almost an epithet, implying something evil, strange, to be shunned and avoided. In fact, the word itself is apparently derived, from "slumber," as slums were once thought by the majority to be "unknown, back streets or alleys, wrongly presumed to be sleeping and quiet."[1] Emotional attitudes toward the slum are still reflected in population definitions and value-laden terms that emphasize the seamy aspects of the slum, its filth and squalor, its poor social conditions, and the presence of vicious characters. The slum, for example, has been described as a "street, alley, court, etc., situated in a crowded district of a town or city and inhabited by people of a low class or by the very poor; a number of these streets or courts forming a thickly populated neighborhood or district of a squalid and wretched character."[2] Because the term has been used in such value-laden and derogatory contexts, its use has often been avoided in recent years, in the United States at least. Other terms of a more genteel nature have come into use, for example, "blighted area," "renewal area," "deteriorated area," "gray area," "lower class neighborhood," "low income area," and "inner core area." Still, as Hunter has said, "slum" is a "good, old fashioned word that carries real meaning."[3]

Housing Conditions

Of all the characteristics of a slum, the physical conditions have been emphasized most often. Slums have commonly been defined as those portions of cities in which housing is crowded, neglected, deteriorated, and often obsolete. Many of the inadequate housing conditions can be attributed to poorly arranged structures, overcrowding, and inadequate maintenance.⁴ In developing countries, many cities have large squatter areas, shanty towns built of scrap materials on unauthorized land and providing minimal protection from the elements.

In terms of physical conditions and housing standards, it is important to keep in mind the comparative nature of the definition. A slum should be judged physically according to the general living standards of a country. Certainly slum housing in New York City or Chicago would be regarded as adequate, or even good, in many parts of the world. Even limited availability of running water, flush toilets, electricity, and cooking facilities may be enough to exempt certain "slum" areas from classification as slums, at least in the physical sense, in other parts of the world.

. . .

The United States Census Bureau classifies poor dwellings as dilapidated or deteriorated. Dilapidated housing does not provide safe and adequate shelter, and deteriorating housing needs more repair than would be provided in the course of regular maintenance.⁵ According to the 1960 Census, the United States had 3,684,000 urban-slum housing units, of which 1,173,000 were "dilapidated urban units."⁶ According to one estimate, this figure means that 12,500,000 persons lived in slum areas.⁷ If slums in the United States were to be defined according to such standards as dilapidated housing, lack of adequate sanitary facilities, overcrowding, and location in extremely undesirable surroundings, it has been estimated that one-sixth of the urban population, or more than five million families, could be said to reside in a slum environment.⁸

There is a world-wide tendency to stress the physical aspects of the slum and to define it in these terms alone. A study of Houston, Texas, for example, showed that in the five census tracts with the highest delinquency rates, 65.5 per cent of the occupied dwellings units were in need of major repair or had no private bathrooms, whereas in the five tracts with the lowest rates, only 3.9 per cent of the units were in similar condition.[9] The coefficient of correlation between delinquency rates and the percentage of poor housing was .75 ± .06; between delinquency rates and overcrowding the correlation was .85 ± .04. The explanation of such a relationship, however, is more likely to be a slum way of life, which promotes deviant behavior. Careful analysis of the high deviation rates in the slums fails to show that bad housing explains them, although poor housing may encourage a slum way of life. Rather, low economic status and discrimination force people to live in low-rent areas where certain values prevail. Some studies have attempted to show that improved housing also means improved general social conditions, including lower incidence of delinquency, but this result by no means always follows. Morris found, for example, that, even after the construction of new government housing projects in an English city, the rates of delinquency remained high.[10] He concluded that an area's physical characteristics bear little relation to its crime and delinquency, except indirectly as a determinant of the social status of the area.

The importance of distinguishing the physical from the social aspects of the slum has been emphasized. One writer has pointed out that the "slum problem" differs from the "renewal problem." The latter is concerned with how to construct, maintain, and rebuild those parts of a city in which buildings have become deteriorated, or in which the facilities, although still in sound structural condition, have become so obsolete that they cannot be brought up to standards of health, comfort, or efficient operation. The slum problem, on the other hand, is "basically a problem of the attitudes and behavior of people and of the indifference of the community to the neglect and victimization of the underprivileged."[14] Obsolescence per se is not harmful, and the designation of an area as a slum for this reason alone "is merely a reflection of middle-class standards—and middle-class incomes."[12]

In Tokyo the proportion of dwellings listed as slums is much smaller than that in New York City. On the other hand, the average Tokyo "non-slum dweller" lives under physical conditions much inferior to those of the average New York slum dweller. His home is often made of shoddy materials, is not connected to a sewage system, has no central heating, and does not have bathing facilities. Such differences in the definition of the extent of slums cannot be explained only by differences in the standard of living. As Glazer says: "the main explanation is that Tokyo does not have as large a social problem population as New York. In a variety of ways, the slums of any city will tend to equal the number of people defined as social problems, regardless of the quality of design or construction."[13]

A slum may be an area overcrowded with buildings, buildings overcrowded with people, or both. Density does not always result in unfortunate social consequences; the issue is primarily one of overcrowding.[14] Congestion, however, may be so great that a judgment about the physical conditions of the buildings must often be made in terms of the high density per block, acre, or square mile. It has been pointed out, for example, that, if New York City's total population density were as high as that in some of Harlem's worst blocks, the entire population of the United States could fit into three of New York City's boroughs.[15] Whyte stressed the importance of overcrowding as a criterion for measuring slum conditions when he described how he chose Boston's North End for his well-known sociological study of "street corner society":

I made my choice on very unscientific grounds: Cornerville best fitted my picture of what a slum district should look like. Somehow I had developed a picture of run-down three-to-five-story buildings crowded in together. The dilapidated wooden-frame buildings of some other parts of the city did not look quite genuine to me. To be sure, Cornerville did have one characteristic that recommended it on a little more objective basis. It had more people per acre living in it than any other section of the city. If a slum meant overcrowding, this was certainly it.[16]

Some Indian slum areas, like those of Delhi, have 400,000 people to the square mile. In the Bombay tenements, ten people commonly live in a room ten by fifteen feet. In Panama, slum shelters bulge at the seams with as many as twenty people in a room fifteen by fifteen feet, sleeping in relays. In Kingston, Jamaica, nine people may live in a single tiny hut six by ten feet. In Accra, Ghana, occupancy per single house in 1960 was 19.3 people, and it was even higher in Kumasi. Migration into some cities of the Far East has created living conditions without any vestige of privacy or room for motion. In Hong Kong, five or six human beings share single cubicles measuring forty square feet.[17]

People who live under such crowded conditions obviously have little privacy, a factor that may be of great importance, especially in its effects upon interpersonal relations. Frazier states that overcrowded housing probably explains why so many Negroes congregate on the streets of Negro neighborhoods. "So far as the children are concerned, the house becomes a veritable prison for them. There is no way of knowing how many conflicts in Negro families are set off by the irritations caused by overcrowding people, who come home after a day of frustration and fatigue, to dingy and unhealthy living quarters."[18] The ill effects of this feature of slum life are partially mitigated, however, through the greater use of outside space, including front stoops and sidewalks, hallways, alleys, and lanes. Most studies of lower-class and slum life have shown the importance of peer-group relations developed under these very conditions, where slum streets, sidewalks, lanes, and alleys become important places for promoting such contacts.[19] Hartman refers to this factor as an interplay of slum dwellers between "inside and outside," both in physical and social senses.[20] The middle class places a higher value on privacy, which tends to encourage orientation toward individual responsibility and achievement.

Neighborhood Facilities
Poor slum housing is invariably associated with poor facilities and community services. Along with shabbiness and

dilapidation, the park facilities are inadequate, the schools are of poor quality, and other public facilities are often insufficient. Streets and sidewalks often go unrepaired, and rubbish and garbage are infrequently collected, adding to the undesirable environment. These services may be especially neglected in slums inhabited by minority groups in the United States.[21] In developing countries, this lack of facilities and services is often stressed in defining slums. The slums in India have been described as chaotically occupied, unsystematically developed and generally neglected, overpopulated and overcrowded with ill-repaired and neglected structures, insufficiently equipped with proper communications and physical comforts, and inadequately supplied with social services and welfare agencies to deal with the needs and social problems of families who are "victims of biological, psychological and social consequences of the physical and social environment."[22]

.   .   .

Poor Sanitation and Health

Slums have generally been dirty and unclean places. In fact, the United Nations, which has been concerned more with the slums of developing countries, has defined them largely in terms of physical deterioration, stressing particularly unsanitary conditions and lack of sufficient facilities like water and latrines.[23] These factors have resulted in high death and disease rates, which have always been typical of slum areas where overcrowding and the presence of rats, cockroaches, and other pests complicate the problems of health and sanitation. One United States estimate is that, on the average, the slum areas of a city that contain about 20 per cent of its residential population will have 50 per cent of all its diseases.[24] The infant-mortality rate of any community is reputed to be the best single index of its general health. In 1961 this rate for Harlem was 45.2 per 1,000 live births, as compared to 25.7 for New York City, and in Cleveland's Hough area the infant deaths are almost double those of the rest of the city.[25] In the slum areas of developing countries, the rates of disease, chronic illness, and infant mortality are exceptionally high. There is little application of proper sanitation and health practices.

Deviant Behavior

A high incidence of deviant behavior—crime, juvenile delinqency, prostitution, drunkenness, drug usage, mental disorder, suicide, illegitimacy, and family maladjustment—have long been associated with slum living. In the Western world, particularly the United States, the slum is closely associated with delinquency and crime. Hunter's survey of the evidence led him to estimate that in slums accommodating 20 per cent of the population of an American city there occur approximately 50 per cent of all arrests, 45 per cent of the reported major crimes, and 55 per cent of the reported juvenile delinquency cases.[26] Numerous studies made over a period of several years in Chicago, for example, have revealed that conventional crime, delinquency, mental disorder in general and schizophrenia in particular, suicide, prostitution, vagrancy, dependency, illegitimacy, infant mortality, and high death and disease rates are largely concentrated in the slums.[27] A 1960 study of Milwaukee showed that the slum, or innercore area of the city, which had 13.7 per cent of the population in 1957, had 38 per cent of the arrests for burglary, 69 per cent of the aggravated assaults and 47 per cent of other assaults, 60 per cent of the murders, 72 per cent of the arrests for commercial vice, 22 per cent of the drunkenness, and 67 per cent of the narcotics arrests.[28] Similar findings have been reported in such cities as Cleveland, Jacksonville (Florida), and Indianapolis. A slum area in Cleveland, which contained only 2.5 per cent of the city's population in its 333 acres, was responsible for 6.8 per cent of its delinquency, 21 per cent of its murders, and 26 per cent of its houses of prostitution.[29] The rates for nearly all twenty-nine types of crime known to the police in Seattle and arrests for these crimes, during the period 1949–1951, showed a decline as one moved through six one-mile concentric zones from the center of the city. Slum areas were higher in twenty-three of twenty-nine crimes and were particularly high in robbery, prostitution, rape, gambling, and common drunkenness.[30] Two detailed studies of criminal homicide in the United States, one in Houston and the other in Philadelphia, have shown concentrations in lower class slum areas.[31] In Houston, more than 87 per cent of all criminal homicides occurred in four lower-class areas, not far apart, located near the city center.[32]

Studies by Shaw, McKay, and Thrasher in Chicago several decades ago demonstrated the much higher rates of juvenile delinquency within slum districts.[33] Furthermore, the Chicago slum areas also had had much higher delinquency rates in both 1900 and 1920, even though their ethnic composition was almost entirely different. Whether slum areas were occupied successively by Swedes, Germans, Poles, or Italians, the rates were high, as they are today with a primarily Negro or Spanish-speaking population. Similar findings have been reported in the United States for eight other large metropolitan areas and eleven other cities, all widely separated geographically, including Boston, Philadelphia, Cleveland, Richmond, Birmingham, Omaha, and Seattle.[34] In 1960, ninety-seven health areas of New York City, comprising 27 per cent of the population, accounted for 51 per cent of the juvenile delinquency.[35] In a recent study of drug addiction among juveniles in New York City, the highest rates were found in the slums.[36] A study of Croydon, a large English town near London, revealed that the highest rates for delinquency were concentrated in areas populated by unskilled and semi-skilled workers' families.[37] Indications are that, with the growth of urbanization, the cities of developing countries are beginning to face similar problems in the slums.[38] Studies of Kanpur and Lucknow in India showed that juvenile delinquency, juvenile vagrancy, and crime are primarily associated with slum areas.[39]

The existence of unconventional values in slum areas accounts for the high rates of such deviant behavior as delinquency. Yet it should be recognized that not all those residing in slum areas become deviant. In any slum area, there exist simultaneously conventional value systems carried through certain individuals, schools, churches, the police, and other sources.[40] The interaction of conventional and such unconventional value systems as those of delinquency and crime may have differential impacts on individuals.[41]

Research in Chicago and in seven other United States cities on the residences of patients admitted to state and private mental hospitals, particularly for schizophrenia, has revealed much higher admission rates from the slum areas of the cities.[42] A New Haven study of all patients of psychiatrists or psychiatric clinics or in psychiatric institutions on December 1, 1950, revealed that those in the lowest classes had the highest rates of diagnosed mental disorder.[43] Those in the lowest class had almost twice the expected percentage based on total population; schizophrenia was almost two and a half times as great. A survey of the prevalence of mental disorder among the adult population in midtown New York City re vealed a higher rate among the lower class; in fact, 32.7 per cent of the lowest class was classified as "impaired," compared with only 17.5 per cent of those from the highest status group, for those with "severe symptom formation" or "incapacitated," 14.7 per cent compared with 5.7.[44] The validity of this and the other studies depends, of course, upon the research procedures and criteria used to determine "mental health," "mental disorder," "neuroses," and "psychoses."

The Culture of the Slum

Culture might be defined as a system of symbols or meanings for normative conduct standards, having three distinct properties: It is transmittable, it is learned, and it is shared. The slum has a culture of its own, and this culture is a way of life. This learned way of life is passed from generation to generation, with its own rationale, structure, and defense mechanisms, which provide the means to continue in spite of difficulties and deprivations. One writer has commented on the slum: "It is because people themselves produce blight, or more correctly, the cultural patterns operating through people produce blight. This distinction between people themselves and the cultural patterns operating through people is an important one, because people themselves produce neither slums nor well-kept neighborhoods. It is the habits, customs,

behavior patterns people have learned and which they hold
that move them to act in particular ways."[45]

This slum culture affects virtually every facet of the lives
of most of the world's slum dwellers. It is largely a synthesis
of the culture of the lower class and of what Lewis has referred to as the culture of poverty.[46] Nearly all slum dwellers
are of the lower class, and, with few exceptions, they live at
the poverty level, but not all lower class or poor urban people
live in slums. The culture of the slum has a number of characteristics that vary only in degree.[47] Although these cultural
patterns are typical of the slum from an over-all perspective,
they vary in detail from slum to slum, from ethnic group to
ethnic group, from society to society. Each individual in the
slum is influenced in different degrees by the general slum
culture.[48] Furthermore, certain people may live in a slum area,
and may even be poor, yet remain removed from the slum
culture. Members of higher social classes, for example, may
reside in a slum, as they do in some Asiatic cities, yet not
become part of its way of life. Others, like students and artists
may simply seek cheap housing in the slum and never become
part of it. In addition, certain groups, like the Jews in Europe
and the Japanese-Americans in the United States, have often
resided in slum areas but have not necessarily shared the
values of most of those who live there.

Life in the slum is usually gregarious and largely centered
in the immediate area, where are found friends, shops,
and possible credit. There is little privacy, and confusion and
noise seldom abate; life, however, has more spontaneity, and
behavior, whether in the home or on the street corner, is more
unrestrained than in middle-class areas. Toughness is often
regarded as virtuous, and frequent resort to violence to settle
disputes is common. Initiation into sexual experiences,
whether by marriage or otherwise, comes early, and middle-
class standards of sex conduct are not widely observed. Above
all, there is a greater tolerance of deviant behavior, a higher
rate of delinquency and crime, and an ambivalence toward
quasi-criminal activities committed against the "outside
world." Slum dwellers generally display apathy about their

conditions, apathy associated with intolerance of conventional ambitions. Often accompanying this sense of resignation there is an attitude of "fatalism" toward life.[49]

Throughout the slums, such attitudes have led to the development of generalized suspicion of the "outside world," which includes government and politicians, welfare groups, and the upper and middle classes generally. Slum people often fail adequately to utilize those very agencies, both public and private, that could be helpful to them, such as the health department, schools, and even the police. These services are often feared as possible dangerous sources of interference in everyday living. Such fears are frequently confused by the people's own failure to understand modern health or educational services or even the proper use of such public facilities as schools, playgrounds, and parks.

Miller has outlined six focal concerns of lower-class culture, focal concerns that apply to most slum areas, particularly those of the Western world.[50] First, there is concern over "trouble," an attempt to avoid it and in other cases to seek it. The second is a concern with "toughness," in that lower-class men often feel the need to demonstrate physical powers, "masculinity," and bravery. "Smartness" centers on the capacity to outsmart, outfox, outwit, dupe, "take," or "con" another, as well as on the ability to avoid being "taken" oneself. "Excitement" and the search for thrills characterize many features of lower-class life; examples include the use of alcohol and often narcotics, gambling, and the recurrent practice of taking a "night on the town." Much emphasis is placed on "fate" or luck by many who feel that they have little control over the forces affecting their lives. "Autonomy" is the final concern of lower-class culture: External controls and retrictions on behavior and authority that seem coercive and unjust are bitterly denounced, although often actually desired.

Unemployment, underemployment, and low wages are the rule in the slums. There is a constant struggle for economic survival. Work patterns are likely to be irregular, and lack of stable employment often contributes to unstable family patterns. There is an almost complete absence of savings or even of the desire to save, and there is little ability to plan for the future or to defer present gratification of the senses. Food reserves are often nonexistent, and personal possessions are frequently pawned, or local money lenders are visited. Any treatment of the slum solely as a product of poverty, however, is far too simple. "Poverty" is both an absolute and a relative term. In an absolute sense, it means a lack of resources for specified needs; in a relative sense it refers to the extent of these resources in comparison to what other individuals in the society have. As societies vary in the degree of poverty characterizing them, individuals and the slums themselves vary in the degrees to which they are "poor." Slum people in the United States have a higher standard of living than many in higher social classes in other parts of the world. For example, the radio, television, electricity, processed foods, and other material possessions that slum dwellers generally have in the United States today would have been considered luxuries years ago, and they are still not available to large numbers of people in many countries. A slum person in the Western world may have many more material goods than a slum person in India has: A poor urban family today may have technological possessions and education superior even to those of the upper socioeconomic classes in the eighteenth century. In other words, poverty must be defined in terms of the aspirations and expectations of a culture and its capacity to produce these goods, and in these terms as an explanation of slum life it has serious limitations.

The social aberration among the poor of the slums, as well as their apathy, is a product of their being the poorest, rather than of their being "poor," and their alienation, apathy, and withdrawal from the general society appear to be maximum under urban slum conditions. In rural areas, the relative effects of poverty are counterbalanced by stronger traditions and group ties. In areas of extensive urbanization and also industrialization, where traditional and primary-group ties are weakened, the lack of power and status among the poor, particularly those in urban areas, is much greater.

General categorizations of the relation of poverty to lower-class life, however, are too broad. Sydney Miller has suggested, using as criteria family stability and job security,

that there actually are four types of lower class: the stable
poor (both familial and economic stability); the strained
(economic stability and familial instability); the copers (economic instability and familial stability); and the unstable
(economic instability and familial instability).[51] Such a classification makes it possible to consider cultural variations in
the lower class. In any event, the lower class, which is associated with slum living, should not be identified with, or confused with, the "working class." The working class, made up
of communities of semiskilled and skilled workers, has more
stability of employment, although the orientation may largely
be toward "getting by." The working class is more concerned
with educational improvement than is the lower class but
not so much as is the middle class.[52] Organized family life
plays an important role in the working class.[53] Although the
working class is not concerned with manners and proper behavior to the same extent as is the middle class, it does not
generally have so high an incidence of deviant behavior as
does the lower class.

Apathy and Social Isolation

A slum also has an image in the eyes of the larger community. There is a societal reaction to slum dwellers. The
nonslum dweller often associates the physical appearance
and difficult living conditions of the slum with belief in the
"natural inferiority" of those who live in the slums. As a slum
is an inferior place, those who live there are also inferior.
This reaction has important conquences in the social isolation of slum dwellers and their exclusion from power and
participation in urban society. Those who live in the slum
lack an effective means of communication with the outside
world because of apathy, lack of experience in commu-
nicating with outsiders, and their own powerlessness to make
their voices heard. The common denominator of the slum is
its submerged aspect and its detachment from the city as a
whole. "The life of the slum is lived almost entirely without
the conventional world."[54] The local politician often becomes
the only "ambassador to the outside world," one who unfortunately tries to manipulate it, frequently for his own
benefit.[55]

Inevitably the slum dweller's conception of himself comes to reflect the attitudes of outsiders toward the slum and its inhabitants. Slum dwellers realize that they live under conditions that are physically, although not necessarily socially, inferior to those of the middle class. Sometimes they take actions that they hope can improve their lot, but far more often they apathetically accept the situation, do what they can with what they have, and experience little or no control over their surroundings. A research study of midtown Manhattan, for example, reported that lower-class tenement dwellers tend not to plan ahead, have feelings of futility, and express a fatalistic outlook on life.[56] In a New Haven study, the lower class was described as fatalistic, tending to accept what life brought.[57]

Slum people feel relatively powerless to alter their life situations.[58] This powerlessness is accompanied by long-standing patterns of behavior and beliefs that reflect acceptance of this weakness. As conditions of success, a person tends to see chance rather than effort, luck rather than planning, and favoritism rather than ability. One writer refers to this outlook as the "feel" of a slum, the "feel" when an outsider is in a slum, or the "feel" of things when one lives in the slum.[59]

The attitude of the slum dweller toward the slum itself, toward the city of which the slum is a part, toward his own chances of getting out, toward the people who control things, toward the "system," this is the element which as much as anything else will determine whether or not it is possible to "do something" about slums. This is what makes slums a human problem rather than a problem of finance and real estate.[60]

A slum dweller reported:

Survival for us depends on staying on good terms with the rich people and the law. Whenever I think about myself and the kids, I am reminded what my father used to say, "We are the ones who are told what to do, when and how" around here. This town takes us for granted. Most people think the people down here [the tannery flats] are too ignorant to do anything and don't care; I guess they're right."[61]

Not all slum dwellers feel inferior or rejected, however. Studies of the more settled Italian slums in Boston have demonstrated that the residents found many satisfactions in their neighborhood and did not want to be moved from it. Firey, for example, found that the physical undesirability of the North End was outweighed by the advantages of living with people of similar backgrounds.[62] Whyte stated that, although the North End was a mysterious, dangerous, and depressing place to an outsider, it provided an organized and familiar environment for those who lived there.[63] Seeley lived in the Back of the Yards in Chicago in the early 1940s, and he discovered that its inhabitants had many advantages not found in "better" parts of the city: possibilities for fulfillment of basic human needs and outlets for aggressiveness, adventure, sexual satisfaction, strong loyalties, and a sense of independence. When the slum inhabitants were taken "slumming" into middle-class neighborhoods, they did not envy the residents.[64] In the West End of Boston, Gans found much the same attitudes reported by Firey and Whyte for the North End. Residents were satisfied with their neighborhoods and did not want to leave them for the suburbs or central-city locations that offered "improved" conditions.[65]

THE SOCIAL ORGANIZATION OF THE SLUM

As slum dwellers are largely part of lower-class culture, they develop characteristic styles of life within their environments in the same manner as does the middle class. The fact that their patterns of life differ does not necessarily imply that one is "better" or more acceptable as a "standard" of life, as many authorities on social problems unfortunately seem to suggest through their use of middle-class standards as measuring rods or "core culture" with which to compare other class cultures.[66] This tendency has led to some erroneous assumptions about the life of slum inhabitants. For example, one such belief or assumption has been that the slum is composed of a "disorganized" population whose members neither know nor care about others living in the immediate vicinity.[67] Because delinquency, violence, sex patterns, the spontaneity and enjoyment of sensual pleasure, and such various other norms of behavior as lack of emphasis on good sanitation, neat housing, and industriousness differ from the norms of the middle class, they have been attributed to or are said to constitute "disorganization."

Detailed descriptive studies of slum communities often reveal high degrees of organization, with systematic and persisting features of social behavior.[68] Rather than being "disorganized," the slum often simply has its own organization, usually a type judged by the middle class to be unconventional. Miller states that lower-class culture is a cultural system in its own right, with its own integrity, set of practices, focal concerns, and ways of behaving, systematically related to one another rather than to corresponding features of middle-class culture.[69] Whyte has pointed out that, in the American slum, behavior may be as highly organized and social controls as effective as in middle-class suburbia but that the slum resident may not always conform to middle-class standards of proper conduct and respectability.[70] Formal governmental controls may be ineffective, and police and other government authorities may be held in disrespect, but they are replaced by some degree of informal control based on age, sex, occupation, or ethnic group. Sanitation, health, and child-care beliefs and practices may also reflect a highly organized system, though one contrary to both scientific and middle-class beliefs. Delinquent gang activity in the slums can be viewed as the lower-class boys' "positive effort to achieve status, conditions or qualities valued within the actor's most significant cultural milieu."[71] In fact, Cloward and Ohlin have theorized that slum-gang delinquency in the United States has become more aggressive and violent as a result of the disintegration of traditional slum organization due to massive slum-clearance or renewal programs, which have displaced entire slum-neighborhood populations.[72] The original residents have been dispersed throughout a community, and people who are strangers to one another have been assembled in housing projects. These residents are not only new and alien, but they commonly lack patterns of social organization that might bind them in community life. In addition, traditional slum patterns change because of de-

clines of the urban political machines, which have meant
the loss of important integrating structures and of significant
channels for social ascent for the urban lower class.

Although some slums lack unity, disunity cannot be assumed to be a general phenomenon of the slum. Rather, each
slum neighborhood must be examined in the light of its own
subculture. In each case, the particular subculture will be the
dominant influence on the life patterns of the respective slum
inhabitants, shaping their lives through the pressures of
environmental and family backgrounds, cultural traditions,
and major life concerns. Zorbaugh described the rooming-
house slum as a district of little social interaction among
neighbors, as people constantly move in and out without ever
really becoming part of the neighborhood.[73] Ethnic slums in
the United States, on the other hand, may maintain their
common cultural ties through their lodges, neighborhood
shops, and taverns, which serve as meeting places. As ethnic
slums split up and the more upwardly mobile residents move
away, a breakdown in the effectiveness of the neighborhoods
as units of social control results, and the continuity of neighborhood traditions is broken.[74] Furthermore, although ethnic
and racial groups may live in close association with one another, there may be considerable isolation from other ethnic
groups living geographically close by.[75]

Upper- and middle-class areas in the city are, however,
quite different from slum areas in ecology, social structure,
and, above all, the ability to participate in and utilize effectively the resources of the larger city. Middle- and upper-class
groups, particularly in the Western world, live in neighborhoods, but their actual participating areas, where they shop,
visit, and pursue recreational and cultural activities, are generally much larger. The world of slum people is much more
fixed. It is centered in smaller areas that tend to create resentment and suspicion of the outside urban communities.
Slum dwellers spend most of their time in the immediate
neighborhoods: Their friends and relatives live there, whatever recreation they have is there, and what credit they can
get is also there. Slum dwellers thus remain more fixed in
residence, although in certain types of slum there may be con-

siderable mobility, mainly, however, to other slum areas in the same city.

THE FUNCTION OF THE SLUM

Throughout history, the slum has met various needs and has served several useful functions for slum residents. In particular, it has provided cheap housing for the poor, has fostered group associations, has educated people in urban ways of life, and has given some of its residents an element of anonymity. One could, of course, look at the function of the slum from the point of view of the nonresidents. For example, some people believe that, were slums not profitable to absentee landlords, "slumlords," they might well diminish in extent. For some employers slums have been useful as places where employees could live at lower rentals and therefore on lower incomes.

Housing for the Poor and the Migrant

The most common function of the slum has been to provide housing for the lowest income groups in society. Slums have been havens for penniless rural migrants and immigrants who need a first living base in the city at the lowest possible prices. In areas undergoing industrialization and urbanization, migrants to the cities in the past and today have found their first homes, at rents they could afford or as squatters, in the city slums. Living in the slums has made it possible for low-income families to save enough for other purposes, as in the case of Italian immigrants who desired to save enough money to enable their families to join them or eventually to provide better lives for themselves and their children.[76] Similarly, the Jewish immigrants to New York's Lower East Side slum tried to save in order to send money to their families to pay their passages to this country.[77] Then there are those who, by living in the slums, have managed to build up small businesses or to save enough money by renting out rooms to be able to move to more suitable neighborhoods.[78] In developing countries, however, where vertical class mobility is severely restricted, the older and more settled slums and the large colonies of squatter shacks that spring up in and around large cities often become more or less permanent habitations for the poor. With low rents or no rents at all, their meager existences can be stretched indefinitely.

Group Associations

In many countries, the slums serve as places where group living and associations on the basis of villages, regions, tribes, or ethnic or racial groups may develop. The appearance of a slum can easily be quite misleading to an outsider. What the middle-class observer often sees as a neighborhood of filthy, dilapidated and overcrowded dwellings is often viewed quite differently by those who live there and understand the neighborhood and its residents. In the West End of Boston, for example, the low rents, the sentiments of the people, and their identification with the neighborhood, as well as their strong kinship ties, built an attachment to a slum or low-rent neighborhood that cannot be fully understood by a person with middle-class values.[79] Whyte found an organized way of life in the slums, which offered many satisfactions to its residents.[80] Firey also found a strong identification with the Italian communities and its distinctive values among many of the Boston North Enders. For those who most fully identified themselves with the Italian values, the overcrowded and run-down housing was more than offset by the advantages of living with similar people in an Italian neighborhood. The fact that many of these people could have moved out had they so desired tended to demonstrate the invalidity of the conception of the slum as a "product of compulsion rather than design."[81]

Satisfaction for residents of the ethnic or regional slum arises from the fact that, for them, the residential area is often the setting for a vast and interlocking set of social networks and from the fact that physical area has meaning for them as an extension of their homes, various parts of which are delimited and structured on the basis of a sense of belonging.[82] A feeling of belonging in or to a slum area is thus, in some cases, an important factor in the attitudes of slum dwellers toward their environments. It is especially important in the slums of Asian and African cities.

Education for Urban Life

The slum performs a function as a type of "school" to educate newcomers to the city. It gives them a place to become oriented upon arrival, to find first jobs, and to learn the ways of city life. This function is particularly important in developing countries, where the contrast between village and urban life is often great. As many immigrants of the past lived in the slums for periods of adjustment before moving on to better neighborhoods, so today, in large cities of the United States, the slums house the migrants from rural areas, the Negroes from the South, the Puerto Ricans, and the Mexicans.

Demand for Anonymity

An important function of the slum is that of offering a place of residence to those who prefer to live anonymously. The urban slum has harbored both those on the way up and those on the way down, and this dual character of the slum's social function has often been overlooked.[83] The slum accepts people who may be rejected elsewhere, and this function is important in preserving conformity in the remainder of the city. Some of the deviant behavior found in the slum does not originate there but in more fashionable neighborhoods. After defeat in personal life, a person may drift to the slum.[84] The Skid Rows of the large cities of the United States provide an example of the anonymity offered people in all kinds of circumstances. Skid Row residents include migratory workers, "bums," criminals, chronic alcoholics, and workers in illegal enterprises.[85] Only in the city, where rapid change is taking place, and often only in the slums of the city, can the disfranchised and deviant find genuinely important roles.[86] In addition, the artist often finds his start here, as do the poet, the jazz musician, and the radical. The slum also satisfies certain demands for vice and illegal activities like gambling, prostitution, and black-market trades. These demands call forth supplies, and the question is not whether or not, but where, the supplies will be found.[87] This accumulation of various deviant groups in slum areas should not necessarily be viewed as serving no social function or as a highly disturbing or dysfunctional element, for deviant groups may play important roles in the introduction of innovations in any society.[88]

THEORIES OF THE SLUM

Several hypotheses have been advanced to explain the continued existence of slums. Changes in urban land-use patterns and lack of housing, which lead to overcrowding and improper maintenance, have commonly been emphasized.

Changes in Urban Land-Use Patterns

According to one theory, largely derived from a study of cities in the United States, the slum develops within the zone surrounding the central business district.[89] Early in the development of a city, this area is the home of the upper classes, a fashionable residential district. With the expansion of commercial and industrial ventures, the neighborhood becomes infiltrated with industrial, storage, and wholesale operations, and the more well-to-do move farther out, away from the city center. Low-income workers, including recently arrived poor regional ethnic, and racial groups, then move in and become the exclusive inhabitants of these areas. Because the owners receive insufficient rental income to maintain their buildings properly, conditions decline, and, because of overcrowding, carelessness, and destructiveness by the occupants, the neighborhood becomes a slum. Zorbaugh has described the growth of the slum on the near North Side of Chicago:

One alien group after another has claimed this slum area. The Irish, the Germans, the Swedish, the Sicilians have occupied it in turn. Now it is being invaded by a migration of the Negro from the South. It has been known successively as Kilgubbin, Little Hell, and, as industry has come in, as Smoky Hollow. The remnants of these various successions have left a sediment that at once characterizes and confuses the life of this district. . . .

It is an area in which encroaching business lends a speculative value to the land. But rents are low; for while little business has actually come into the area, it is no longer desirable for residential purposes. It is an area of dilapidated dwellings, many of which the owners, waiting to sell the land for commercial purposes, allow to deteriorate, asking just enough in rent to carry the taxes. . . .

The city, as it grows, creates about its central business district a belt of bleak, barren, soot-begrimed, physically deteriorated neighborhoods. And in these neighborhoods, the undesirable and those of low economic status, are segregated by the unremitting competition of the economic process in which land values, rentals, and wages are fixed.[90]

The slum develops into an area of high land values but cheap rents, a curious contradiction that results from the land's being held "in pawn," so to speak, on the assumption that the central business district will expand, bringing into the area new business firms, manufacturing establishments, and high-priced rental units like hotels and apartment hotels. The landowners, who seldom live in the area, do not wish to improve slum housing as it will eventually be torn down. This fact and the rather undesirable location result in cheap rentals, yet the land remains so high-priced that, when an occasional apartment hotel is erected, it must be of high-rise proportions to be profitable.

A modification of this theory based on city growth is that of the city pattern as a pie, divided into wedge-shaped sections. According to this theory, industrial areas follow river valleys, water courses, and railroad lines out from the center, and workingmen's houses cluster along them, with factories tending to locate even at the outer fringes of the city. According to the sector view, the best housing then does not fringe the entire city but only parts of it. The main industrial areas of the future may well be located on the outskirts of cities in new industrial towns and suburbs, as they are already beginning to be.[91]

It has been claimed, however, that the pattern of land distribution in which the slum is located in or near the central city represents a generalization fulfilled only in industrial cities, where centralized commercial and industrial activities are necessarily more prominent, and does not apply to "preindustrial" cities.[92] In such cities, formerly common in

Europe and still common in the developing countries of Asia and other parts of the world, the central areas are generally inhabited by the elite, with the slums located on the peripheries where "houses toward the city's fringes are small, flimsily constructed, often one-room, hovels into which whole families crowd." The disadvantage of distant locations are borne by the poorest, who must travel the farthest to gain access to the city's facilities. This pattern of slum development is seen today in the extensive squatter or shanty towns that have sprung up around the cities in Asia, Africa, and Latin America to which large numbers of rural people have migrated. In some instances, they are located closer to the cities on unoccupied or undesirable land. After surveying seven sociological studies of Latin American cities, Schnore found that the cities do not follow the zonal pattern that North American cities supposedly do. One of his conclusions is that "it is evident that an accretion of jerry-built peripheral slums still characterizes most of the larger cities of the region. Living conditions and levels of health and sanitation in these out-lying slums are generally described as extremely low, and municipal officials seem powerless in their efforts to turn the tide."[94]

Housing Shortages and Maintenance

The continuing existence of slums has also been explained by the fact that "their inhabitants cannot afford good housing and because private enterprise will not supply it at prices they can afford."[95] The blame for their existence, according to Colean, must be shared by the landlords, the tenants, and the community: the landlords because of their indifference to their property and their willingness to profit from overcrowding; the tenants because they are too poor, too ignorant, or too indifferent to maintain the dwellings properly; and the community at large because it allows slums to develop and to persist and fails to support government efforts to enforce decent standards.[96] One theory of slums advanced by an English writer lists four factors: the physical surroundings of the house, the physical conditions of the house, the owner, and the tenant.[97] His suggested means of improving or eliminating the slum demonstrates emphasis on the physical environment as a perceived cause of slum conditions. The three essential tools for "slum-breaking" are foresight in construction, careful maintenance by owner and tenant, and expert supervision by the authorities.[98]

A relatively recent theory of slum growth and development emphasizes the role of current urban-renewal projects in creating new slums in areas where old slums have been eliminated. The main point of this theory is that slum clearance reduces the number of dwellings available to low-income families and that, as a result, they cannot bargain with landlords of the prospective dwellings to obtain repairs and improvements as conditions of rental. As slum clearance continues, tenants in low-rent nonslum housing will have a harder time convincing landlords to spend funds for maintenance. If economic growth, full employment, or the lowering of racial discrimination toward job applicants should raise the real income of a neighborhood's population, however, housing quality would tend to improve.[99]

APPROACHES TO THE SLUM PROBLEM

Over the centuries, many groups have lived in the slums and have left; others have stayed on. The slums of most cities, however, not only have continued for centuries but also in many instances have grown in size; or new slums have been created. In this sense slums are self-perpetuating, either replenished from within or established through migration from outside the city. Several traditional approaches have been developed to deal with the slum problem, including charity measures, public and private services to slum dwellers, and slum clearance. Considering the nature of slum life and the enormity of its extent in most major cities, these measures have often offered only limited possibilities of dealing with the slum way of life in the final analysis.

Because slums have been so impervious to change and because the slum has been regarded as primarily a physical problem, one approach has been the destruction of the slum through clearance and renewal programs. Within a new physical environment, it has been hoped, slum problems might disappear. So far slums have not been amenable to such a simple solution. In fact, the problems of slum dwellers have even been accentuated by this method. In developing countries, where urban housing is perennially in short supply, the entire scheme has always been surrounded by an aura of unreality. Social workers from outside the slums have also offered various services through settlement houses and welfare centers, as many humanitarians or liberally oriented people have believed that the slum dweller needs outside help through charity, philanthropy, or other form of "uplift." Efforts have been directed toward ameliorating slum problems rather than toward eliminating the slum. In spite of such services through the years, slums have generally continued to resist efforts to change them, and they remain largely unaffected by the multitude of agencies and services offered, even in developing countries. Quite recently, the idea has developed in the United States that the slum problem stems basically from a lack of economic and educational opportunities and that, given a chance by government agencies to better themselves, the people of the slums will individually respond and take advantage of these services.

Another approach is to place emphasis on enlisting the slum dwellers themselves in an effort to bring about more rapid and at the same time more permanent changes. Recognizing the essential nature of most slum problems, this approach involves developing greater community consciousness, participation in a wider community, and self-help on the part of the slum dweller. This approach, relying upon indigenous leadership to bring about change and supplemented by some financial and technical assistance from the outside, has been termed "urban community development." Various experiments along these lines have been undertaken recently in the slums of developed and developing countries. . . .

Part II

The Distribution of City Crime

Introduction

ONE WAY of relating crime to city life is by statistics, showing the urban geography of crime and its correlations with other attributes of city populations. This is one form of what sociologists call a "structural analysis," for it interrelates characteristics of large groups and their settings, rather than describing separately the acts of the individuals who comprise these groups. Such an analysis can be done in many ways, from simple to complex, depending on the data available, and the refinements of knowledge sought.

The research reports presented here illustrate the diverse strategies of data collection and analysis that have been employed in the statistical study of crime in the city. They are arranged in a sequence which is, roughly, according to the knowledge of statistics required to understand them fully, from the most easily followed to the most difficult. However, the most technical articles, such as Gordon's review of multiple correlation studies, have been considerably abbreviated here, on the assumption that most of the readers of this volume are not sufficiently trained in mathematical statistics to comprehend all details of the original. It is hoped that this sampling of diverse research methods will spur the student to achieve a greater mastery of such statistical methods; if he is curious about further details of these studies he should examine the original articles, which include some analysis, interpretation and qualification, as well as some data, that are omitted here.

It will be noted that these studies differ considerably in the types of data on crime which they employ. For example, some refer exclusively to "delinquency," while others speak of "crime," and the first article refers to both. "Crime" is a legal term which designates all types of behavior for which

persons may lawfully be punished in a society. "Delinquency"
is another legal term, in many respects of even broader and
more complex reference than "crime." First of all, delinquency includes any criminal acts committed by persons
designated as "juvenile" because they are below a specific
age, usually 18. However, it also encompasses a variety of
behavior not prohibited to adults but which may lead to state
intervention if committed by juveniles, on the assumption
that these forms of behavior are conducive to crime. For
example, running away from home, truancy from school, and
being otherwise disobedient to parents or teachers are forms
of behavior which adults can pursue with impunity, but
which may lead to a juvenile's being brought into court and
perhaps even committed to a correctional institution. Finally,
it should be noted that an immense amount of discretion is
left to the courts in determining whether a specific act should
be called "delinquency." Even the age boundary is flexible in
most states, so that there is a range in age—for example, 14
to 18—in which a person committing a criminal act may
either be adjudged delinquent or be tried as an adult criminal,
as the court sees fit. Each of these two alternatives gives the
court a different choice of methods for trying to protect society by restricting the offender's freedom—and for trying
to reform the offender.

In addition to the distinction between crime and delinquency, there is a tremendous variety of behavior en-
compassed within the term "crime." Most often connoted as
"criminal" are predatory acts, those which have a clearly
identifiable victim, such as theft, assault, burglary, forgery,
rape, and murder. Sometimes these are distinguished im-
perfectly as "serious crime" or "felonies," for they are the
acts which elicit most of the severe penalties imposed by the
courts. State penalties are much less severe but much more
frequent for crimes which have no clear victim, such as disorderly conduct and public drunkenness.

The preceding paragraphs differentiated offenses on the
basis of the most frequently employed official distinctions,
but it should be noted that most crime never comes to the
attention of official agencies. This includes many crimes

(already described) which are never reported to the police, as well as the much less frequently reported illegal service and illegal consumption crimes, such as off-track horserace gambling, prostitution, and the sale or possession of narcotics. Finally, there is a large variety of illegal misrepresentation in selling, falsification of expense and tax accounts, collusion in bidding, and other "white collar crimes" which have become common practices in much business activity; they could be lawfully punished, but they seldom are prosecuted. The reports presented here thus differ not only in whether they are concerned with delinquency or with crime as a whole, but they also include some studies based on official statistics and some based on other types of evidence on the distribution of crime or delinquency.[1]

Karl Christiansen of the University of Copenhagen presents the unusually complete and accurate official statistics of his native Denmark, and summarizes statistical studies in many other countries, to show the interrelationships of both urbanization and industrialization to crime and delinquency. Reiss and Rhodes present an exhaustive analysis of the relationship between social class and delinquency in an urban area, using both official statistics (delinquency cases reported to the juvenile court) and interviews during which schoolboys admitted committing various delinquent acts. Clark and Wenninger compare delinquency rates in three types of urban school districts and in one rural area by unsigned questionnaires. It should be pointed out that in a separate study, Clark and Tifft demonstrated rather conclusively, by using a lie-detector, that such self-reports are quite reliable and complete.[2]

All of the remaining articles rely exclusively on official statistics, but of different types. Eberts and Schwirian rely on "crimes known to the police." This is the most complete official record of the criminality in a city, especially for predatory crimes, since officials know about crimes mostly from those victims who seek help. Robins and Hill used police and juvenile court records to procure lifetime delinquency rates for a group of Negro boys selected initially from records of admission to the first grade in ghetto schools, then traced in official records throughout their childhood and adolescence. They show that in this setting the correlates of early delinquency are different from the correlates of delinquency that begins at a relatively older age. Sarah Boggs is concerned with the geographical relationship between residences of urban criminals and the location of their crimes, so she uses both crimes known to the police and "crimes cleared by arrest," since only for the latter can she know the residences of the offenders. Gordon summarizes studies based on the home addresses of delinquents who have records in juvenile courts; he is concerned with the ecological correlates of delinquency.

In reviewing the conclusions of these studies there may be some merit in considering them in reverse order, for this reveals that complex statistical methods do not necessarily yield the most complex conclusions. In a highly technical analysis, most of which we have not included here, Gordon demonstrates that all of the studies he surveyed made serious errors in their use of the complex statistical procedure known as factor analysis, and in their rather arbitrary choices of indexes and cutting points for the variables they were investigating. He concludes that, contrary to the claims of some, all these studies show only that an urban neighborhood's official delinquency rate is most consistently a function of the poverty in the neighborhood.

The study by Boggs is unique for it relates crime to the criminal opportunities available in the neighborhood where the crime occurs, which is considered separately from the neighborhood where the criminal resides. Different kinds of crime occur in different kinds of neighborhoods. Sarah Boggs explains the location of crime as primarily a function of either the profit in crime in a particular area or the familiarity of offenders with the neighborhood. Again, a highly complex statistical procedure yields rather simple conclusions.

Robins and Hill find that early delinquency of Negro ghetto boys is most closely related to family status and to school adjustment, but not to the absence of a father from the home. However, these correlates of early delinquency were not found related to delinquency after age 15, when problems of adolescence and of race may become more significant.

The study by Eberts and Schwirian is distinguished by its concern not just with poverty as a variable related to crime, but with relative deprivation—an individual's sense of his own poverty. They assume that this sense of deprivation reflects the disparity of income distribution in a community more than the actual poverty there, and they find that this disparity is, indeed, a correlate of crime. Crime rates are highest in a given metropolitan area either when the proportion of the population earning unusually high incomes or the proportion earning unusually low income is greatest; crime is lowest when incomes are most evenly distributed. This relationship of crime to disparity of income distribution occurs especially in large metropolitan areas, in those with high non-white populations, and in those where the largest proportion of whites and the smallest proportion of non-whites are in white-collar jobs.

Clark and Wenninger checked findings by other researchers who concluded that self-admitted delinquency by juveniles in small cities is not significantly associated with the occupational status of the parents. They found this to be the case within any separate neighborhood, but they found delinquency more frequent and qualitatively different in a neighborhood of predominantly low occupational status and low income, as compared with neighborhoods where the occupational status was either mixed or predominantly high. Clark and Wenninger also found distinctly lower rates and different types of delinquency in a poor rural area.

Reiss and Rhodes also found that delinquency varies inversely with the average occupational status of an urban neighborhood, especially for neighborhoods homogeneous with respect to social class. However, they found that the delinquents oriented to criminal careers were almost exclusively located in the lowest status areas, although most delinquents in all areas were more oriented to delinquency as a peer-group activity than as a career. These, and additional details, provide interesting tests for prevailing theories of delinquency, as do the Clark and Wenninger findings.

The Christiansen study employs essentially a natural history approach, the first step in science,[3] which is an attempt to classify and chart without complex theory. The Reiss and

Rhodes, Clark and Wenninger, Robins and Hill, and Eberts and Schwirian studies represent the hypothetical and deductive stage in science, whereby complex theories are formulated from which objective tests are deduced and carried out.[4] The Boggs study and those reviewed by Gordon represent still another stage—made especially feasible by the computer— which greatly reduces the labor of statistical analysis. The multifactor statistical methods employed by them were not just designed to test theories on interrelationships, but also to "fish for them." Although more or less extensive and systematic theorizing may determine the selection of variables for study by these methods, the search for statistical interrelationships is mechanical, and *ad hoc;* theories must often be developed speculatively to account for the relationships which the statistical computations reveal.

INDUSTRIALIZATION AND URBANIZATION IN RELATION TO CRIME AND JUVENILE DELINQUENCY

Karl O. Christiansen

F R O M A crimino-political point of view, the most urgent social and psychological problems that have arisen since the Second World War have been the increases in crime and juvenile delinquency. Most of the European countries, the United States of America, Australia, and countries of Asia and Africa, have reported great increases in the rate of juvenile delinquency and crime, and the newspapers have given much prominence to these phenomena. Hooliganism, teen-age violence and youth riots have frequently been reported in newspapers and periodicals. Some of these reports undoubtedly exaggerate the situation, but it cannot be denied that, since the Second World War, juvenile delinquency has shown an upward trend in most countries.

· · ·

The relationship between industrialization and urbanization, on the one hand, and the rate of criminality on the other, provides a challenging area of inquiry, and an analysis of this relationship could perhaps shed some light on the factors contributing to the increase in juvenile delinquency.

· · ·

Abbreviated with permission of the author and publisher from *International Review of Criminal Policy*, No. 16 (October, 1960), United Nations ST/SOA, series M/16, pp. 3–8.

Industrialization is a term generally used to connote development characterized by an increasing utilization of mechanical power in production, transportation and other economic activities. Up to 1770 industrialization was a rather slow process, but during the last one hundred and fifty years it has been accelerated to a remarkable degree; yet we are most probably still at the beginning of a far-reaching evolution.

One measure of industrialization is the percentage of manpower available for work in factories. Also it should be borne in mind that in many countries nowadays a relatively large part of agricultural work has been taken over by machines. This means that the process of industrialization has not only helped to draw people to industrial centres, but has also enabled an ever smaller proportion of the population to grow the food for all the rest.

Urbanization is a more complex and less precise term. It may roughly be defined as the development towards a higher concentration of the population in towns and cities. So far, industrialization has been an important factor in the trend towards urbanization, but it has not been the only influence at work.

Some seven or eight thousand years ago, or even earlier, the first big cities arose in the rich valleys of the Nile, Tigris, Euphrates and Indus. Important to this development were the existence of rich agricultural hinterlands, of means of transportation, manufacturing and—consequently—of intense urban division of labour, military protection or military compulsion, concentration of religious services in the cities and—even in those early days—some recreation and entertainment facilities.

From a purely demographic point of view, urbanization may be defined in such a way as to be measurable by the density of the population, the size of the population in absolute figures, and the size of the area.[1] In most studies, however, the distinction between rural and urban areas is made arbitrarily in terms of the absolute population alone. . . .

Moreover, the term "urbanization" is used in different senses. For instance, when sociologists and criminologists speak of urbanization they do not only or primarily refer to the high concentration of a large number of people within a given area. To them "urban" and "urbanized" are terms which connote *a certain way of life*. Urbanization is the corresponding development towards such a way of life. It is not a demographic concept, but a sociological one, and is more specifically a concept drawn from the sociology of cultural changes.

. . .

Investigations of the relationship between industrialization, and urbanization on the one hand and delinquency on the other may be conducted along three main lines.

LONG-TERM VARIATIONS IN CRIME RATES

It is a well-established fact that industrialization and urbanization have increased to a considerable degree in many countries for more than a hundred years. Over the same period, the long-term trend of delinquency and crime in the same countries has shown a corresponding increase, although short-term variations (for instance, periods of depression or war) may have interfered now and then to disturb the picture. This correlation may yield some support to the hypothesis that increasing urbanization will cause an increase in crime, but a statistical correlation is certainly not absolute proof, and long-term variations in the crime rates may be otherwise explained. During a period of five to ten decades, other factors which have not been observed or analysed may influence the development.

. . . In Denmark during the last hundred years, the proportion of people living in cities has increased from 20 per cent in 1840–50 to 50 per cent in 1950–55. During the same period, the crime rate has increased from 180 to 340 per 100,000 population. The trend of crime has taken a much more irregular course, however, than the trend of urbanization.

. . .

. . . Urbanization reduces the possibilities of social control, and it is generally assumed that the urbanized citizen will therefore yield more easily to illegal temptations than does his rural counterpart. This poses questions as to whether temptations to the commission of crime have increased with the growth of industrialization and urbanization, and what new forms such temptations have assumed. In general, it may be asked what relationship exists between industrialization, urbanization and temptations to crime.

It would not be surprising if there were found to be a positive relationship between urbanization and industrialization on the one hand, and the growth of temptations to crime on the other. For instance, the possibilities of stealing vehicles may be compared over periods of time.

An increase in the temptations to crime may also form part of the explanation of the considerable increase in juvenile delinquency in many countries after the last war. The increase has also been explained in some countries as being an after-effect of the war, inasmuch as the juvenile offenders of today are those children who were brought up during the war under conditions of great social disorganization. Family life was virtually destroyed and hence many of these young people grew up with little education, supervision and control. Further, many of the parents of these children were themselves the products of the disorganization of the First World War and themselves suffered from a poor upbringing.

COMPARISONS OF CRIME RATES IN URBAN AND RURAL SOCIETIES

To compare crime rates in urban and rural societies is another and more convincing way of studying the problem. With a few exceptions, statistical studies have shown that the frequency of crime and delinquency is several times higher in cities than in rural areas and furthermore—although with more exceptions—that the larger the city the higher the rate that may be expected. The following figures, for example, are quoted from Danish criminal statistics.

Male Crime Rates per 100,000 of the Male Population over 15 Years of Age

	Copenhagen	Provincial Towns	Rural Areas
1939	623	492	198
1955	679	614	221

It appears that the difference in crime rates between the capital and the provincial towns has lessened, while the difference between rural and urban areas remains considerable. This development may perhaps be explained by the larger proportion of urbanized people now living in the provincial towns as compared with before the war, or by their higher degree of urbanization.

The rate of criminality for the urban areas is, however, much higher than that for the rural areas even though the latter has also increased.

The juvenile delinquency rates in Denmark in 1955 for males show roughly the same rural-urban differences.

Male Delinquency Rates in 1955 per 100,000 of the Population in the Respective Male Age-Groups

Age Group	Copenhagen	Provincial Towns	Rural Areas
18-20	1,882	1,932	598
21-24	1,603	1,684	616

The explanation of these differences is not easy. Reckless, in his studies of societies with frequent and infrequent crime,[2] notes that

societies with low crime and delinquency rates are societies of relative isolation, with little mobility of population, little change, homogeneity of population in race and culture, little institutional disorganization, minimum differentiation in classes and social groups, a single system of customary rules or a single code of customs, and a high degree of control over their members

and that the societies with the highest crime rates are

those that seem to have large-scale outside contacts, to manifest great mobility, flux and change, to contain a heterogeneous population in race and culture as well as considerable differentiations in class levels and specialized social groups, to present several systems of norms for conduct as manifest by the clash of the rules of the dominant legal and moral order with the behaviour standards of many subdominant groups, and to exercise at best a limited social control over the behavior of individuals.

Clinard[3] mentions mobility, impersonal relations, differential association, non-participation in community organizations, organized criminal culture, and a criminal social type as urban characteristics. Most of these factors may be considered as different aspects of urbanization in the sociological meaning of the term.

To put it briefly, one could say that the sociological explanation of the difference between cities and rural districts with respect to delinquency and crime has stressed two main points: the degree of isolation, and the degree of homogeneity of the population from both a biological and a sociological point of view.

Psychiatrists tend to explain the urban-rural differences in law-breaking and other social deviations by differences in specific personality traits which are supposed to characterize people in rural and urban societies. This hypothesis, however, is based also on data from the third type of investigation and will therefore be discussed below.

COMPARISONS OF DIFFERENT AREAS WITHIN A CITY

During the last thirty years a number of ecological investigations have been carried out in the United States and in several other countries. These investigations show that the rates of delinquency and crime vary widely in different neighbourhoods, and that the rates are generally highest in the centre or near the centre of the city.

The classical studies in this field are two investigations carried out in Chicago by Shaw and McKay (1929 and 1942).[4] The latter investigation is based on an analysis of statistics on juvenile delinquency. The following conclusions were reached: (1) Delinquency is very unevenly distributed in the city of Chicago—namely, from zero in one neighbourhood to 26 per cent of the juveniles in another neighbourhood against whom penal complaints had been lodged in a single year. In several other areas, more than one-fifth of the boys had been arrested in one year. (2) Delinquency is highest in the low-rent areas near the central part of the city. Delinquency rates are also high near commercial and industrial sub-centres. (3) The delinquency rate decreases with the distance from the centre. (4) High juvenile delinquency areas also have high crime rates in the adult age-groups. (5) Areas with high delinquency rates for boys also have high rates for girl delinquency. (6) One of the striking facts is that the same neighbourhoods had remained the most delinquent ones throughout a thirty-year period in spite of radical changes in nationalities and racial composition of the population. When German and Swedish immigrants at the beginning of this century moved into the centre of the city their children had high rates of delinquency. Twenty to thirty years later these immigrants were replaced by Poles and Italians, whose delinquency rates very soon reached the same level.

Ecological studies in a number of other American cities have revealed a more or less similar pattern of distribution of delinquency and crime.

Sutherland points out that two principal interpretations of the concentration of delinquents near the industrial and commercial centres of large American cities have been presented.

The first is in terms of social organization in the neighbourhood. The areas of concentration in large American cities, and especially Chicago, where the problem has been studied most intensively, are areas of physical deterioration, congested population, decreasing population, economic dependency, rented homes, foreign and Negro population, and few institutions supported by the local residents. Lawlessness has become traditional; adult criminals are frequently seen and have much prestige. . . . Delinquencies begin here at an early age and maturity in crime is reached at an early age. Boys fourteen or fifteen years of age steal automobiles and commit robberies with sawn-off shotguns. . . . At the same time the anti-delinquent influences are few, and organized opposition to delinquency is weak. Parent-teacher associations do not exist, nor do other community organizations which are supported principally by the people of the neighbourhood. Because the population is mobile and heterogeneous, it is unable to act with concert in dealing with its own problems.[5]

Psychiatrists and some psychologists will argue that in such areas the population is segregated on the basis of rent-paying ability, and that this involves a selection of the constitutionally inferior. In such areas three types of resident are found: recent immigrants, remnants of the earlier residential groups, and failures in the better residential districts who have been forced to move back into the cheaper rent areas. Here also is found the highest incidence of backward children, of feeble-minded and insane persons, and most psychopaths. Consequently, delinquency and crime are characteristics of the population living in such areas.

Sutherland, in his discussion of these different points of view, emphasizes that the most important finding is that the delinquency rate remained practically constant over a thirty-year period in spite of an almost complete change in the national composition of the population.[6] This would indicate that the delinquency rate is a function related to the area rather than to the type of people who reside there.

·   ·   ·

The statistics that have been presented previously indicate that there are significant rural-urban differences in the volume of crime committed. The question then arises as to whether there are qualitative differences as well, and whether there are significant differences in the type of crime committed in towns and rural districts.

A number of investigations show that offences against property are *relatively* more frequent in cities than in the country. On the other hand, crimes of violence and sexual crimes are *relatively* more frequent in rural areas. It is necessary to stress the word "relatively." It means that if, for instance, 100 criminal acts are committed in towns and cities in Denmark, more than 80 of these will be offences against property and only 10 to 15 will be crimes against the person. Of 100 criminal acts committed in rural areas in Denmark, only about 75 will be property offences and about 20 will be crimes of violence and sexual crimes. However, as the crime rates are three times higher in urban than in rural areas, the rates for all these different offences will be higher in the cities.

Among the crimes against property, theft prevails in all parts of the country, while fraud, embezzlement and similar offences are much more frequent in the cities than in the rural districts.

.   .   .

A modest but rather safe conclusion which could be drawn from the studies on urbanization and crime is that it is not unlikely that the long-term trend of delinquency and crime, which is clearly on the increase, may be considered as partly related to industrialization and urbanization. Nevertheless, the rise in juvenile delinquency after the war cannot be wholly explained in this way. Influential factors of another type also play an important role.

It may, however, be predicted that countries where the process of industrialization and urbanization continues—and this holds true of most if not all countries of the world—have to expect a further increase in crime and delinquency.

.   .   .

THE DISTRIBUTION OF JUVENILE DELINQUENCY IN THE SOCIAL CLASS STRUCTURE

Albert J. Reiss, Jr. and Albert Lewis Rhodes

A NUMBER of theories of deviating behavior and juvenile delinquency posit social class variation in rates of delinquency, particularly gang delinquency, such that the lowest social stratum has the highest delinquency rate.[1] The validity of this postulate is questioned by some who maintain that middle and high status persons have a much higher rate of delinquency than is shown in a statistical test of the hypothesis.[2] These critics demonstrate that the data of law enforcement or judicial agencies give biased estimates of a true rate of delinquency in the population. They suggest that the delinquency life chances are equal for all socioeconomic status groups. The apparently higher rate of the low socioeconomic status group is due solely to the fact that agencies of social control are more likely to classify them as delinquents.[3] This paper is an attempt to shed some light on this disagreement by providing evidence on variation in white male delinquency rates among the social classes of the Nashville, Tennessee Standard Metropolitan Area.

Abbreviated with permission of the authors and publisher from *American Sociological Review*, Vol. 26, No. 5 (October, 1961), 720–731. Published by the American Sociological Association.

This paper was read at the American Sociological Association Meetings, New York City, August 29, 1960. The research was performed pursuant to a contract with the United States Office of Education, Department of Health, Education, and Welfare.

THE STUDY

Nine thousand two hundred thirty-eight white boys, 12 years old and over, and registered in one of the public, private or parochial junior or senior high schools of Davidson County, Tennessee during the 1957 school year comprise the base population. . . .

Limiting the population of boys to those still in school does not bias our conclusions about differentials in delinquency rates among social categories, but it does not permit us to estimate precisely the magnitude of these differences. The rate of delinquency is higher for out-of-school than for in-school boys since out-of-school boys are on the average older, of lower IQ and social status than are in-school boys. Below it is shown that the rate of delinquency is higher for older boys, lower status boys, and dropouts. The rate for out-of-school boys and hence the rate for all adolescent boys must be higher than the observed rate for in-school boys alone. Confidence in the observed differences presented in this paper is therefore justified since the inclusion of the out-of-school groups would increase the magnitude of the observed differences.

A cross-section sample of boys age 12–16 was also selected, since almost all boys in the county from this age group are still in school. Self-reports of delinquent acts were secured from each of these boys by means of a personal interview. A boy from this sample was classified as a delinquent person if on the basis of these self-reports, his acts would have classified him as a delinquent person by juvenile court criteria of delinquency or, if he had been classified as a delinquent person by the court. This cross section sample provides the data for the final section of the paper.

Three status groups were defined in terms of the occupation of the head of the household.

Low Status. All laborers, including farm laborers, operatives and kindred workers, service workers (except protective service workers), and peddlers and door-to-door salesmen.

Middle Status. All craftsmen, foremen and kindred workers, clerical and kindred workers, protective service workers, managers and proprietors of small business, sales workers of wholesale and retail stores, and technicians allied to the professional services.

High Status.   All managers, officials, and proprietors, and professional, and semiprofessional workers not included in the middle status category, and sales workers in finance, insurance, and real estate.

. . . In some tables, data are reported for only two status positions to increase the number of cases within subgroups created by the detailed breakdown of other variables cross-classified with status. The dichotomous class of *white collar status* includes all "high status" and "middle status" subjects *except* craftsmen, foremen, and kindred workers and protective service workers while *blue collar status* includes these exceptions plus all "low status" subjects.

Delinquency rates of residential areas were calculated for the in-school population of an area. These delinquency rates are based on the combined total of official and unofficial cases known to the juvenile court.

The social status structure of residential areas in the United States varies considerably. Some are quite homogeneous in class status while others tend to be more representative of the class structure of American society. Residential areas, therefore, vary considerably in opportunities for cross-class contacts, institutional access to legitimate and illegitimate means, and so on. . . .

The operational definition of the social status structure of a residential area is the distribution derived from aggregating the data for the ascribed status position of pupils in schools. Seven types of social status context were defined in this way. More than one school is included within each of the contexts.

1. *Upper and Upper Middle Status Context:*   Approximately 60 per cent of all student have fathers classified as old or new professionals, managers, officials and proprietors, and 90 per cent are from white collar origins (6 schools).
2. *Balanced Upper and Lower Middle Status Context:*   Approximately 90 per cent are from white collar origins with roughly an equal balance between top and bottom white collar occupations (6 schools).

3. *Crosscuts Social Status Structure: Overrepresentation at Top Context:*   Crosscut criterion,[4] plus 15 per cent more than expected in the top two occupation groups of the six major white-collar occupation groups (7 schools).

4. *Crosscuts Social Status Structure: Overrepresentation at Center Context:*   Crosscut criterion, plus 15 per cent more than expected in the two "center" occupation groups of the six major white-collar occupation categories (4 schools).

5. *Representative of All Schools Context:*   Within 2 per cent of the distribution for all schools (4 schools).

6. *Crosscuts Social Status Structure: Overrepresentation at Bottom Context:*   Crosscut criterion, plus 15 per cent more than expected in the bottom two of the four major blue-collar occupation groups (7 schools).

7. *Lower Social Status Context:*   Approximately 75 per cent are in blue collar occupations with 50 per cent in the lowest of the four major blue-collar occupation groups (5 schools).

.   .   .

VARIATION IN DELINQUENCY RATES BY SOCIAL STATUS STRUCTURES AND RESIDENTIAL RATES OF DELINQUENCY

Sociological theories which maintain that delinquency is primarily a lower class phenomenon differ in their explanatory use of the social class concept. The cultural transmission-differential association theorists view delinquency as behavior which is learned from other delinquents in residential areas where there is an established delinquent culture and organization. Although they usually describe the residential areas supporting a delinquent culture as "lower class," "slum" or "disorganized" areas, it can be inferred from their theory that delinquency rates should be high for *all* social class groups resident in high delinquency areas of a city.[5] Albert K. Cohen defines the social class variable as generating a delinquent gang subculture. His "status frustration" hypothesis holds that subcultural delinquency is a reaction-formation against a middle-class organized status dilemma in which the lower-class boy suffers status frustrations in competition with middle status boys. The delinquent subculture provides a solu-

tion to these problems when boys who are similarly frustrated
interact together, by conferring status on the frustrated boys.[6]
Following Cohen's reasoning, one would deduce that: (1)
lower status boys, regardless of their residential location,
should generate subcultural delinquency (and perhaps the
highest rate of all delinquency as well) if they interact and,
(2) that the rate of subcultural delinquency among low
status boys who interact should be higher in areas and
schools where they are in direct competition with middle
status ones (the competition is presumably more intense)
and the lowest in the monolithic low-status area. A test of
these hypotheses and the deductions from them is made
below.

The effects of social class status stem from two principal
sources so far as the adolescent in our society is concerned.
One source is the status of his family in the larger society,
e.g., whether he is middle or lower class, regardless of where
he resides. This is sometimes referred to as his mass society
status position. The other major effect of status is the status
structure of the school and residential community. It may be
one thing to be a low status boy in a primarily low status
school or community and quite another to be one in a school
which crosscuts the class structure or in one of a primarily
high status composition. The first status component is referred to as his *ascribed social status* since his status position
is that of the family status in the social structure. The second
component is referred to as the *social status structure* of the
school (and usually therefore of the residential community
in American cities). The purpose of our investigation is to
learn whether both of these components independently affect
the rate of delinquency consistent with deductions from the
Cohen and differential association theories and, in turn,
whether the effect of the rate of delinquency of an area is independent of both status components in delinquency.

Variation in delinquency rates for the ascribed social status
position of boys and the social status structure of schools is
described in Table 1. Delinquency rates, in general, vary inversely with the prestige component of the social status structure of the school (except for the Crosscut: Center schools)

TABLE 1. *Rate of Delinquency per 100 White School Boys Calculated Separately for All Offenses[a] and All Offenses with Traffic Offenses Excluded, by Occupational Status of Father and Status Structure of the School*

Status Structure of the School	Occupational Status of Father											
	High			Middle			Low			Total[b]		
	Sub-total	All Offenses	Excl. Traffic	Sub-total	All Offenses	Excl. Traffic	Sub-total	All Offenses	Excl. Traffic	Number	All Offenses	Excl. Traffic
Upper and upper middle	292	3.8	0.7	109	2.8	0.0	6	0.0	0.0	434	3.2	0.5
Balanced middle	389	6.2	2.6	310	5.8	2.0	35	0.0	0.0	749	5.6	2.2
Crosscut: top	567	6.5	3.9	1039	5.9	3.7	372	5.9	4.4	2119	6.1	3.8
Crosscut: center	117	9.4	6.3	446	10.1	6.0	217	9.6	5.8	797	9.7	5.8
Representative of all	160	2.5	1.9	446	6.3	5.3	294	8.5	6.9	965	6.2	5.2
Crosscut: bottom	237	5.5	3.4	1026	9.4	7.5	914	9.2	8.4	2267	8.7	7.3
Lower	52	7.7	6.0	423	15.4	13.5	353	16.4	14.5	847	15.6	13.8
Total	1814	5.7	3.0	3799	8.3	5.7	2191	9.6	7.6	9238	7.8	5.6

[a] Includes all official and unofficial court cases of delinquency other than minor traffic offenses (violation of registration and driver's license laws).

[b] The number of cases for which information on father's occupation is not reported can be obtained by subtraction from the total column of each school prestige status context.

and by the ascribed social status of the boy. The range of variation of ascribed social status is less (3.9 per cent) than that for variation in status structures of schools (12.4 per cent), suggesting that the status structure of the school exercises a greater effect on delinquent behavior than does ascribed social status.[7]

The effect of the occupational status structure of the school on ascribed status position is to alter, for an adolescent in any ascribed status group, the life-chances of becoming a delinquent. The occupational structure of the school "virtually eliminates" the *risk* of being a delinquent of court record for low status boys in schools with a predominantly high status student body and substantially increases the *risk* of a low status boy in a predominantly low status school. The average rate of court recorded delinquency is 9.6 for all low status boys, but in the two top status structures it is zero, while in the lowest one it is over 16 per cent. The effect of the status structure is somewhat less for middle status boys and least marked for high status boys. If all traffic offenses are eliminated, however, the results are as striking for the middle and low status boys and somewhat more clearcut for high status ones. The effect of the social structure of a residential community on the rate of delinquency is virtually to double the rate for any status group in the lowest status context and to bring it to its lowest point (approaching zero) in the highest status context.

.   .   .

At each status level delinquents are *over*represented in some stratification context relative to their representation in that context. Thus, twice as many of the delinquents, as of all boys, are drawn from the low ascribed social status position in the lower status structure context. Correlatively, lower class delinquent are *under*represented in the top stratification contexts. There are, in fact, proportionally fewer delinquents of all status levels in the upper status contexts than would be expected from their status context distribution. The delinquency life-chances of a boy in any ascribed status position also varies with the delinquency rate of the residential area,

TABLE 2. *Rate of Delinquency[a] per 100 White School Boys by Occupational Status of Father and Delinquency Rate of Residential Areas*

Delinquency Rate of Residential Area	Occupational Status of Father											
	High			Middle			Low			Total[b]		
	Delin-quents	Sub-total	Rate per 100	Delin-quents	Sub-total	Rate per 100	Delin-quents	Sub-total	Rate per 100	Delin-quents	Num-ber	Rate per 100
0.0– 1.9	0	298	0.0	3	354	.8	2	213	.9	6	898	.7
2.0– 3.9	3	184	1.6	14	461	3.0	11	313	3.5	28	999	2.8
4.0– 5.9	10	382	2.6	43	1075	4.0	47	776	6.1	106	2358	4.5
6.0– 7.9	12	182	6.6	10	103	9.7	5	80	6.3	28	399	7.0
8.0– 9.9	37	481	7.7	54	726	7.4	30	290	10.3	124	1564	7.9
10.0–11.9	14	114	12.3	44	424	10.4	30	271	11.1	94	874	10.8
12.0–13.9	15	130	11.5	42	322	13.0	10	103	9.7	69	566	12.2
14.0–15.9	2	34	5.9	25	184	13.6	20	138	14.5	49	374	13.1
16.0–17.9	11	80	13.8	49	308	15.9	40	237	16.9	101	635	15.9
18.0 and over	3	37	8.1	52	299	17.4	43	222	19.4	101	566	17.8
Total	107	1922	5.6	336	4258	7.9	238	2644	9.0	707	9238	7.7

[a] Includes all official and unofficial court cases of delinquency other than minor traffic offenses (violation of registration and driver's license laws).

[b] The number of cases for which information on father's occupation is not reported can be obtained by subtraction from the total column of each school prestige status context.

as examination of Table 2 shows. In both the low and high rate delinquency areas, the probability that a boy will be a delinquent varies inversely with his status position. This means that in low and in high delinquency areas, the low status boy has the greatest chance of becoming delinquent, although, to be sure, his chances are only one in a hundred in the low delinquency area, while they are one in five in the high delinquency areas. The relationship is less clear for the areas with "average" rates of delinquency where the probability of being a delinquent is almost as great for high as low status boys.

The joint effects of the delinquency rate of an area and its social status structure on the delinquency rate of ascribed status positions must be investigated to clarify the effect of these variables on the delinquency life-chances of a boy. Within each ascribed status group, the delinquency rate usually rises with the delinquency rate of the area regardless of the social status composition of the area. . . . In every status stratification context, the chances that a high, middle or low status boy will be a delinquent are greater if he resides in a high than in a low delinquency rate area. Both the occupational stratification of the area and the delinquency rate of residential areas, then, are independent sources of variation in the rate of delinquency for ascribed social status groups.

.   .   .   .

IMPLICATIONS FOR DELINQUENCY THEORY

At this point we have several empirical findings that may be related to the major theories of delinquency causation. First, it is clear that there is no simple relationship between ascribed social status and delinquency. Both the status structure of an area and the extent to which delinquency occurs as a cultural tradition affect the delinquency life-chances of a boy at each ascribed status level. While the life-chances of low ascribed status boys becoming delinquent are greater than those of high status ones, a low status boy in a predominantly high status area with a low rate of delinquency has almost no chance of being classified a juvenile court delinquent. In this latter situation, the delinquency life-chances of a high status boy are greater than for low status boys.[8]

Likewise, there does not seem to be much evidence that the lower class boy is more likely to be delinquent the more he is subjected to pressure from middle-class norms. The more the lower class boy is in a minority in the school and residential community,[9] the less likely is he to become delinquent.[10] What seems more apparent is that the largest proportion of delinquents for any status group comes from the more homogeneous status areas for that group and that the delinquency life-chances of *all* status groups tend to be greatest in the lower status area and in the high delinquency rate areas.

Examination of the data in Table 2 lends some support to Miller's thesis that delinquency (violative behavior) is normative in lower class culture while conformity (nonviolative behavior) is normative in middle class culture. Yet a number of facts in the table do not support Miller's position as he has formulated it.[11] The more important of these are: (1) delinquency does not appear to be normative in all lower class areas if the rate is taken as an indicator of a norm; (2) substantial numbers of delinquents come from residential areas where the majority of residents are from other than the lower class; (3) high status boys in the three top status contexts have somewhat higher delinquency rates than middle or low status boys. It is possible for Miller to rationalize these exceptions with his more general formulation. He holds that lower class culture is seldom found in its pure form in most residential areas. Consequently, the rate in a residential area is not a simple function of class culture, but of both the relative prevalence of the classes in an area and the extent to which the class culture of each is diffused to the other.

The third major conclusion which seems warranted at this point is that the factors related to where a family of a given ascribed status will live are important in predicting the delinquency life-chances of a boy of any ascribed status. The evidence seems to be consistent with what we already know but have not generally incorporated in our theory—that lower class status is not a necessary and sufficient set of conditions in the etiology of any type of delinquency. Rather, we know there are some lower class areas of large American cities that consistently produce a high volume of all delinquency and most of the systematically organized career delinquency, while other lower class areas, particularly rural ones, do not. The theoretical problem is: *why should delinquency be so widespread in some lower class areas, and not in others?* Cloward and Ohlin suggest that variation in the availability of both legitimate and illegitimate opportunity structures is crucial in determining the delinquency orientation of lower class boys in status dilemmas.[12] There probably are other community conditions as well which account for these differences.

SUBCULTURAL DELINQUENCY

Gang delinquency is generally viewed as a lower class phenomenon, although Cohen and Short suggest that only some subcultural forms of gang delinquency are a distinctly lower class phenomenon.[13] An attempt was made to learn whether the "parent delinquent subculture" is largely a lower class phenomenon. It is difficult, however, to test for the hypothesized distribution given lack of precision in the theoretical formulation, for this, in turn, generates problems of operationalization.

A two per cent sample of white boys, ages 10 to 16 (158 cases) and their first two sociometric choices was selected and interviewed intensively on their career orientations and delinquency history. The interview population was classified into seven major types of conforming-deviating behavior using eight major variables: (1) achievement orientation in school and vocational aspirations; (2) conforming or deviating behavior score of sociometric choices; (3) whether or not the sociometric choices were reciprocated; (4) whether or not time was spent with peers in the evening; (5) the quality of supervision offered in leisure situations; (6) the usual type of delinquent offense committed by the boy and his associates in delinquent acts; (7) the pattern of delinquent activity; (8) the teacher's rating of the boy's behavior in the school and community. Chart 1 briefly outlines the ideal typical characteristics for defining each of the seven conforming-deviating subtypes.

Cohen characterizes the delinquent subculture as having a non-utilitarian, malicious, and negativistic emphasis. Participants in the gang have a versatile content to their delinquent offenses. The group, rather than the individual, is autonomous. The study design operationalized each of these characteristics of the subculture but the measures generally failed to achieved sufficient discrimination to isolate such a subtype.[14]

The "most delinquent" person in the classification schema developed for this study is based on the conception of the career delinquent as advanced by E. W. Burgess, Clifford Shaw and E. H. Sutherland, among others. The career delinquent is one whose achievement orientation is that of the adult criminal. He is a member of a gang that maintains contacts with adult criminals. Most career oriented delinquents probably would be classified as participants in Cohen's parent delinquent subculture, but the class would not exhaust his subcultural category.

The other major type of group delinquent in this investigation is called the peer oriented delinquent, since these boys are essentially peer oriented and peer directed in their goals and activity. Though the boys do band together in delinquent activity, the delinquency is primarily a consequence of orientation toward other group goals. The "lone delinquent" is classified as a non-conforming isolate.

Conformers are divided into four subtypes; two subtypes are classified primarily on the basis of their achievement orientation, one on the absence of peer affiliation, and a fourth on the basis of overconformity to social norms.

The social class distribution of each of the conforming-deviating subtypes is presented below. There is a sizeable sampling error for the estimates, since there are but 158 cases representing a two per cent random sample of the population of boys. Nevertheless, several predicted findings

CHART 1. Classification of Seven Types of Conformers or Deviators Based on Eight Principle Criteria of Classifcation

Type of Conformer or Deviator	Achievement Orientation	Sociometric Choices	Reciprocation of Sociometric Choices	Time with Peers in Evening	Leisure Time in Supervised Situations	Usual Delinquent Offenses	Content of Delinquent Offenses	Teacher's Rating
Organized career delinquent	Low	Delinquent peers and adult criminals	Yes	Regularly	None	Serious	Versatile	School behavior problem or trouble maker
Peer oriented delinquent	Low	Delinquent peers	Yes	Regularly	None	Petty (some serious)	Versatile	Poorly motivated and school behavior problem
Conforming nonachiever	Low	Conforming peers	Yes	Occasionally	Mostly	Minor infractions	Conventional infractions	Poorly motivated or conformer
Conforming achiever	High	Conforming peers	Yes	Occasionally	Always	Rare	—	Conformer

	Any level	Few or none	No reciprocation	Never	Alone or family only	Serious or petty	Specialized or versatile	School behavior problem or trouble maker
Nonconforming isolate	Any level	Few or none	No reciprocation	Never	Alone or family only			
Conforming isolate	Any level	Few or none	No reciprocation	Never	Alone or family only	None	—	Poorly motivated or conformer
Hyperconformer	High	Other hyperconformers	Yes	Rare	Always	None	—	Conformer

emerge from the data: (1) There is more frequent and serious delinquent deviation in the lower than in the middle stratum when the self-reports of delinquent deviation by boys are examined; this is true in fact for all classes of deviators—career and peer oriented delinquents, nonconforming isolates and conforming nonachievers; (2) The career oriented delinquent is found only among lower class boys; (3) Peer oriented delinquency is the most common form of delinquent organization at both status levels; (4) The major type of lower status boy is a conforming nonachiever while the conforming achiever is the major type in the middle class; (5) Conformers are more likely to be isolates than are non-conformers; the lone delinquent is infrequent in a population of boys.

	Per Cent
Career Oriented Delinquent	
Blue-collar	1.3
White-collar	0.0
Peer-Oriented Delinquent	
Blue-collar	4.5
White-collar	1.3
Conforming Nonachiever	
Blue-collar	31.3
White-collar	3.3
Conforming Achiever	
Blue-collar	12.0
White-collar	29.3
Hyperconformer	
Blue-collar	3.9
White-collar	2.0
Nonconforming Isolate	
Blue-collar	0.6
White-collar	0.6
Conforming Isolates	
Blue-collar	8.6
White-collar	1.3

One other important finding emerges from these comparisons. Conforming isolates are more frequent in the blue- than in the white-collar stratum. If it is assumed that in many lower class areas, the pressures of groups are toward nonconforming activities then at least in these communities isolation from the group may be a price of social conformity. There is much more support for group organized conventional behavior in middle class areas.

SOCIO-ECONOMIC CLASS AND AREA AS CORRELATES OF ILLEGAL BEHAVIOR AMONG JUVENILES

John P. Clark and Eugene P. Wenninger

U N T I L recently almost all efforts to discover characteristics that differentiate juveniles who violate legal norms from those who do not have compared institutional and non-institutional populations. Though many researchers still employ a "delinquent" or "criminal" sample from institutions,[1] there is a growing awareness that the process through which boys and girls are selected to populate our "correctional" institutions may cause such comparison studies to distort seriously the true picture of illegal behavior in our society. Therefore, conclusions based upon such studies are subject to considerable criticism[2] if generalized beyond the type of population of the particular institution at the time of the study. Although the study of adjudicated offenders is important, less encum-

Reprinted with permission of the authors and publisher from *American Sociological Review*, Vol. 27, No. 6 (December, 1962), 826–843. Published by the American Sociological Association.

The total project of which this paper is a part was sponsored by the Ford Foundation and the University of Illinois Graduate Research Board. Professor Daniel Glaser was very helpful throughout the project and in the preparation of this paper.

bered studies of the violation of legal norms hold more promise for those interested in the more general concept of deviant behavior.

Though it, too, has methodological limitations, the anony-
mous-questionnaire procedure has been utilized to obtain results reflecting the rates and patterns of illegal behavior
among juveniles from different social classes, ages, sexes,
and ethnic groups in the general population.[3] The results of
these studies have offered sufficient evidence to indicate that
the patterns of illegal behavior among juveniles may be dramatically different than was heretofore thought to be the
case.

Some of the most provocative findings have been those that
challenge the almost universally-accepted conclusion that the
lower socio-economic classes have higher rates of illegal behavior than do the middle or upper classes. For example,
neither the Nye-Short study[4] nor that of Dentler and Monroe[5]
revealed any significant difference in the incidence of certain
illegal or "deviant" behaviors among occupational-status
levels—a finding quite at odds with most current explanations of delinquent behavior.

Although most of the more comprehensive studies in the
social class tradition have been specifically concerned with
a more-or-less well-defined portion of the lower class (i.e.,
"delinquent gangs,"[6] or "culture of the gang," or "delinquent
subculture"[7]), some authors have tended to generalize their
findings and theoretical formulations rather specifically to
the total lower class population of juveniles.[8] These latter
authors certainly do not profess that *all* lower class children
are equally involved in illegal behavior, but by implication
they suggest that the incidence of illegal conduct (whether
brought to the attention of law enforcement agencies or not)
is more pervasive in this class than others because of some
unique but fundamental characteristics of the lower social
strata. For example, Miller has compiled a list of "focal concerns" toward which the lower class supposedly is oriented
and because of which those in this class violate more legal
norms with greater frequency than other classes.[9] Other
authors point out that the lower classes are disadvantaged in

their striving for legimate goals and that they resort to deviant means to attain them.[10] Again, the result of this behavior is higher rates of illegal behavior among the lower socio-economic classes.

Therefore, there *appears* to be a direct conflict between the theoretical formulations of Miller, Cohen, Merton, Cloward and Ohlin, and those findings reported by Nye and Short and Dentler and Monroe. This apparent discrepancy in the literature can be resolved, however, if one hypothesizes that the rates of illegal conduct among the social classes vary with the type of community[11] in which they are found. Were this so, it would be possible for studies which have included certain types of communities to reveal differential illegal behavior rates among social classes while studies which have involved other types of communities might fail to detect social class differences.

Whereas the findings and formulations of Merton, Cohen, Cloward and Ohlin, and Miller are oriented, in a sense, toward the "full-range" of social situations, those of Nye-Short and Dentler-Monroe are very specifically limited to the types of populations used in their respective studies. It is important to note that the communities in which these latter studies were conducted ranged only from rural to small city in size. As Nye points out, "They are thus urban but not metropolitan."[12] Yet, most studies of "delinquent gangs" and "delinquent subcultures" have been conducted in metropolitan centers where these phenomena are most apparent. Perhaps, it is only here that there is a sufficient concentration of those in the extreme socio-economic classes to afford an adequate test of the "social class hypothesis."

In addition to the matter of social class concentration and size, there is obviously more than one "kind" of lower class and each does not have rates or types of illegal behavior identical to that of the others. For example, most rural farm areas, in which occupations, incomes, and educational levels are indicative of lower class status, as measured by most social class indexes, consistently have been found to have low rates of misconduct—in fact lower than most urban middle class communities.

Therefore, to suggest the elimination of social class as a significant correlate to the quantity and quality of illegal behavior before it has been thoroughly examined in a variety of community situations, seems somewhat premature. Reiss and Rhodes concluded as a result of study of class and juvenile court rates by school district that "it is clear, that there is no simple relationship between ascribed social status and delinquency."[13] In order to isolate the factor of social class, to eliminate possible effects of class bias in the rate of which juvenile misbehavior is referred to court, as well as to vary the social and physical environs in which it is located, we chose in this study to compare rates of admitted illegal behavior among diverse communities within the northern half of Illinois. Our hypotheses were:

1. Significant differences in the incidence of illegal behavior exist among communities differing in predominant social class composition, within a given metropolitan area.
2. Significant differences in the incidence of illegal behavior exist among similar social class strata located in different types of community.
3. Differences in the incidence of illegal behavior among different social class populations within a given community are not significant.

THE STUDY

The data used to test the above hypotheses were gathered in 1961 as part of a larger exploratory study of illegal behavior (particularly theft) among juveniles, and its relationship to socio-economic class, type of community, age, race, and various attitudinal variables, such as attitude toward law, feelings of alienation, concept of self, and feelings of being able to achieve desired goals. Subsequent reports will deal with other aspects of the study.

A total of 1154 public school students from the sixth through the twelfth grades in the school systems of four different types of communities were respondents to a self-administered, anonymous questionnaire given in groups of from 20 to 40 persons by the senior author. Considerable precaution was taken to insure reliability and validity of the responses. For example, assurances were given that the study was not being monitored by the school administration; questions were pretested to eliminate ambiguity; and the administration of the questionnaire was made as threat-free as possible.

The four communities represented in the study were chosen for the unique social class structure represented by each. The Duncan "Socio-Economic Index for All Occupations,"[14] was used to determine the occupational profile of each community by assigning index scores to the occupation of the respondents' fathers. The results are summarized in Table 1.

The overwhelming majority of the respondents comprising the *rural farm* population live on farms, farming being by far the most common occupation of their fathers. Many of the fathers who were not listed as farmers were, in fact, "part-time" farmers. Therefore, though the Duncan Index would classify most of the residents in the lower class, most of these public school children live on farms in a prosperous section of the Midwest. The sixth, seventh, and eighth graders were drawn from schools located in very small villages. Grades 9–12 were drawn from the high school which was located in open-farm land.

The *lower urban* sample is primarily composed of children of those with occupations of near-equal ranking but certainly far different in nature from those of the rural farm community. The lower urban sample was drawn from a school system located in a very crowded and largely-Negro area of Chicago. The fathers (or male head of the family) of these youngsters are laborers in construction, waiters, janitors, clean-up men, etc. Even among those who place relatively high on the Duncan Scale are many who, in spite of their occupational title, reside, work, and socialize almost exclusively in the lower class community.

As Table 1 demonstrates, the occupational structure of the *industrial city* is somewhat more diffuse than the other communities, though consisting primarily of lower class occupations. This city of about 35,000 is largely autonomous, al-

TABLE 1. *Duncan Socio-Economic-Index Scores Based on Occupation of Father*

| | Type of Community | | | | |
Score	Rural Farm %	Lower Urban %	Industrial City %	Upper Urban %
(1) 0–23	75.9	40.4	36.4	5.7
(2) 24–47	9.9	15.5	19.3	4.8
(3) 48–71	4.7	12.5	22.9	43.9
(4) 72–96	1.5	4.2	10.0	34.6
(5) Unclassifiable[a]	8.0	27.4	11.4	11.0
Total	100 (N = 274)	100 (N = 265)	100 (N = 280)	100 (N = 335)

[a] This category included those respondents from homes with no father and those respondents who did not furnish adequate information for reliable classification. The 27.4 per cent figure in the lower urban community reflects a higher proportion of "father-less" homes rather than greater numbers of responses which were incomplete or vague in other ways.

though a small portion of the population commutes daily to Chicago. However, about two-thirds of these students have fathers who work as blue-collar laborers in local industries and services. The median years of formal education of all males age 25 or over is 10.3.[15] The median annual family income is $7,255.[16] The population of this small city contains substantial numbers of Polish and Italian Americans and about fifteen per cent Negroes.

Those in the *upper urban* sample live in a very wealthy suburb of Chicago. Nearly three-fourths of the fathers in these families are high-level executives or professionals. The median level of education for all males age 25 or over is 16 plus.[17] The median annual family income is slightly over $20,000—80 per cent of the families make $10,000 or more annually.[18]

With two exceptions, representative sampling of the public school children was followed within each of these communities: (1) those who could not read at a fourth grade level were removed in all cases, which resulted in the loss of less than one-half per cent of the total sample, and (2) the sixth-grade sample in the industrial city community was drawn from a predominantly Negro, working class area and was, therefore, non-representative of the total community for that grade-level only. All the students from grades six through twelve were used in the rural farm community "sample."

MEASURE OF ILLEGAL BEHAVIOR

An inventory of 36 offenses was initially assembled from delinquency scales, legal statutes, and the FBI Uniform Crime Reports. In addition to this, a detailed list of theft items ranging from candy to automobiles, was constructed. The latter list was later combined into two composite items (minor theft, and major theft) and added to the first list, enlarging the number of items in this inventory to 38 items as shown in Table 2. No questions on sex offenses were included in this study, a restriction found necessary in order to gain entrance into one of the school systems.

All respondents were asked to indicate if they had com-

TABLE 2. *Percentage of Respondents Admitting Individual Offenses and Significance of Differences Between Selected Community Comparisons*

Offense	Community				Significance of Differences[a]		
	(1) Industrial City N=280	(2) Lower Urban N=265	(3) Upper Urban N=335	(4) Rural Farm N=274	(1–2)	(2–3)	(3–4)
1. Did things my parents told me not to do.	90	87	85	82	X	X	X
2. Minor theft (compilation of such items as the stealing of fruit, pencils, lipstick, candy, cigarettes, comic books, money less than $1, etc.)	79	78	80	73	X	X	X
3. Told a lie to my family, principal, or friends.	80	74	77	74	X	X	X
4. Used swearwords or dirty words out loud in school, church, or on the street so other people could hear me.	63	58	54	51	X	X	X
5. Showed or gave someone a dirty picture, a dirty story, or something like that.	53	39	58	54	1	3	X
6. Been out at night just fooling around after I was supposed to be home.	49	50	51	35	X	X	3

7. Hung around other people who I knew had broken the law lots of times or who were known as "bad" people.	49	47	27	40	X	2	4
8. Threw rocks, cans, sticks, or other things at passing car, bicycle, or person.	41	37	33	36	X	X	X
9. Slipped into a theater or other place without paying.	35	40	39	22	X	X	3
10. Major theft (compilation of such items as the stealing of auto parts, autos, money over $1, bicycles, radios and parts, clothing, wallets, liquor, guns, etc.)	37	40	29	20	X	2	3
11. Gone into another person's house, a shed, or other building without their permission.	31	16	31	42	1	3	4
12. Gambled for money or something else with people other than my family.	30	22	35	26	X	3	3
13. Got some money or something from others by saying that I would pay them back even though I was pretty sure I wouldn't.	35	48	26	14	2	2	3
14. Told someone I was going to beat-up on them unless they did what I wanted them to do.	33	28	24	32	X	X	4

TABLE 2 (Continued)

Offense	Community (1) Indus-trial City N=280	(2) Lower Urban N=265	(3) Upper Urban N=335	(4) Rural Farm N=274	Significance of Differences[a] (1-2)	(2-3)	(3-4)
15. Drank beer, wine, or liquor without my parents permission.	38	37	26	12	X	2	3
16. Have been kicked out of class or school for acting up.	27	28	31	22	X	X	3
17. Thrown nails, or glass, or cans in the street.	31	29	21	17	X	X	X
18. Used a slug or other things like this in candy, coke, or coin machines.	24	35	18	12	2	2	3
19. Skipped school without permission.	24	36	18	11	2	2	3
20. Helped make a lot of noise outside a church, or school, or any other place in order to bother the people inside.	17	37	18	15	X	2	X
21. Threw rocks, or sticks or any other thing in order to break a window, or street light, or thing like that.	24	26	22	16	X	X	3
22. Said I was going to tell something on someone unless they gave me money, candy, or something else I wanted.	23	28	17	19	X	2	X

		(1)	(2)	(3)	(4)	(5)	(6)	(7)
23.	Kept or used something that I knew had been stolen by someone else.	29	36	15	16	X	2	X
24.	Tampered or fooled with another person's car, tractor, or bicycle while they weren't around.	26	13	19	24	1	3	X
25.	Started a fist fight.	26	22	15	18	X	2	X
26.	Messed up a restroom by writing on the wall, or leaving the water running to run onto the floor, or upsetting the waste can.	18	33	14	17	X	2	X
27.	Hung around a pool hall, bar, or tavern.	21	18	10	23	X	2	4
28.	Hung around the railroad tracks and trains.	16	13	23	16	X	3	3
29.	Broken down or helped to break down a fence, gate, or door on another person's place.	15	14	8	8	X	2	X
30.	Taken part in a "gang fight."	12	18	7	7	X	2	X
31.	Ran away from home.	12	12	8	7	X	X	X
32.	Asked for money, candy, a cigarette or other things from strangers.	12	12	6	7	X	2	X
33.	Carried a razor, switch-blade, or gun to be used against other people.	8	16	3	4	2	2	X

TABLE 2 (Continued)

Offense	Community				Significance of Differences[a]		
	(1) Indus- trial City N=280	(2) Lower Urban N=265	(3) Upper Urban N=335	(4) Rural Farm N=274	(1-2)	(2-3)	(3-4)
34. "Beat up" on kids who hadn't done anything to me.	8	5	5	6	X	X	X
35. Broke or helped break up the furniture in a school, church, or other public building.	8	4	2	8	X	X	4
36. Attacked someone with the idea of killing them.	3	6	1	3	2	n	n
37. Smoked a reefer or used some sort of dope (narcotics).	3	4	1	3	X	n	n
38. Started a fire or helped set a fire in a building without the permission of the owner.	3	2	1	3	X	n	n

[a] Code: X=No significant difference

1, 2, 3, or 4=significant differences at .05 level or higher. The numbers indicate which of the communities in the comparison is higher in incidence of the offense.

n=too few offender cases to determine significant level.

82

mitted each of these offenses (including the detailed list of theft items) *within the past year*, thus furnishing data amenable to age-level analysis.[19] If the respondents admitted commission of an offense, they so indicated by disclosing the number of times (either 1, 2, 3, or 4 or more) they had done so. The first four columns of Table 2 reveal the percentage of students who admitted having indulged in each specific behavior one or more times *during the past year*.

Specific offense items were arranged in an array from those admitted by the highest percentage of respondents to those admitted by the lowest percentage of respondents. Obviously the "nuisance" offenses appear near the top while the most serious and the more situationally specific fall nearer the end of the listing.[20] Several offenses are apparently committed very infrequently by school children from the sixth to twelfth grades regardless of their social environs.

FINDINGS

In order to determine whether significant differences exist in the incidence of illegal behavior among the various types of communities, a two-step procedure was followed. First, each of the four communities was assigned a rank for each offense on the basis of the percentage of respondents admitting commission of that offense. These ranks were totaled across all offenses for each community. The resultant numerical total provided a very crude over-all measure of the relative degree to which the sample population from each community had been involved in illegal behavior during the past year. The results were (from most to least illegal behavior): industrial city, lower urban, upper urban, and rural farm. However, there was little over-all difference in the sum of ranks between upper urban and rural farm and even less difference between the industrial city and lower urban areas.

In the second step the communities were arranged in the order given above and then the significance of the difference between adjacent pairs was determined by applying the Wilcoxon matched-pairs signed-ranks test. Only those comparisons which involve either industrial city or lower urban versus upper urban or rural farm result in any significant differences.[21] This finding is compatible with the above crude ranking procedure.

On the basis of these findings the first hypothesis is supported, while the second hypothesis received only partial support. Lower urban juveniles reported significantly more illegal behavior than did the juveniles of the upper urban community, and the two lower class communities of industrial city and lower urban appear to be quite similar in their high rates, but another lower class area composed largely of farmers has a much lower rate, similar to that of the upper urban area.

Much more contrast among the rates of juvenile misconduct in the four different communities, than is indicated by the above results, becomes apparent when one focuses on individual offenses. As the last column in Table 2 reveals, and as could be predicted from the above, there are few significant differences in the rates on each offense between the industrial city and lower urban communities. The few differences that do occur hardly fall into a pattern except that the lower urban youth seem to be oriented more toward violence (carrying weapons and attacking persons) than those in the industrial city.

However, 16 of a possible 35 relationships are significantly different in the upper urban-rural farm comparison, a fact that could not have been predicted from the above results. Apparently, variation in one direction on certain offenses tends to be neutralized by variation in the opposite direction on other offenses when the Wilcoxon test is used. There are greater actual differences in the nature of illegal behavior between these two communities than is noticeable when considered in more summary terms. (It might be pointed out here, parenthetically, that this type of finding lends support to the suggestion by Dentler and Monroe that the comparison of criterion groups on the basis of "omnibus scales" may have serious shortcomings.)[22]

Rural farm youngsters are more prone than those in the upper urban area to commit such offenses as trespassing, threatening to "beat up" on persons, hanging around taverns

and being with "bad" associates—all relatively unsophisticated acts. Although some of the offenses committed more
often by those who live in the upper urban community are
also unsophisticated (throwing rocks at street lights, getting
kicked out of school classes, and hanging around trains),
others probably require some skill to perform successfully and
probably depend on supportive peer-group relationships. For
example, these data reveal that upper urban juveniles are
more likely than their rural farm counterparts to be out at
night after they are supposed to be at home, drink beer and
liquors without parents' permission, engage in major theft,
gamble, skip school, and slip into theaters without paying. In
addition to their likely dependence upon peer-groups, perhaps
these offenses are more easily kept from the attention of
parents in the urban setting than in open-farm areas.

The greatest differences between rates of illegal conduct
occur between the lower urban and upper urban communities, where 21 of a possible 35 comparisons reach statistical
significance, the lower urban rates being higher in all except
five of these. Although the upper urban youngsters are more
likely to pass "dirty pictures," gamble, trespass, hang around
trains, and tamper with other people's cars, their cousins in
the lower class area are more likely to steal major items,
drink, skip school, destroy property, fight, and carry weapons.
The latter offenses are those normally thought to be "real
delinquent acts" while the upper urban offenses (with the exception of vehicle tampering) are not generally considered to
be such.

To summarize briefly, when the rates of juvenile misconduct are compared on individual offenses among communities, it appears that as one moves from rural farm to upper
urban to industrial city and lower urban, the incidence of
most offenses becomes greater, especially in the more serious
offenses and in those offenses usually associated with social
structures with considerable tolerance for illegal behavior.

While most emphasis is placed here on the differences, one
obvious finding, evident in Table 2, is that in most of the
nuisance offenses (minor theft, lying to parents, disobeying
parents, swearing in public, throwing objects to break things

or into the streets) there are no differences among the various communities. Differences appear to lie in the more serious offenses and those requiring a higher degree of sophistication and social organization.

The Reiss-Rhodes findings tend to refute theories of delinquent behavior which imply a high delinquency proneness of the lower class regardless of the "status area" in which it is found.[23] In view of this report, and since Nye-Short and Dentler-Monroe were unable to detect inter-class differences, inter-class comparisons were made within the four community types of this study. Following the technique employed by Nye and Short, only those students age 15 and younger were used in these comparisons in order to neutralize the possible effects of differential school drop-out rates by social classes in the older categories.

With the exception of the industrial city, no significant inter-class differences in illegal behavior rates were found within community types when either the Wilcoxon test was used for all offenses or when individual offense comparisons were made.[24] This finding supports hypothesis #3. It could account for the inability of Nye-Short and Dentler-Monroe to find differences among the socio-economic classes from several relatively similar communities in which their studies were conducted. It is also somewhat compatible with the Reiss and Rhodes findings. However, we did not find indications of higher rates of illegal conduct in the predominant socio-economic class within most areas, as the Reiss and Rhodes data suggested.[25] This may have been a function of the unique manner in which the socio-economic categories had to be combined for comparison purposes in this study. These findings, however, are logical in that boys and girls of the minority social classes within a "status area" would likely strive to adhere to the norms of the predominant social class as closely as possible whether these norms were legal or illegal.

Within the industrial city the second socio-economic category (index scores 24–47) was slightly significantly lower than either extreme category when the Wilcoxon test was used. Since the largest percentage of the sample of the industrial city falls in the lowest socio-economic category (0–23) and since this category evidences one of the highest rates of misconduct, the finding for this community is somewhat similar to the Reiss-Rhodes findings.

CONCLUSIONS

The findings of this study tend to resolve some of the apparent conflicts in the literature that have arisen from previous research concerning the relationship between the nature of illegal behavior and socio-economic class. However, some of the results contradict earlier reports.

Our findings are similar to those of Nye-Short and Dentler-Monroe in that we failed to detect any significant differences in illegal behavior rates among the social classes of rural and small urban areas. However, in keeping with the class-oriented theories, we did find significant differences, both in quantity and quality of illegal acts, among communities or "status areas," each consisting of one predominant socio-economic class. The lower class areas have higher illegal behavior rates, particularly in the more serious types of offenses. Differences among the socio-economic classes within these "status areas" were generally insignificant (which does not agree with the findings of Reiss and Rhodes), although when social class categories were compared across communities, significant differences were found. All this suggests some extremely interesting relationships.

1. The pattern of illegal behavior within small communities or within "status areas" of a large metropolitan center is determined by the predominant class of that area. Social class differentiation within these areas is apparently not related to the incidence of illegal behavior. This suggests that there are community-wide norms which are related to illegal behavior and to which juveniles adhere regardless of their social class origins. The answer to the obvious question of how large an urban area must be before socio-economic class becomes a significant variable in the incidence of illegal behavior is not provided by this study. It is quite likely that in addition to size, other considerations such as the ratio of

social class representation, ethnic composition, and the prestige of the predominant social class relative to other "status areas" would influence the misconduct rates. The population of 20,000 of the particular upper urban community used in this study is apparently not of sufficient size or composition to provide for behavior autonomy among the social classes in the illegal behavior sense. There is some evidence, however, that an industrial city of roughly 40,000 such as the one included here is on the brink of social class differentiation in misconduct rates.

2. Though the juveniles in all communities admitted indulgence in several nuisance offenses at almost equal rates, serious offenses are much more likely to have been committed by lower class urban youngsters. Perhaps the failure of some researchers to find differences among the social classes in their misconduct rates can be attributed to the relatively less-serious offenses included in their questionnaires or scales. It would seem to follow that any "subculture" characterized by the more serious delinquencies, would be found only in large, urban, lower-class areas. However, the data of this study, at best, can only suggest this relationship.

3. Lastly, these data suggest that the present explanations that rely heavily on socio-economic class as an all-determining factor in the etiology of illegal behavior should be further specified to include data such as this study provides. For example, Cohen's thesis that a delinquent subculture emerges when lower class boys discover that they must satisfy their need for status by means other than those advocated in the middle class public schools should be amended to indicate that this phenomenon apparently occurs only in large metropolitan centers where the socio-economic classes are found in large relatively-homogeneous areas. In the same manner, Miller's theory of the relationship between the focal concerns of the lower class culture and delinquency may require closer scrutiny. If the relationship between focal concerns to illegal behavior that Miller has suggested exists, then those in the lower social class (as determined by father's occupation) who live in communities or "status areas" that are predominantly of some other social class, are apparently not participants in

the "lower class culture;" or, because of their small numbers, they are being successfully culturally intimidated by the predominant class. Likewise, those who are thought to occupy middle class positions apparently take on lower class illegal behavior patterns when residing in areas that are predominantly lower class. This suggests either the great power of prevailing norms within a "status area" or a limitation of social class, as it is presently measured, as a significant variable in the determination of illegal behavior.

RESEARCH QUESTIONS

At least three general questions that demand further research emerge from this study.

1. What dimension (in size and other demographic characteristics) must an urban area attain before socio-economic class becomes a significant variable in the determination of illegal behavior patterns?

2. What are the specific differences between lower class populations and social structures located in rural or relatively small urban areas and those located in large, concentrated areas in metropolitan centers that would account for their differential illegal behavior rates, especially in the more serious offenses?

3. The findings of this study suggest that the criteria presently used to determine social class levels may not be the most conducive to the understanding of variation in the behavior of those who fall within these classes, at least for those within the juvenile ages. A substitute concept is that of "status area" as operationalized by Reiss and Rhodes. For example, the differentiating characteristics of a large, Negro, lower-class, urban "status area" could be established and would seem to have greater predictive and descriptive power than would the social class category as determined by present methods. Admittedly, this suggestion raises again the whole messy affair of "cultural area typologies" but area patterns of behaviors obviously exist and must be handled in some manner. Research effort toward systematically combining the traditional socio-economic class concept with that of cultural

area might prove extremely fruitful by providing us with important language and concepts not presently available.

METROPOLITAN CRIME RATES AND RELATIVE DEPRIVATION

Paul Eberts and Kent P. Schwirian

THE PURPOSE of this study is to investigate the association between certain aspects of community structure, specifically . . . sources of relative deprivation, and total rates of criminal activity within American metropolitan communities.

· · ·

The 212 communities listed as SMSA's in 1960 comprise our population of cases; complete data, however, were obtained for 200 metropolitan areas.

. . . Most structural variables in urban crime rate research have been demographic indicators of socio-economic status, race and ethnicity, community size and living and housing conditions. The theory underlying the use of these variables has been what we might call the "urban-disorganization" perspective. Accordingly, urbanism is seen as a prime causal factor in crime. While we use certain urbanism variables as controls in our analysis, the theoretical perspective underlying our work is not the conglomerate of the "urban-disorganization" model but, rather, a more specific "relative deprivation" model . . .

Abbreviated with permission of the author and the publisher from *Criminologica*, Vol. V, No. 4 (February, 1968), 43–52. Published by the American Society for Criminology.

This is a revision of a paper presented at the American Sociological Association Meetings, 1966, Miami Beach, Florida.

. . . Status disparities present in a social system, particularly those affecting lower class populations, will produce . . . frustrations or relative deprivations in the lower class population, which will result in . . . anti-social and criminal behavior (as indexed by . . . rates of crime).

. . .

VARIABLES

The independent variable of this study is . . . relative deprivation. By this we mean a condition of the social structure which results in discrepancies in social position leading to a relative deficit for people in the lowest segment of the community's population relative to the position of other segments of the population.

The term relative deprivation as used originally by Stouffer and associates in *The American Soldier*[1] refers specifically to "promotional prospects" or "chances for advancement" among non-commissioned officers in the Military Police and the Air Force. In this study, we use the concept, relative deprivation, to refer to the range of deprivations existing in the social system, and more specifically, the extent to which one segment of the population feels disadvantaged in its position relative to other segments of the population in the same community.

Since we have assumed that lowest class people are . . . [most] immediate gratification oriented we also assume that their reference system is bound in both time and place. . . .

Thus we postulate that in communities with higher percentages of people in the highest income categories relative to those in the lowest income categories, the relative economic aspirations of people in the lowest classes are raised so that frustrations [are] more keenly felt by them. We further postulate that this frustrating relative positional deficit produces aggressive behavior among the population members experiencing the deprivation, and that a certain amount of these aggressive reactions will be translated into higher crime rates in these populations. Thus structural relative deprivations will produce higher crime rates.

Two structural sources of relative deprivation are explored here; one is a general social status deprivation and the other involves the relative economic prosperity of whites and non-whites in the local community. Our measure of general social status deprivation is the ratio of the number of persons in the community earning $10,000 or more a year to those earning $3,000 or less a year. This gives us an approximate indication of the relative concentration of those doing well economically to those doing poorly. An index value of less than 1.0 indicates a greater concentration of the population in the lowest income category while a value of greater than 1.0 indicates a greater concentration of the population in the higher income category.

For the purpose of our analysis the metropolitan areas were trichotomized on this index. SMSA's with an index value of 1.25 or larger are classified as having a relatively large upper class while those with a value between 1.24 and .86 are classified as having a fairly balanced class structure and those with an index of .85 or less are classified as having a relatively large lower class. Of the 200 SMSA's 59 have a large upper class, 40 have a balanced class structure, and 101 have a large lower class.

In terms of the relative deprivation hypothesis, we would expect to find higher crime rates in those communities with a large upper class than in those with a balanced class structure. We suggest that as the size of the upper income population exceeds that of the lower group, the lower income population perceives itself as being relatively more deprived of local economic rewards than in communities where the populations are of a more equal size. Thus they are a poor minority surrounded by a relatively prosperous majority. We expect this frustration to be manifest in aggressive behavior against other members of the community.

According to the relative deprivation hypothesis we would expect to find metropolitan areas with a balanced class structure having higher crime rates than those with an unbalanced, larger lower class. They certainly have a larger and more visibly affluent upper class to induce deprivational perceptions in the lowest class. But, on the other hand, as the current fads in the sociology of poverty would seem to suggest, it may be that massive poverty and generally poor economic conditions in those communities with a large lower income population would magnify other frustrations which result in aggressive and/or anti-social behavior.

If there is this type of culture of poverty effect then we would expect a curvilinear association between crime rates and the class structure index. If there is no such effect then we would expect a fairly linear association between the class structure index and crime rates.

The second aspect of relative deprivation explored here is the relative status standing of local whites and non-whites. We suggest that as the status gap between whites and non-whites widens non-whites experience greater relative status deprivation which leads to higher rates of local crime. The focus here is upon the occupational distribution of the two populations with the specific indicator being the percentage of each in white collar occupations. Non-white occupational data could be obtained from the 1960 census for only 166 of our 200 SMSA's (that is, those with a fairly large non-white population).

The measurement of the occupational gap between the two populations is somewhat complicated by the race factor. In the United States today even with increasing fair employment practices by race, whites and non-whites generally do not compete in the same labor market locally. In most communities the vast majority of white collar jobs are reserved for whites only. Thus to determine how well whites and non-whites are doing occupationally for any one metropolitian area, each population must be viewed in terms of how well each population is doing in *all* metropolitan areas. For each metropolitan area we first classified the whites as being either above or below the median percentage of white collar whites for all metropolitan areas, and then we classified the non-whites as being either above or below the median percentage of white collar non-whites for all metropolitan areas.

The metropolitan areas were then grouped in terms of the relative standing of their whites and non-whites. Sixty-two of the SMSA's have occupationally high whites and non-whites. Thirty-seven have relatively low whites but high non-whites. Twenty-two have occupationally high whites and low non-whites and 45 have both whites and non-whites occupationally low.

Of the four categories we expect crime rates to be highest where the whites are occupationally high but the non-whites are occupationally low. Here is where the gap between the two populations is the greatest and here is where the relatively poorer status of the non-whites is probably the most salient. Additionally, it is also probable that in those communities where both whites and non-whites are experiencing a rather high rate of white collar employment that those left behind in the blue collar jobs or who are unemployed may experience greater relative deprivation, which may then be translated into aggressive criminal behavior. We expect the crime rates to be lower in those communities where the non-whites are high but the whites low on the occupational measure and in those communities where both groups are low.

Out data analysis consists of testing the relative deprivation hypothesis for the two structural sources of relative deprivation. Three control variables are introduced into the analysis and they are: percentage of the SMSA population non-white, total population size of the metropolitan area, and the regional location of the SMSA.

FINDINGS

The measure of relative deprivation viewed in its relationship to crime is the general social status measure indexed by the ratio of those with incomes of $10,000 and over to those with incomes below $3,000 Table 1 presents the median total crime rate for the three categories of class structure. From the table it may be noted that the data generally support the relative deprivation hypothesis. For the total 200 SMSA's the median crime rate is highest for those metropolitan communities with a large upper class and lowest for those with a more balanced class structure. The general curvilinear pattern discussed before seems to characterize the overall association.

The next step in the analysis is to ascertain if the association between class structure deprivation and total crime holds when other structural characteristics of the communities are controlled. Three structural controls introduced into the analysis are: population size, percent of local population non-white, and regional location. In Table 1 it may be noted that each of the control variables is related to the crime measure. The median total crime index is higher for large SMSA's than for small, for those communities with large percentages of non-whites than for those with small percentages, and for those SMSA's located in the South than for those located elsewhere.[2] However, within each category of the control variables crime rates are still highest where the class structure is of the large upper class type than when the class structure is either balanced or of the large lower class type.

The curvilinear pattern of association found for the total 200 communities holds for both the large and the small SMSA's.

However, when percent non-white population is controlled the curvilinear pattern holds for those SMSA's with a high percentage of non-whites but becomes linear for those communities with a low percentage of non-whites. Also, when region is controlled the curvilinear pattern holds for those SMSA's in the South but becomes linear for those located elsewhere.

Thus the data in Table 1 show the relative deprivation hypothesis to be supported since regardless of control variable the median total crime rate is highest in those metropolitan communities where the class structure is of the large upper class type. Also, the linear pattern of association predicted by the deprivation model holds in both large and small communities and is manifest in those communities with a small percentage of non-whites and in those located outside of the South. Interestingly, the curvilinear pattern which

TABLE 1. Class Structure and Median Crime Rates in Metropolitan Areas[a]

Class Structure[b] (N$10,000/N3,000)	All SMSA's	Population Size		SMSA's Controlled for: Percent Non-White		Region	
		Large	Small	High	Low	South	Non-South
Large Upper Class	1260(59)	1285(36)	960(23)	1390(25)	945(34)	1405(2)	1040(57)
Balanced	895(40)	845(19)	950(21)	1060(14)	875(26)	1110(6)	855(34)
Large Lower Class	1160(101)	1435(28)	1115(73)	1230(64)	810(37)	1210(65)	820(36)
Total SMSA's	1055(200)	1260(83)	970(117)	1280(103)	860(97)	1240(73)	940(127)

[a] The rate is the number of crimes per 100,000 inhabitants
[b] The number in parentheses is the number of SMSA's in each category.

TABLE 2. Occupational Prosperity by Race and Median Crime Rate for Metropolitan Areas

Percent White Collar By Race	All SMSA's	Population Size		SMSA's Controlled for: Percent Non-White		Region	
		Large	Small	High	Low	South	Non-South
High Whites + High Non-Whites	1250(62)	1360(40)	1095(22)	1380(31)	950(31)	1405(13)	1050(49)
High Whites + Low Non-Whites	1420(22)	1485(8)	1275(14)	1390(17)	1580(5)	1450(19)	1100(3)
Low Whites + High Non-Whites	970(37)	940(17)	1055(20)	1295(16)	890(21)	1160(4)	950(33)
Low Whites + Low Non-Whites	960(45)	1025(10)	940(35)	1170(30)	730(15)	1030(25)	830(20)
Total SMSA's	1140(166)	1290(94)	920(72)	1260(75)	1040(91)	1230(61)	960(105)

represents the deprivation factor complicated by the "culture of poverty" factor appears for those SMSA's with a large percentage Negro and for those located in the South.

The second indicator of relative deprivation explored here is the comparative occupational prosperity of local whites and non-whites. The deprivation hypothesis leads us to expect the highest crime rates where the occupational gap between the two populations is greatest. The data in Table 2 show this to be the case. For the total 166 SMSA's the median crime rate where the whites are high occupationally and the non-whites low is 1,420. The second highest median is 1,250 and is for those communities where both groups are doing well occupationally. Earlier we suggested that the rates would be high in this category since those individuals not doing well occupationally would experience great relative deprivation since they are surrounded by prosperous populations of whites and non-whites.

Since we have already shown that crime rates are related to other structural community characteristics including population, percentage non-white population, and region, we controlled for these structural characteristics to see if the pattern of association found for the total 166 communities held. In Table 2 the data show that in all of the categories of the control variables the median total crime rate is highest where the whites are high and the non-whites low on the occupational measure and second highest where both groups are high occupationally. Thus, the control variables do not alter the basic pattern of association and the relative deprivation hypothesis is thereby supported by the data.

SUMMARY

It has been the purpose of this paper to explore the relationship between two structural sources of relative deprivation and total crime rates in American metropolitan communities. Generally, the data show that even when basic structural variables are controlled, crime rates are highest when one segment of the population . . . experiences a status deficit relative to a comparatively more economically or occupationally advantaged segment of the local population. In this study crime rates were shown to be highest where the low income population is a distinct local minority and where the occupational gap between the whites and non-whites is the greatest.

.   .   .

Perhaps the clearest implication of this work for crime control lies in the fact that increased consideration must be given to the social structural conditions producing crime if lower crime rates are to be achieved. Control attempts which focus upon constraint or rehabilitation of individual criminals and attempts aimed only at strengthening local police forces are treating the symptoms or results of social conditions and not the underlying causes of aggressive and anti-social behavior.

ASSESSING THE CONTRIBUTIONS OF FAMILY STRUCTURE, CLASS AND PEER GROUPS TO JUVENILE DELINQUENCY

Lee N. Robins and Shirley Y. Hill

PROBLEMS IN RESEARCH INTO SOCIAL FACTORS IN DELINQUENCY

Looking back over the research thus far into social factors that contribute to delinquency, we find that two principal kinds of data have been analyzed: first, descriptions of the social environments of children seen in juvenile courts,

Abbreviated by special permission of the authors and *The Journal of Criminal Law, Criminology and Police Science* (Northwestern University School of Law), Vol. 57, No. 3, 325–331. Copyright 1966.

clinics serving juvenile courts, and reformatories; and second, census tract data from high and low delinquency areas. The first method directly contrasts family histories of delinquents with family histories of non-delinquents, while the second method contrasts family patterns in high and low delinquency areas. If we allow ourselves to make the inference from the census tract data that differences in family patterns between high and low delinquency areas are parallelled by differences in the social and family patterns of delinquents and non-delinquents, there is much overall agreement in the results obtained by these two methods. The first, or case history, method, beginning with Healy's 1915 study of *The Individual Delinquent*, has consistently found delinquents' families to be more predominantly lower class and more frequently disrupted than families of non-delinquents, and has found that the delinquent himself associates with other delinquents. The census tract method, beginning with Shaw, Zorbaugh, McKay and Cottrell's 1929 *Delinquency Areas* has found that high delinquency areas include predominantly low income families, few married men, and many women in the labor force, affirming that delinquency is associated with low social status and disrupted homes. While there is no direct evidence in the census data concerning the delinquent's peer group associations, by definition, high delinquency areas should provide each individual delinquent with more potential contacts with other delinquents than should low delinquency areas.

Inspired by these repeated correlations between delinquency and class, family structure, and association with other delinquents, efforts to curb delinquency through manipulating social environments have consisted of assults on these three factors: The poor housing and low income associated with lower class status have been ameliorated through public housing and welfare funds; parents have been advised to avoid divorce for the sake of the children; and "good influences" have been provided through community recreation programs and social work to offset or interrupt the influence of the delinquents' "bad companions." But to date, the effectiveness of these techniques has not been demonstrated.

Children who live in housing projects continue to be delinquent.[1] Children of unhappily married parents are at least as likely to be delinquent as children of divorced parents.[2] And providing predelinquents with a "good friend" in the Cambridge-Somerville project,[3] or the good influence of a social case worker in the Washington, D.C., public elementary schools[4] or in New York's "Vocational High,"[5] did not improve their outcome as compared with the outcome of a control group of predelinquents.

Perhaps because delinquency was not prevented by manipulating the social environment, newer research has begun to question the causal importance of low social class and broken homes. There has been less criticism of the differential association theory, which proposes that children become delinquent as a result of associating with delinquents, although good evidence *for* it is not available. No test of the differential association theory has yet shown that the making of delinquent friends *precedes* the onset of delinquent behavior. Without this essential bit of evidence, it is as reasonable to say that delinquents *choose* each other as friends as to argue that having delinquent friends causes delinquency.[6] The influence of the broken home on delinquency has been challenged as important only as an indirect measure of family disorganization or unhappy marriage of the parents.[7] The influence of social class on delinquency has been challenged by two kinds of research: (1) the finding that delinquent acts that do *not* lead to police action are less closely associated with class status than is official delinquency;[8] and (2) the finding that in some cities indicators of social class (occupation, rent, education) typical of high delinquency areas do not remain related to delinquency rates when other census measures such as percent non-white and foreign-born and number of working women, number of children under five, and number of multiple-dwelling units are held constant.[9]

While newer research has questioned the causal connection between social variables and delinquency, it has not yet solved some of the methodological problems that make the two methods so far used unable to produce more definitive answers. The basic methodological problems in census tract research are the so-called "ecological fallacy" and the limitations of working with data for a single year. The "ecological fallacy" is a consequence of the fact that census data by tracts are not available for sub-populations identified by age, sex, or delinquency. As a result, there is no way of being sure that the description of the census tract as a whole is a valid description of the class and family distributions of the population at risk (i.e., children from about 8 to 17 years of age). Nor can one tell whether the characteristics of the tract as a whole are more or less characteristic of delinquent than of non-delinquent populations within the tract.[10]

.   .   .

The unsolved methodological problems in the case history technique concern the selection of control groups and the necessity for assuming that social factors found to discriminate delinquents from control subjects existed *prior* to the occurrence of the initial delinquency, and so could reasonably be thought of as causes. One obvious way to provide a control group for the delinquents is to select a random sample of a city's population of children within the ages of risk. But such a control sample will differ from the delinquents along so many variables, all or most of which are intercorrelated, that it becomes impossible to hold all the relevant variables constant while the effect of a particular variable is studied . . .

The alternative, then, is to select a control sample matched with the delinquents along some variables, as the Gluecks have done.[11] Their problems with this method epitomize the difficulties inherent in the case history method. The sample they designed held constant age, sex, IQ, ethnic background, and social level of the area lived in, so that they could study family and personality factors in delinquency. While this technique did allow them to study family and personality factors that would have been obscured by class and nationality variables, having matched their cases on social class and ethnicity, they could no longer compare the contribution of these variables with the contribution of family and personality factors. It also became impossible to learn whether family relationships have similar effects in all ethnic groups and at all social levels. Because ordinary random sampling is an inefficient way to provide a matched sample of non-delinquents (necessitating the interviewing of many cases who are later rejected because they do not match), the Gluecks found their control subjects in the public schools, in whose records could be found data concerning the variables on which children could be matched. But by using the schools as a source, they eliminated boys no longer attending school. This introduced an unintended difference between their delinquents and their control subjects: their control subjects did not include drop-outs, while their delinquents did. As a result of the intrinsic problems that matched control groups pose, the Gluecks were unable to use class or ethnic variables or persistence in school in developing their prediction tables, thus discarding the best established correlates of delinquency. Also, of course, since they compared family relationships and personality factors in children *already* delinquent with such factors in the control group, they could not be sure the differences they found could have been found *before* the occurrence of delinquency.

The two common techniques so far used in research then have two drawbacks in common: (1) A failure to provide a control group that can be used to test simultaneously the major theories concerning social factors in delinquency, and (2) a failure to obtain information about delinquent and control groups *prior* to the onset of delinquency.

AN ALTERNATIVE METHOD: THE COHORT OF SCHOOL ENTRANTS

One method that seems to solve some of the problems in both case history and census tract techniques is the use of a cohort of school children. It is a method which provides a random sample of delinquents, so that one may investigate the full spectrum of juvenile police contact, from the child released with a warning to the reformatory inmate, or any portion of that spectrum; it provides a built-in control group, which is not only statistically appropriate but is made up of children with whom the delinquent are *known* to have had an opportunity to interact; and finally, it obtains information *prior* to the first police contact.

The method is simple: One selects all cases entering a city's first grade in the public schools for a year far enough in the past that all children will have passed the upper limit of juvenile court age. Children who left the school system for other cities or who died in childhood must then be discarded, since their risk of exposure to the police of the city is diminished by the years of their absence. But no children are discarded because of retention in a grade, transfer to special schools, or dropping out of school. Consequently, neither school success nor persistence plays a role in the child's chances of appearing in the sample. Police and juvenile court records are then checked against this roster of school children to identify the delinquents. Obviously a wide variety of categorizations of delinquency are possible here, from a simple "record-no record" dichotomy to identification by type of disposition or by number and types of offenses.

Against the chosen measure or measures of delinquency can be tested all the variables available from school records. While family and class data in school records are obviously less complete than they are in juvenile court records or than individual interviews could provide, and less complete than the reports of family constellation, income, and housing data in census reports, a surprising amount of social class and family material is available. The presence or absence of the father can be inferred from the name of the guardian. If the first name is masculine and the last name is the same as the child's, one can assume that the child lives with his own father. In all other instances, one can assume that the father is missing.[12] The occupation of the guardian can be used as a measure of the social class status of the family. The child's place of birth and the number of addresses can furnish a measure of the family's stability. The surname provides a rough clue to ethnic identification. The address at school entry or at a specified age can be used to locate the family in a census tract, allowing the use of all the census data used in tract analysis. The social data obtained at the time of registration for the first grade, unlike data collected for juvenile delinquents appearing in court or census tract data for high and low delinquency areas, will almost always have been collected before any of the children became known to the police. There is no difficulty, then, in establishing the time sequence between family characteristics and first official delinquency or between neighborhood lived in and delinquency.

Because delinquents and non-delinquents entered the same schools at the same ages, one can treat the population of each school as a sub-population of functioning peers. And there is no question but that the child actually had an opportunity to interact with these peers. Nor can the child's association with these peers be explained entirely by mutual attraction. Children are *assigned* to schools which turn out to have high or low delinquency rates. If in "high-delinquency" schools it takes fewer predisposing personal and social factors to produce delinquency than it does in "low-delinquency" schools, we can at last offer substantial evidence that exposure to other delinquents increases the risk of delinquent behavior.

. . .

AN APPLICATION OF PARTS OF
THE SUGGESTED METHOD

As part of a study of childhood variables associated with the criminality and occupational mobility of Negro men, it has been possible to explore the use of certain parts of this method. The available data allow the study of the emergence of juvenile offenses in a cohort of 296 Negro boys selected at the time of their entry into public school as related to social variables recorded in their school records and to their school performance. It will *not* be possible to treat children from a given school as a set of peers, because, to meet the requirements of the larger study, only boys fulfilling certain criteria with respect to intelligence test scores, place of birth, length of school attendance, and completeness of records were accepted, and children entering school over a five-year period were included. Therefore, the children from a given school comprise selected parts of classes entering over a five-year period, rather than a single first grade cohort. . . .

RESULTS

Twenty-six percent of our sample of 296 had a police or Juvenile Court record before the age of 17. Fourteen percent had a record before age 15. Twelve percent had their first record at age 15 or 16.

.　　　.　　　.

Four variables in the school records were tested for relationship to the occurrence of delinquency: school retardation, apparent truancy, guardian's occupation, and father's presence or absence. The criteria used to dichotomize these variables can be found in footnote 13. Truancy and guardian's having a low status occupation were found to be related to delinquency at a statistically significant level, and school retardation was close to significance. About a third of the boys with truancy, retardation, or a lower status guardian eventually became delinquent, compared with one-fifth of the remainder. Surprisingly, no relationship was found between father's presence or absence and delinquency.

Since the sample selection method had eliminated correlations between school problems, class status, and father's presence, school problems and class are independent of each other as predictors of delinquency. When truancy was tested holding retardation constant, truancy was still found to be predictive of delinquency ($\chi^2 = 6.34$, df $= 2$, p $< .05$). When retardation was tested, holding truancy constant, no significant relationship was found. The small relationship between school retardation and delinquency apparently resulted in part from the fact that retardation is a frequent concomitant of truancy. Retardation, nevertheless, seemed to make a small contribution, since the presence of retardation, in the absence of truancy and very low status, still showed a (non-significant) relationship to delinquency (11% with

TABLE 1. Family and School Performance Factors in Delinquency

	Juvenile Delinquency		
	Ever	Before 15	After 15 (of Those Not Previously Delinquent)
Total Delinquents	26% (296)[a]	14% (296)	14% (256)
Guardian's Occupation			
Low: Unemployed, domestic or laborer. (SEI = 10 or less)	31% (148)	18% (148)	14% (121)
High: All others (SEI = 11+)	20% (148)	9% (148)	14% (135)
	$x^{2b} = 3.98, p < .05$	$x^2 = 4.88, p < .05$	n.s.
Elementary School Retardation			
Moderate or severe	33% (94)	23% (94)	12% (72)
No serious retardation	22% (202)	9% (202)	15% (184)
	$x^2 = 3.31, p < .10$	$x^2 = 10.32, p < .01$	n.s.
Elementary School Truancy			
Moderate or severe	35% (127)	20% (127)	19% (102)
No extended truancy	19% (169)	9% (169)	11% (154)
	$x^2 = 5.71, p < .02$	$x^2 = 6.35, p < .02$	n.s.
Father Present	26% (155)	17% (155)	10% (128)
Father Absent	26% (141)	9% (141)	18% (128)
	n.s.	$x^2 = 3.58, p < .10$	n.s.

[a] Figures in parentheses are the total number of cases on which percentages are based.
[b] Two-tailed test with correction for continuity.

none of the three variables *vs.* 31% with retardation only), and its presence also added a small amount to the effect of low status in the absence of truancy (22% with low status only; 28% with low status and retardation). The additive effect of lower class status and truancy can be seen in the fact that with neither, 14% were delinquent, with one only, 25%, and with both, 42% ($\chi^2 = 14.31$, df $= 2$, p $< .001$).

. . . The rate of early delinquency (delinquent before 15) in Table 1 is based on the total sample of children studied, but the rate of late delinquency (first offense at 15 or 16) is based on the sample of children *not* delinquent before age 15.

While school retardation had been not quite significantly related to the total delinquency rate, it was the variable most highly related to *early* delinquency. Almost one-fourth of children held back in elementary school had juvenile offenses before 15, as compared with only one-eleventh of those with regular progress. Truancy and guardian's low status occupation also predicted early delinquency, as they had the overall delinquency rate. Whether or not the father was in the home was still not quite significant, but early delinquency was more common when the father was *present* than when he was absent. Neither truancy nor retardation was significant when holding the other constant. Again cumulating significant predictors gave striking results. With none of the predictors present, only 3% were delinquent before age 15; with all three, 36% were ($\chi^2 = 21.27$, df $= 3$, p $< .001$).

None of the four variables in the elementary school record significantly predicted delinquency in children who had not yet acquired a police record by their fifteenth birthday.

A corollary to the finding that late delinquency was not predicted by the three variables that predicted early delinquency is that these variables not only predicted the *occurrence* of delinquency but the *age* at which it would first occur if it occurred at all. Delinquents with all three predictors were under 15 years of age at the time of their first offense in 83% of cases. With only two predictors, 55% of the delinquents were less than 15 at the time of their first offense. With only one predictor, 44% of the delinquents

were less than 15; and delinquents with none of these predictors had a first offense before 15 in only 25% of cases
($\chi^2 = 6.85$, df = 2, p < .05).

An absence of low status, retardation, and truancy in
elementary school, therefore, permits two predictions: that
few children will be delinquent at all, and that the excep-
tional child who is delinquent will come to police attention
after age 15.

. . .

URBAN CRIME PATTERNS

Sarah L. Boggs

A NEW approach to a long neglected problem is to construct crime occurrence rates on the basis of environmental
opportunities specific to each crime category. Using these
crime-specific occurrence rates, one can determine whether
crime targets in certain areas are exploited at higher rates
than targets in other neighborhoods. The first question is
whether the rate in each offense category is associated with
the presence of offenders who commit these crimes, and the
second, whether the social-structural characteristics of resident populations vary among different offense areas.

Abbreviated with permission of the author and publisher from
American Sociological Review, Vol. 30, No. 6 (December, 1966),
899–908. Published by the American Sociological Association.

This paper is based on "The Ecology of Crime Occurrence in
St. Louis: A Reconceptualization of Crime Rates and Patterns," unpublished Ph.D. dissertation, Washington University, 1964. I gratefully
acknowledge the contributions of David J. Pittman, whose concerns
with the problem of developing valid crime occurrence rates created
the impetus and guidelines for this study. The study was financed in
part by the Crime Research Center of the Social Science Institute,
Washington University.

Environmental opportunities for crime vary from neighborhood to neighborhood. Depending on the activities pursued in different sections of the city, the availability of such targets as safes, cash registers, dispensing machines, people and their possessions varies in amount and kind. These differing environmental opportunities should be reflected in the occurrence rates.[1]

If opportunities in the offenders' own neighborhoods are exploited at high rates, then the variables traditionally associated with the prevalence of offenders in the social structure, namely low social class, non-white status, and anomie will also be associated with crime occurrence.[2] But if crime targets in other areas are more intensively exploited than they are in offenders' neighborhoods, then these structural characteristics may not appear in high-occurrence areas.

CRIME OCCURRENCE RATES

Evidence provided by previous criminological studies leads to the conclusion that areas where offenders reside are not likely to be areas where the most crime occurs. On the whole, the highest crime occurrence rates are to be found in the central business districts of urban areas,[3] while the highest criminal offender rates are found in lower-class, non-white, anomic neighborhoods.[4] Thus, crime occurrence rates cannot be explained by the same factors that account for the prevalence of offenders.

The discrepancy between criminal offender and crime occurrence rates is in part the result of the standard method of constructing occurrence rates. Conventionally, these rates are computed as the number of crimes that have occurred in an area relative to the number of people residing in that area. A valid rate, however, should form a probability statement, and therefore should be based on the risk or target group appropriate for each specific crime category. The rate of residential burglary, for example, should be stated as the number of residences that were burglarized in relation to the number of residences that could have been burglarized, not the number of people residing in the area. Since the number of events, or the numerator, varies with the type of crime, the denominator should likewise vary so that the whole number of exposures to the risk of that specific event is incorporated as the base.

As a consequence of the invalid method conventionally used, spuriously high crime occurrence rates are computed for central business districts, which contain small numbers of residents but large numbers of such targets as merchandise on display, untended parked cars on lots, people on the streets, money in circulation, and the like. Although many crimes do take place in such areas, valid occurrence *rates* would be low relative to the number of potential targets or environmental opportunities for crime.

When crime occurrence is measured correctly, the rates indicate the degree to which people and property in neighborhood stores, filling stations, restaurants, homes, and so forth are exploited in areas where business and commerce are less concentrated.

For the purposes of uniform crime reporting, offenses are divided into Index and Non-Index Crimes. For Index Crimes, including criminal homicide, forcible rape, robbery, aggravated assault, burglary, grand larceny, and auto theft, both the place of occurrence of the crime and the place of residence of the offender are recorded.[5] These are the offenses used in this study.

For many of the offense categories, the risk groups used as denominators for the crime-specific rates have not been counted directly, but approximated by various methods. A business-residential land-use ratio was developed as a base for business robbery, non-residential burglary, and grand larceny, since these offenses occur primarily in connection with the conduct of business and commerce. A count of the number of businesses classified by the degree of crime risk would be a more sensitive measure for these offenses; the number of businesses estimated by this land-use measure is only a first approximation.

Pairs of persons, computed by the formula $N(N-1)/2$, were the base for criminal homicide and aggravated assault, since these offenses involve both a victim and assailant. The

TABLE 1. *Frequency, Median Number, and Rates of Index Crime Occurrence for 128 Census Tracts, St. Louis City, 1960*

Index Crime Category	Frequency of Occurrence Total	Median	Standard Rates per Resident Population: Median	Crime-Specific Rates per Environmental Opportunities: Median
Criminal homicide-Aggravated assault	2195	5	9	12
Forcible rape	269	1	1	3
Robbery:				
Highway	1409	3	8	23
Business	554	2	5	62
Miscellaneous	194	0	0	—ᵃ
Residential burglary:				
Day	2606	10	21	60
Night	2573	13	28	82
Non-residential burglary:				
Day	1272	5	10	114
Night	4172	21	43	597
Grand larceny	4146	17	34	444
Auto theft:				
Permanent retention	3042	20	34	2
Joy riding	917	5	10	.5

ᵃ Base not revised.

rationale is that other things being equal, the greater the number of pairs of persons, the greater the opportunities for criminal homicide ,and aggravated assault.

Untended parked cars are the most likely targets for auto theft, and this risk group was estimated by the amount of space devoted to parking. People on the public streets, either pedestrians or occupants of vehicles, are the targets for highway (street) robbery. In the absence of a daytime census of population, number of square feet of streets was substituted as the crime-specific base.

More direct measures were used for the remainder of the offense categories. Miscellaneous robbery is a residual category composed primarily of robberies of persons in and around their homes, therefore the resident population is an appropriate base. Since women are the victims of forcible rape, the number of resident females served as the revised base. The number of occupied housing units is the base for residential burglary rates.

The 23,349 Index Crimes the police recorded as occurring in the City of St. Louis in 1960, along with the various risk-

TABLE 2. *Rank Order Correlation Between Crime-Specific and Standard Crime Occurrence Rates for 128 Census Tracts, St. Louis City, 1960*

Index Crime Category	Rank Order Correlation[a]
Non-residential night burglary	−.078
Grand larceny	−.107
Non-residential day burglary	−.230
Auto theft for joy riding	.015
Auto theft for permanent retention	.266
Business robbery	.330
Highway robbery	.768
Residential night burglary	.856
Residential day burglary	.924
Forcible rape	.969
Criminal homicide-Aggravated assault	.997

[a] Kendall's *Tau.*

group measures, were allocated to the 128 census tracts in the City so that crime-specific and standard occurrence rates could be computed for each of the offenses for each of the census tracts.[6]

The most radical differences between the rates were among the business crimes, for which rank order correlations between the two sets of rates were quite low (see Table 2).[7] Contrary to the traditionally high standard crime occurrence rates, rates of non-residential burglary, grand larceny, auto theft, and business robbery are low for business areas when the rates are computed on the basis of the environmental opportunities.

Illustrative of this pattern is the non-residential night burglary category. On the basis of crime-specific rates, tracts with small resident populations but much business and commerce ranked among the lowest in the City, although the standard rates for the same tracts were among the highest in the City (see Table 3).

.   .   .

CRIME OCCURRENCE AND URBAN SOCIAL STRUCTURE

Interpretation of the crime factors requires an examination of the characteristics of residential populations, to see whether the variables traditionally associated with the presence of offenders in urban areas are also associated with crime occurrence. That is, do high rates of crime occur among residential populations characterized as lower-class, non-white, and anomic? Social area analysis, based on the dimensions of social rank, urbanization, and segregation,[8] is used here to answer this question. These dimensions have been used before to predict the prevalence of offenders, as well as other social phenomena, and the anticipated relationships have appeared.[9]

As an index of social class, the social rank dimension differentiates population aggregates (census tracts) according to educational and occupational status. The segregation

TABLE 3. *Rates, Rate Bases and Rank of Selected Census Tracts for Non-Residential Night Burglary, St. Louis City, 1960*

Census Tract	Frequency of Occurrence	Resident Population	Ratio of Square Feet of Business to Residential Land Use	Rate per 10,000 Population	Rate per 10,000 sq. ft, Business-Residential Land Use Ratio	Rank on Crime-Specific Rates	Rank on Standard Rates
5E	37	11,121	5.4	33	68,518	1	75
11C	90	9,025	20.5	100	43,904	2	21
17B	26	13,466	6.4	19	40,625	3	102
2B	12	8,779	3.7	14	32,432	4	107.5
21B	155	11,248	47.9	138	32,359	5	16
18B	36	259	6,456.5	1390	56	122	1
8F	12	147	3,982.0	816	30	124	2
25C	119	1,571	27,280.9	757	40	123	3
25D	39	561	81,376.5	695	5	127	4
22C	21	321	9,768.9	654	21	126	5

dimension, in the original social area schema, distinguished subordinate populations generally, including foreign-born residents. For the present study, however, the index has been re-defined as the percentage Negro.[10]

The urbanization index is based on the fertility ratio, proportion of single-family dwelling units, and proportion of women in the labor force. A "life style" continuum is assumed, with home and family-centered neighborhoods at the low end and apartment house neighborhoods, characterized by childless or small families and unrelated individuals at the other. Wirth's "urbanism as a way of life" is the ideal-typical characterization of "high urban" neighborhoods. On the grounds that highly urbanized neighborhoods permit only a limited development of informal shared norms for regulating conduct, the urbanization component is used here as an indirect measure of anomie.[11] It seems particularly relevant to crime occurrence. Because residents of highly urban neighborhoods have only limited acquaintance with one another, strangers and perhaps potential offenders can go unnoticed and unsuspected in such areas.[12] The lack of knowledge about the lives of other residents and the absence of common interests among neighbors create indifference, and in the extreme, prevent interference even when a crime is observed.[13]

. . . Although the degree of association between the structural variables and the occurrence rates is only moderate, it suggests certain patterns. The salient characteristic of the homicide-assault and residential burglary occurrence rates is that they are directly associated with the percentage Negro in the census tract, regardless of its social rank or urbanization. Social rank considered separately is moderately associated with these crime rates, but the Negro population concentrated in the low social ranks accounts for this.

The positive association between occurrence rates and both social rank and percentage Negro indicate that the targets for the majority of business crimes that comprise Factor II are located in "Gold Coast and slum" neighborhoods where subordinate Negro and high-rank populations live in close proximity. In several of these offense categories—auto theft, grand larceny, and highway robbery—urbanization shows the predicted positive association with crime occurrence.

The combination of highway and miscellaneous robbery occurrence from Factor IV is inconsistent. Highway robbery occurrence follows a pattern very similar to that of business crimes, while miscellaneous robbery, like forcible rape occurrence (both are in Factor III) is apparently unrelated to variations in social rank, urbanization, and percentage Negro.

INTERPRETATION OF CRIME OCCURRENCE FACTORS

Factor I. The higher occurrence rates in high-offender neighborhoods, for homicide-assault and residential burglary, suggest that familiarity between offenders and their targets —or victims—is a characteristic shared by these offenses.

The homicide-assault pattern has been found in other studies dealing with similar offense categories. Schuessler's study of occurrence rates, for one, revealed a factor composed of murder, assault, per cent non-white, crowded dwellings, and low income.[14] Bullock's case study of homicides lends further support, for his results showed that homicides were concentrated in Negro neighborhoods; furthermore, the assailants and victims were most likely to be neighbors, and the crime to occur in the block where they lived.[15]

High rates of both homicide and residential burglary in lower status areas have been interpreted in terms of the economic and social deprivations to which subordinate populations are subject. Deprived of legitimate access to money and material goods, members of the subordinated population turn to illegitimate means to obtain valued objects. And, I suggest, familiarity with the neighborhood may precipitate illegitimate entry into other people's houses for purposes of theft. The kinds of knowledge useful to burglars—knowing when the premises are occupied and unoccupied, how to get in and out of the buildings without detection, where to look for objects, when and where police and watchmen are present, etc.—are doubtless more readily known or more easily obtained about their own neighborhoods than about other areas.

Factor II. The combination of business robbery, non-residential day and night burglary, auto theft, and grand larceny in Factor II is very similar to Schuessler's "property crimes" factor.[16] The weak association between offender and occurrence rates and the particular patterns of association with the social structural variables found here suggest that the most intensively exploited business crime targets are those located in high-rank neighborhoods adjacent to offender areas; these targets are potentially more profitable than similar targets in low-rank areas. Merchandise displayed in stores, for example, is likely to be more expensive, cars are apt to be more valuable, cash registers or "snatched" purses and wallets may contain more money in a high-rank population than in the lower-rank neighborhoods likely to be occupied by the offenders.

Factor III. Forcible rape and miscellaneous robbery occurrences are apparently randomly distributed among social areas. Here, as in Factor II, target and offender areas are disassociated, but unlike the business crime rates, the occurrence rates of forcible rape and miscellaneous robbery present no distinguishable pattern. This clustering of offenses is similar to Schmid's "Atypical Crime Factor," composed of bicycle theft, indecent exposure, and residential burglary—offenses with occurrence patterns different from the others.[17]

Factor IV. Factor IV is composed primarily of offender variables. That miscellaneous robbery and highway robbery occurrence are correlated with the offender variables here suggests that offender neighborhoods are also subject to high rates of crime occurrence, though the offenders may not reside in the same areas in which they commit their offenses.

SUMMARY AND CONCLUSIONS

This analysis of crime occurrence rates based on environmental opportunities specific to each crime category indicates that areas of exploitation vary. Targets in central business districts are not the most intensively exploited in the city, nor are exploited targets entirely limited to neighborhoods in which the offenders live.

The crime factors extracted from the occurrence and offender rates suggest several different dimensions of crime occurrence. One is familiarity between offenders and their targets as evidenced by the exploitation of particular types of targets in offender neighborhoods. Profit is connoted by the business crime patterns, where targets in areas of high social rank adjoining offender areas appear to provide abundant illegitimate opportunities. . . .

ISSUES IN THE ECOLOGICAL STUDY OF DELINQUENCY

Robert A. Gordon

EVER SINCE its appearance in 1954, Lander's *Towards an Understanding of Juvenile Delinquency* has drawn much attention.[1] The major thesis of Lander's study, based upon multivariate analyses of ecological data, was that juvenile

Abbreviated with permission of the author and publisher from *American Sociological Review*, Vol. 32, No. 6 (December, 1967), 927–944. Published by the American Sociological Association. The most technical portions of this article have been deleted here. These sections show that all of the studies reviewed misused multivariate statistical procedures, and were also affected by calculation artifacts due to their choices of cutting points on some of the indices they employed as key variables. See also the letters of commentary on this article in the August, 1968 issue of this journal.

Work on this paper was supported by Research Grant MH 10698–01, from the National Institute of Mental Health. The present version was part of a longer paper, "Issues in Multiple Regression and the Ecological Study of Delinquency" (Department of Social Relations, Johns Hopkins University, 1966).

delinquency rates over a four-year period in the city of Baltimore were related in only a superficial sense to census tract variables indicative of socioeconomic status. Lander claimed to show that, in actuality, the juvenile delinquency rates in question were not related to socioeconomic status at all, but rather to the variables: percentage of homes owner-occupied, and percentage nonwhite. Since these latter variables seemed to him to be more identifiable with degrees of social integration than with degrees of socioeconomic status, Lander was led to conclude that his data favored an "anomie theory" explanation of delinquency rather than one based upon some kind of economic determinism.

Both types of theory have a long tradition in sociology, and both have their special adherents. It was only natural that the overall reaction to Lander's study be one of ambivalence. On the one hand, the study appeared to support the existence of the more elusive and therefore more glamorous variable, anomie. On the other hand, it denied a relation with the most concrete and most solidly established of all sociological variables, namely, socioeconomic status. This denial ran counter both to much statistical evidence and to intuition, and thus placed in doubt one of the few strong relations with delinquency that sociologists had been able to identify. As a result, sociologists have been at once fascinated with and suspicious of Lander's conclusion.

The two most ambitious re-examinations of Lander's findings to appear thus far have been by Bordua and by Chilton.[2] Bordua, employing data for Detroit, raised a number of questions concerning the original study, in the course of attempting to replicate some of Lander's analyses. Somewhat cautiously, he concluded that the Lander interpretations were essentially confirmed for Detroit. Chilton incorporated both Lander's and Bordua's data into an almost total replication, adding data for a third city, Indianapolis. On the basis of his analysis, he severely questioned the utility of Lander's anomie explanation. His main criticism, and potentially the most damaging one, was that Lander had confused the signs of the factor loadings of four of his variables, and that, as a result, his factor analysis could no longer support the interpretation that his variables gave rise to an anomie factor and a socio-economic factor, with delinquency being more closely related to the anomie factor. This criticism alone would probably have been sufficient to discredit Lander's theory and to remove whatever doubt that theory had raised concerning the proposition that delinquency and socioeconomic status were related. At a time when resources are being committed on an unprecedented scale against poverty, partly on the justification that social ills such as crime and delinquency have a socioeconomic basis, it is certainly important that sociologists be correct about the facts of this particular relationship. Unfortunately Chilton's criticism of Lander on this point, and on other points as well, is mistaken. However, there are other important faults in Lander's procedures that completely invalidate his conclusions. The purpose of this paper, therefore, is to describe these mistakes, and others appearing in the studies by Bordua and Chilton, so that this particular erroneous challenge to the hypothesis of a relationship between delinquency and socioeconomic status may finally be laid to rest.

.   .   .

THE CONSTRUCT VALIDITY OF ANOMIE

Campbell and Fiske have proposed certain criteria to be satisfied whenever it is claimed that a particular set of measurements represents a particular theoretical construct.[3] Among these is the simple but powerful requirement that different measurements of the same construct correlate more highly with one another than with measurements of alternative constructs.

If one studies the correlation matrices for all three sets of data—Lander's, Bordua's and Chilton's—it can be seen that the putative anomie variables (nonwhite and homes owner-occupied) do not constitute a genuine construct in terms of this criterion, although the SES variables do.[4] For Detroit and Indianapolis, the anomie variables split apart, in that their highest correlations are not with each other. For Detroit, the variable most correlated with nonwhite is foreign born (−0.73), and with homes owner-occupied, it is substandard housing (−0.64); for Indianapolis, nonwhite correlates most with overcrowded (+0.46), and homes owner-occupied with overcrowded (−0.56). Thus, in not a single instance out of four possible ones does an anomie variable have its highest correlation with another anomie variable in the other two cities. However, in all three replications each SES variable always has its highest correlation with another SES variable.

Furthermore, the correlation between the two anomie variables declines drastically. Whereas it was −0.76 for Baltimore, it drops to −0.43 for Detroit and to −0.26 for Indianapolis. In contrast, the mean absolute correlations between the four SES variables are 0.77, 0.60, and 0.79 for the three cities, respectively. We see, therefore, that in two of the cities the anomie variables are substantially more highly correlated with other variables than they are with each other. Thus, quite aside from the question of whether nonwhite and homes owner-occupied approximate our intuitive conception of what is meant by anomie, there is no evidence whatsoever that these two variables jointly define any theoretical construct at all that is uniquely different from what is measured by other variables in the analysis.

. . .

CONCLUSION

Barring the appearance of surprising new data, there should no longer be any question about the ecological relations among these variables—particularly the one between SES and official delinquency rates. We have seen, for Baltimore, that when the optimal cutting points are used, the more traditional SES indexes of education and rent approach within a few points the correlations of the other indexes with delinquency. It is not unlikely that other data will continue to show this separation of a few points and perhaps, as a result, generate speculation as to its cause. In closing, therefore, it is worthwhile to call attention to possible reasons why the correlations observed between education and rent, on the one hand, and delinquency on the other, might be depressed slightly below those of the other variables that have been studied. Probably the most important of these reasons is the failure of measures like education and rent to be calibrated in the same way for Negroes and for whites.

In the case of education, the gap that widens between the performances of Negro and of white children as they progress through public school means that formally equivalent amounts of schooling, in years, do not imply equal competence in the competition for socioeconomic status.[5] This would be especially true for Negroes whose education was received in the rural South prior to their moving to those cities in which they were found at the times of the 1940 and 1950 censuses.[6] On top of this, the validity of formal education as an index of SES is further undermined by discrimination in employment. Thus Levenson and McDill, whose data are recent, report that even when there is good reason to believe that education is constant in quality, Negro high school graduates trained for a given vocation have substantially lower earnings than their white counterparts, although employment rates for the two groups are practically the same.[7]

Indexes based on rent present similar problems. In their analysis of 1950 Chicago data, the Duncans report that artificial restrictions upon his access to the housing market force the Negro to pay more than the white for housing of a given quality. They state:

One thing seems quite clear: non-whites get less desirable housing for a given rent than do whites . . . a much larger proportion of non-whites than of whites occupy dwelling units that either lack a private bath, are in a dilapidated structure, or fail to meet acknowledged housing standards in both these respects. In 1950, over half, or 53 per cent, of non-white households, as against 15 per cent of white households, lived in units with no private bath or which were dilapidated. This difference prevailed despite the fact that non-white median rental was only slightly below white median rental. . . .

. . . Partly in order to pool incomes and partly because of the limited housing supply. Negroes resort to doubling-up of families and incorporation of non-family members into their households . . . and the Negro household must more often endure a crowding of the dwelling unit to a degree that is generally recognized as undesirable.[8]

The import of these passages concerning the validity of rent as opposed to either substandard housing, overcrowding, or by implication owner-occupancy, as an index of socioeconomic status is clear. Shevky and Bell have also pointed to problems associated with rent as an index, the most important of which is probably the existence of rent controls; at the time of the 1950 census these were still in force, and somewhat spottily at that, thus compounding the difficulty.[9]

We see then that there are reasons for expecting a bit more error in predicting a style-of-life variable that is correlated with race, such as delinquency, from SES indexes based upon formalistic criteria, such as education measured in years, or rent, than from indexes in which present life-style is immanent, such as overcrowding and substandard housing. Until such a time as these reasons can be safely discounted, it would be unwise to conclude on the basis of small differences in correlation that the independent variables in question differ from each other in any fundamental sense.

Finally, it should be emphasized that this paper has been concerned with the empirical issue of whether delinquency is related to socioeconomic status or not, and not with the mechanisms of that relationship. The effect of the revised cutting points on education and rent, and the nature of the variables, such as overcrowding, that already possessed optimal cutting points, indicate that it is the extremely low end of the SES range that is most relevant. The advantage of having this established is that the many known concomitants of low SES become more worthy of investigation in the search for mechanisms.

This finding also contains a warning concerning the conduct of antipoverty programs. It suggests that, in order to decrease delinquency, for example, it is necessary to reach the very bottom-most stratum in every census tract. Simply pumping money into low-income areas may result in helping needy people, but they may not be the ones chiefly responsible for the high social pathology indexes from which intervention against poverty now derives its main political justification. To the extent that programs fail to reach this lowest stratum—however successful they are at assisting the more accessible higher-stratum poor—they will fail to alleviate the more intractable and socially visible consequences of poverty. Certainly there is much to be said, on humanitarian grounds alone, for directing limited resources toward the people best able to take advantage of them. Undoubtedly, this serves to prevent even higher pathology rates in the future. Nonetheless, there remains the possibility that the failure of programs to materially reduce delinquency and eliminate hard-core poverty will trigger political reactions that make it impossible to gain support for efforts that would benefit the very poorest. For these people's own misery to be used to legitimate help for someone else, and in a manner that diminishes their own chances of eventually receiving help themselves, would be the ultimate exploitation.

Part III

Criminogenic Social Processes in City Life

Introduction

THE STATISTICAL studies of the preceding section indicate the components of city populations in which crime is concentrated, but the "social process" reports in this section show *how* and *why* one person engages in crime and another does not. We are concerned here with the meaning of criminal behavior in the life of someone who pursues it; how it reflects his view of himself and his relationships to others.

Toby contrasts and explains the meaning of criminal activity to those who most readily engage in it with its implications for those who most definitely avoid it. The difference, he argues, is primarily a matter of the latter seeing that they have a "stake in conformity." He describes in detail how and why the typical youthful hoodlum fails to develop such a "stake."

Werthman elaborates the Toby picture by tracing "the moral career of the lower-class delinquent gang boy" from the age of 6 or 7 to the late teens or twenties. Here we find much more detail on the actual communications and other activities by which slum boys acquire "identity materials" that give them a "stake in nonconformity." He also shows how the termination of delinquency is a function of the risks and contingencies it comes to involve, for there are fluctuations in the stake in conformity or nonconformity that a youth acquires.

The Burnhams broaden our perspectives of the total slum community, depicting the diverse life of its many age levels and ethnic groups to show that even in one of the highest narcotics and theft-pursuing blocks in New York City, life is not all criminal. On the other hand, Suttles shows that the social consequences of public housing policy in our large cities may be especially conducive to crime.

To prevent our developing the convenient but spurious delusion that the criminal and the presumably noncriminal populations in the city represent two distinct species of life, Lewis points out similarities in the moral concerns of slum "hustlers," delinquent gang members, and legitimate businessmen and statesmen. The implications of these similarities are far-reaching, he contends, both for causal theory in criminology and for practical concerns with reforming offenders.

In the concluding paper, Glaser traces the subcultural factors that must be taken into account to cope successfully with the problem of crimes of individual violence in our cities. Here, more than in the other articles in this section, structural and processual analyses are intermingled and linked.

SOCIAL DISORGANIZATION AND STAKE IN CONFORMITY: COMPLEMENTARY FACTORS IN THE PREDATORY BEHAVIOR OF HOODLUMS

Jackson Toby

THE AMERICAN standard of living is one of the highest of any nation, yet burglary, robbery, car theft, and other forms of larceny are frequent. These predatory crimes are, as a matter of fact, much more numerous than crimes against the person such as murder, rape, and aggravated assault. Furthermore, and this accentuates the paradox, in the United States a thief who steals because he is hungry or cold is a rarity.

THE ROLE OF SOCIAL VIGILANCE

Why should so much stealing occur in a rich country? The age and socio-economic status of arrested offenders provide some clues. American thieves are usually young hoodlums from slum neighborhoods. An explanation of their youth and neighborhood of residence is that people are more prone to act upon their anti-social impulses when external controls over them are weak. Thus, one reason why adolescents are arrested more often than older or younger people is that adolescents are less likely to be under the influence of a family unit; they are becoming emancipated from the family into

Reprinted by special permission of the author and *The Journal of Criminal Law, Criminology and Police Science* (Northwestern University School of Law), Vol. 48, No. 1, 12–17. Copyright 1957.

which they were born but have not yet married and got involved in a new family unit. Similarly, slum dwellers commit more thefts than suburbanites because stealing is not universally frowned on in deteriorated neighborhoods as it is in wealthier communities.[1] In short, predatory crime occurs when social vigilance is reduced.

Case histories of hoodlum type thieves generally support the "social disorganization" explanation of stealing. Commonly, the street-corner rowdy grew up in a chaotic household. His parents exercised ineffectual control over him, not necessarily because of indifference, but because they were overwhelmed by their own difficulties: chronic warfare in the household; death, desertion, or serious illness of the breadwinner; mental deficiency or disease; alcoholism; gambling; promiscuity; too many children for an unskilled father to support or a harried mother to supervise. Such problems not only reduce the effectiveness of parental control but by curtailing income and forcing the family to occupy the least desirable housing, they are indirectly responsible for ineffective community control, too. A slum is a neighborhood where houses are old, overcrowded, and in need of major repairs. But it is also a place where people with incapacitating problems are concentrated. Preoccupied with their difficulties, the residents of a slum are simultaneously ineffective parents and apathetic citizens. The larger the concentration of distracted persons in a community, the less capable the community becomes for united resistance to anything—including crime. "Horse rooms" and "cat houses" are able to locate in slums for the same reason that youngsters are permitted to "hang-out" on street corners: troubled people don't care. Thus, it is no accident when reformatory inmates come from backgrounds where neither family nor neighborhood influences posed a strong obstacle to taking other people's property.

The weakness of parental and community controls cannot, however, account for the fact that girls pass through adolescence and live in slums just as boys do, yet do not steal to the same extent. Nor does the weakness of external controls explain why only a minority of slum youths steal persistently enough to get caught.[2] Others grow up under similar circumstances and seem reasonably law-abiding. More must be involved in the creation of a hoodlum than the lack of vigilance of family and neighbors. What goes on inside the young tough? Is he mentally sick? A small percentage of the thefts which come to the attention of juvenile and criminal courts can be accounted for in this way. The psychiatrist explains how a neurotic need for love may drive a boy to take women's lingerie from clothes lines. More typically, however, the hoodlum is one of a group of friends all of whom steal. Moreover, he does not seem driven by a neurotic compulsion; he steals because his friends expect it of him.

But why? A little can be learned about the motivation of young hoodlums from examining their offenses. For the most part, their thefts are petty and crudely executed. A professional con man or safe-cracker would be ashamed to be suspected of activity so lacking in craftsmanship. They burglarize a grocery store; they drive off a car and "strip" it of radio, heater, and tires; they break into a house while the owner is away and look for valuables; they beat up a drunk on a dark street and take his wallet. Sooner or later they will be imprisoned, for not only are they unskilled in ways of crimes; they are chronically "broke"; they cannot bribe law-enforcement officers nor hire top-notch lawyers. Nor do they ordinarily have friends in high places who will intercede with police or prosecutor. They constitute the proletariat of crime. Unlike the Al Capones, who steal because enormous profits outweigh the risks of apprehension, their material gains are trifling; their risks are overwhelming. It almost seems that they want to spend years in custody; yet no one who has felt the tension in a prison or reformatory can doubt their desire for freedom.

FRUSTRATION AND REBELLION

What possible explanation can there be for such seemingly irrational behavior? When asked why they steal, they say, in effect, "Bad companions," "For excitement," or, "I needed money." Yet other youngsters find nondelinquent friends, different kinds of excitement, and other ways to make money.

Are they indeed "rebels without a cause"? Certainly there is more evidence in favor of the notion that they are hostile to conventional values than that they are for anything. After all, they not only steal; they curse; they destroy property maliciously; they philander; they create public disturbances; they band together in gangs to fight other gangs; and they are insolent to teachers, policemen, social workers. Perhaps they reject conventional values because in terms of conventional values they are failures. They went to the movies and learned that American men should have convertibles and handsome clothes. They also learned, as they got into the teens, that their prospects for legitimate success were poor. Somehow they had been deprived of the chance to "get ahead" and enjoy a luxurious style of life. "Borrowing" flashy cars is, from their point of view, a way of tasting the good things America promised them.

True, in the United States, even slum youths are in no danger of starving. They are well off by comparison with the poor of Europe or Asia. But this is small comfort; they compare their lot with that of the most successful and glamorous Americans, not with downtrodden "foreigners." Relative to movie stars and captains of industry, they feel underprivileged, and it is how they feel that counts. Resentment against a social system has little to do with the objective deprivations it imposes. Resentment arises when deprivations are greater than people believe they ought to be. In the United States, where the ideal is social ascent, poor climbers may be more bitter than poor eaters in other societies. And, paradoxically, the considerable amount of upward mobility in America increases rather than decreases the resentment of those trapped at the bottom. After all, it dramatizes their failure. Faced with the alternative of blaming themselves or of feeling robbed of their birthright, they prefer to believe in injustice.

EDUCATIONAL OBSTACLES TO SOCIAL ASCENT

They are partly right. Youngsters get trapped at the bottom of the socio-economic heap largely because they do poorly at school. In all fairness, however, it should be remembered that the basis for school adjustment is laid in the home and the community. If a child's parents and friends hold education in awe and encourage him to bend every effort to learn from the teacher, he will value gold stars and high grades and being "promoted." If the child is sent to school because the law requires it (and because his mother wants to get him out from under her feet), he may regard the classroom as a kind of prison. Thus, family background is important to the youngster's adjustment in the crucial first years of school. Parents who see to it that their son keeps up with his work in primary school may make it possible later for him to pursue a business or professional career. Parents who permit their boys to flounder in the early grades unwittingly cut them off from the main path of social ascent.

Even an intellectually superior youngster can become a school "problem" if he is not properly motivated in the early grades. Forced to come at set times, to refrain from pinching his neighbors, to keep quiet so that the teacher can instruct the class as a group, he perceives school as a discipline imposed on him rather than an extension and development of his own interests. If no one at home or in the neighborhood makes school effort seem meaningful to him, he lacks the incentive to learn—no matter what his intellectual potentialities. The vicious circle of neglect and failure tightens. Within a few years, he is retarded in basic skills such as reading, which are necessary for successful performance in the higher grades. Whether he is promoted with his age-mates, "left back," or shunted into "slow" programs, the more successful students and the teachers consider him "dumb." This makes school still more unpleasant, and his distinterest increases.

By adolescence, he may well decide that he is fighting a losing battle. Is it surprising that he truants and becomes a disciplinary problem in class? Having learned little in school except how to annoy the teacher, he has neither the prerequisites for further education nor the courage to attempt to make up his deficiencies. It is too late for him to use the educational route to a high standard of living. But what other routes are there? Professional sports? The entertainment world? Politics? The opportunities in these fields are extremely limited. Pathetically, youngsters who think to escape from a pattern of defeat by withdrawing from school and going "to work" find that educational failure is predictive of occupational failure. Except for unskilled labor, high school graduation is required more and more, and college increases occupational prospects further. The youngster who quits school upon reaching the age when state law no longer compels attendance needs lots of luck if his goal is a well-paid job. The early school leaver usually gets unskilled work that offers little chance for advancement: stock clerk, delivery man, soda jerk, pin boy in a bowling alley. (His failure to complete high school, the competition of older and more experienced workers, and the stipulations of the child labor laws make employers reluctant to hire him—unless no one else is available.) He does not get along with supervisors any better than he did with teachers. He changes employment frequently. After several months of frustration, he may lose interest in steady work and instead take odd jobs when pressed for money.

THE GANG: AN ALTERNATIVE TO LOW STATUS

Psychically uncommitted to school or job, such a boy "hangs out" on the street corner with other unsuccessful youngsters. He needs their approval as a compensation for the rejection of school authorities and employers. The price for their approval runs high. He must show that he is not "chicken," i.e., cowardly, by manifesting a reckless willingness to steal, to fight, to try anything once. He must repudiate the bourgeois virtues associated with school and job: diligence, neatness, truthfulness, thrift. He becomes known as a "loafer" and a "troublemaker" in the community. When family and neighbors add their condemnations to those of teachers and employer, all bridges to respectability are burned, and he becomes progressively more concerned with winning "rep" inside the gang. For him, stealing is not primarily a way to make money. It is primarily a means of gaining approval within a clique of outcasts. The gang offers a heroic rather than an economic basis for self-respect. Of course, if a holdup or a burglary nets a substantial amount of money, the hoodlum has the best of both worlds. But for most hoodlums, the income from crime is pitifully small.[3] Only occasionally does a gang member graduate into the ranks of organized crime, as Al Capone did, and thereby become a financial success, Capone was an exception among hoodlums as Rockefeller was among businessmen.

Further insight into the motivation of the hoodlum results from contrasting him with the law-abiding adolescent. Clinical study reveals that the impulses to steal and murder and rape are universal. Apparently, the difference between the law-abiding adolescent and the hoodlum is not that one has impulses to violate the rules of society while the other has not. Both are tempted to break laws at some time or other— because laws prohibit what circumstance may make attractive: driving an automobile at 80 miles an hour, beating up an enemy, taking what one wants without paying for it. The hoodlum yields to these temptations. The boy living in a middle-class neighborhood does not. How can this difference be accounted for? Do shade trees, detached houses, and other economic advantages reduce envy, hatred, maliciousness? Or is it rather that middle-class youngsters have more to lose by giving rein to deviant impulses? What they have to lose should not be measured exclusively in material terms. True, the middle-class youngster has a spacious home to live in, nutritious food to eat, and fashionable clothes to wear; but he usually has social approval in addition. He comes from a "good" family. He lives in a "respectable" neighborhood. He is "neat and clean." Finally, he is likely to be a success in school. His teachers like him; he gets good marks; he moves easily from grade to grade. He has a basis for anticipating that this will continue until he completes college and takes up a business or professional career. If he applied his energies to burglary instead of to homework, he would risk not only the ego-flattering rewards currently available but his future prospects as well.

STAKE IN CONFORMITY

In short, youngsters vary in the extent to which they feel a stake in American society. For those with social honor, disgrace is a powerful sanction. For a boy disapproved of already, there is less incentive to resist the temptation to do what he wants when he wants to do it. Usually, the higher the socio-economic status of the family, the more the youngster feels he has to lose by deviant behavior. For instance, middle-class children are more successful in school, on the average, than lower-class children, although some lower-class youngsters fare better in school than some middle-class youngsters. To determine the stake which a youngster has in conformity it is necessary to know more than the level which his family occupies in the economic system. His own victories and defeats in interpersonal relations can be predicted only roughly from family income or father's occupation.

Some individuals have less stake in conformity than others in every community, but communities differ in the proportion of defeated people. A community with a high concentration of them has an even higher crime rate than would be expected from adding up the deviant predispositions of its individual members. Thus, the small incidence of stealing in suburbs is due not only to the scarcity of youngsters with little stake in conformity but also to the fact that a potential rebel is surrounded in school and in the neighborhood by age-mates who are motivated to compete within the framework of the established social system. They frown upon stealing because they do not need to rebel. On the other hand, in deteriorated neighborhoods, the concentration of defeated persons is greater. Therefore, a youngster needs a larger stake in conformity in the slum than in the suburb in order to resist temptation. In short, there is a social component to stake in conformity; the youngster meets defeat in isolation but does not usually become delinquent unless he obtains the support of his peers. In neighborhoods where most boys feel capable of competing in the educational-occupational status system, those who do not may be unhappy—but are not usually delinquent.

To sum up: the social disorganization approach can explain why community "A" has a higher crime rate than community "B" but not why Joe becomes a hoodlum and Jim does not. The differential stake in conformity of the individuals within a given community, on the other hand, can account for varying tendencies to become committed to an anti-social way of life.

THE FUNCTION OF SOCIAL DEFINITIONS IN THE DEVELOPMENT OF DELINQUENT CAREERS

Carl Werthman

THE MORAL career of the lower-class juvenile gang boy often begins at age 6, 7, or 8 when he is defined by his teachers as "pre-delinquent" for demonstrating to his friends that he is not a "sissy," and it ends between the ages of six-

Abbreviated with permission from an adaptation by Carl Werthman of his "The Function of Social Definitions in the Development of Delinquent Careers," *Task Force Report: Juvenile Delinquency and Youth Crime*, Report on Juvenile Justice and Consultants' Paper, Task Force on Juvenile Delinquency—The President's Commission on Law Enforcement and Administration of Justice (Washington: Government Printing Office, 1967), Appendix J, pp. 155–170. The original adaptation appeared in Donald R. Cressey and David A. Ward, *Delinquency, Crime, and Social Process*, New York: Harper & Row, 1969, pp. 613–632.

The research on which this paper is based was initiated by the Survey Research Center at the University of California in Berkeley on a grant from the Ford Foundation and was later moved to the Center for the Study of Law and Society on the Berkeley campus, where funds were made available under a generous grant from the Office of Juvenile Delinquency and Youth Development, Welfare Administra-

teen and twenty-five when he either takes a job, goes to college, joins the army, or becomes a criminal.[1] Although much
of his behavior during this period can be seen and is seen by
him as a voluntary set of claims on one of the temporary
social identities available to him as a lower class "youth," his
final choice of an adult identity will depend in large measure
on the way his moral character has been assessed, cate-
gorized, and acted upon by his parents, teachers, and officials
of the law as well as on the attitudes and actions he has
chosen in response. How the boys construct their identities,
how adults tend to define and treat them for doing so, and
how the boys respond to these definitions and treatments is
thus the subject of this paper.[2]

THE DYNAMICS OF
CHARACTER CONSTRUCTION

As Erving Goffman has elegantly made clear, there are certain attributes of moral character, particularly those most
prized by gang boys, that can only be claimed by aspirants to
them in social situations where something of consequence is
risked.[3] It is impossible to prove that one is cool, courageous,
or "smart," for example, without a situation in which there
is something to be cool, courageous, or "smart" about, just as
it is difficult to gain a reputation for being "tough" unless the
skills involved are occasionally put to a test.

Claiming title to these character traits can sometimes be
difficult, however, since risky situations do not arise very
often in the course of an average day. In fact, as Goffman
points out, most people manage to arrange their lives so that
matters of consequence such as one's body and money supply
are safely protected, although as a result most people also
encounter few situations in which the most heroic of social
virtues can actually be claimed.

Yet if someone with an adult status actually decides he de-

tion, U.S. Department of Health, Education, and Welfare in cooperation
with the President's Committee on Juvenile Delinquency and Youth
Crime.

sires "action," there is always Las Vegas or a risky job, while a lower-class gang boy is more or less forced to create his own.[4] If he wishes to prove that he is autonomous, courageous, loyal, or has "heart," not only must he take a chance, he must also construct the situations in which to take it; and for most gang boys this means that risky situations must be created from whatever materials happen to be at hand.[5]

Although the various activities defined as "thefts" provide perhaps the best examples of the way gang boys use laws to generate character while they are on the streets, the situations in which laws against theft are broken must be carefully selected to insure that sufficient risk is present. Unlike the professional thief who takes pride in knowing how to minimize the occupational risks of his trade, most younger gang boys create risks where none need be involved.[6] Joyriding, for example, is ideally suited for this purpose. Not only does it require "cool" to get a stolen car started quickly, once the car is started there is also the courage generated by the generous though not overwhelming chance of getting caught. Moreover, given the wide range of risky activities that can be engaged in once the cars are stolen, joyriding is viewed as an abundant source of the anxiety, excitement, and tension that is often referred to as "kicks."

(Did you guys do much joyriding?) Yeah. When I was about thirteen, I didn't do nothing but steal cars. The guy that I always stole with, both of us liked to drive so we'd steal a car. And then he'd go steal another car and we'd chase each other. Like there would be two in our car, two in the other car, and we'd drive by and stick out our hands, and if you touch them then they have to chase you. Or we'd steal an old car, you know, that have the running boards on it. We'd stand on that and kick the car going past. Kind of fun, but, uh, it's real dangerous. We used to have a ball when we'd do that other game with the hands though.

Although joyriding was almost always done at night, the younger gang boys I studied also located two risky daytime situations in which to engage in theft. On Saturday afternoons they would delight in trying to steal hubcaps from a packed parking lot next to a local supermarket, and on special occasions, they enjoyed breaking into gum and candy machines located in a crowded amusement park. In the parking lot, the challenge consisted of making away with the hubcaps without being seen, while in the equally crowded amusement park, the object was to escape from the police after making sure that the theft itself had been observed.

                                   .   .   .

In addition to using the laws against theft, gang boys also use each other to demonstrate moral character—a type of risk-taking activity that Goffman calls a "character game."

I assume that when two persons are in one another's presence it will be inevitable that many of the obligations of one will be the expectations of the other (and vice versa), in matters both substantive and ceremonial. Each participant will have a personal vested interest in seeing to it that in this particular case the rules the other ought to obey are in fact obeyed by him. Mutual dependence on the other's proper conduct occurs. Each individual necessarily thus becomes a field in which the other necessarily practices good or bad conduct. In the ordinary course of affairs, compliance, forebearance and the mechanisms of apology and excuse insure that showdowns don't occur. None the less, contests over whose treatment of the other is to prevail are always a possibility, and can almost always be made to occur. The participants will then find themselves committed to producing evidence that will cause a re-assessment of self at the expense of the assessment that will come to be made of the other. A *character game results.*[7]

Goffman suggests that the stake in most character games is a claim to possess *honor*, honor defined as "the property of character which causes the individual to engage in a character contest when his rights have been violated and when the likely cost of the contest is high."[8] Like other forms of "action," then, character games are played at some risk but also presumably for some reward.

As Short and Strodtbeck have pointed out, fighting is perhaps the classic example of a gang activity that is best understood with this model.[9] After observing gang boys in Chicago for a number of years, these authors concluded that most fights take place either when a *"rep"* for toughness is suddenly challenged or when a challenge to within-group rank appears, either from inside or outside the gang.

Although it is quite true that most older gang boys will only fight when their reputations or ranks are threatened, the younger boys can sometimes be found initiating fights even though they have not been provoked. These fights are consciously sought out or searched for in an attempt to build a reputation where none existed before, and the boys are referred to as "looking for trouble" because they are "coming up." In these situations, also, an attempt is usually made to select the target carefully. Not any rival gang will serve as a suitable object on which to build a rep, and thus . . . a gang invading "rival territory" may decide to go home if the members cannot find boys who are big or important enough to prove a case.

.   .   .

Regardless of whether fights are entered into voluntarily or involuntarily, however, the basic principle involved in this mode of character construction is clear: the fight is defined as a situation in which reputation or rank can be won or lost, and whether a particular fight will be entered into depends on the expected values of the various outcomes, values that can vary considerably from boy to boy. It is no accident, for example, that situations involving violence are often perceived as "turning points" by ex-gang members when contemplating their past careers. Particularly among older boys, it is easy to see how reputations can get so great as to be too risky to defend.[10] Similarly, in areas where it is tacitly understood that certain affronts can only be revenged by attempting to kill the offender, the person offended may simply decide to leave town or the neighborhood rather than risk being sent to jail or killed defending his honor.[11]

The behavior described by Miller as "verbal aggression," also known variously as "ranking," "capping," or "sounding," seems to involve some of the same principles found in fights.[12] As Matza has pointed out, this activity amounts essentially to a process of testing status by insult, and thus honor is the quality of moral character at stake.[13] Goffman has called these encounters "contest contests," situations in which someone forces someone else "into a contest over whether or nor there will be a contest."[14] Like fighting, this activity involves risk and thus can have a bearing on status. Unlike fighting, however, it is not engaged in to demonstrate toughness or courage but rather to display a type of verbal agility that gang boys call "smarts."

Women are a further source of risky activity for gang boys, since status in a gang is also affected by success or failure at "making out." During most of the years spent in a gang, girls are seen primarily as objects for sexual play, and it is not until the age of sixteen or older that they are sometimes treated with anything resembling respect. Ultimately, however, it is marriage that takes most boys out of the gang, thus providing one of the few available legitimate excuses for leaving the streets.[15]

. . .

The gang boy thus aspires to an identity that puts him in a special relationship to risk. When he is around his friends, he often creates the situations in which he chooses to exist, an act of creation that involves selecting out certain features of the social environment and then transforming them into the conditions that allow him to define a self. Taken together, these risky activities can be interpreted as claims to be treated prematurely as "men," a status that gang boys are culturally and structurally forbidden to occupy until the "delinquent career" comes to an end. . . .

THE GENESIS OF AUTONOMY

Although the absence of adult economic responsibilities can be seen as conducive to the development of unconventional identity formations among youth, young people are also legally dependent on adults. A person under age eighteen is always in the custody of someone; and, if he proves to be beyond control by parents, he can always be adopted by the state.

Yet, in most instances, parental power develops into authority.[16] And it is precisely this authority relationship that allows at least the pre-adolescent to define himself as "a child." He implicitly surrenders his autonomy in return for the feeling of being protected and thus he does not exercise the capacity he might otherwise have to make his own decisions.

In addition to securing their own authority, however, parents also have a vested interest in endowing a variety of adult officials with a temporary "title to rule." For example, to ensure that the authority of school personnel is perceived as legitimate, children, are made aware that their parents can be informed of all misadventures. Parents thus become the center of a communications network for other adult authorities; and whether the child is at school or on the streets, he is made to feel none of his behavior can be hidden from his parents.[17]

. . . Although I encountered a great many parents who had come to look upon the trip to jail as "routine" by the time their sons were sixteen, I found none who said that at an earlier point in life they had not hoped for something better. In practically every case it was possible to locate a set of expectations that was perceived by parents either to have broken down or never to have developed, despite the fact that many had also come to view the news of "trouble" as a more or less "normal" event.

. . .

This problem is frequently and simply illustrated among the parents of pre-adolescent and "pre-delinquent" boys, many of whom are described simply as "out of control." In these cases, what parents seem to be describing are situations in which no stable pattern of mutual expectations develops at all. Whatever preferred rules they attempt to establish as ways of ordering the activities of the family are more or less randomly ignored, and thus these parents can rarely count on their sons either to be at school, at home for meals, or sometimes even in bed. For example:

(How do you handle Melvin when he gets into trouble?) Well, we figure that weekends are the main times he looks forward to —parties and going out. So we'd say, "You can't go out tonight." You know, we'd try to keep him from something he really wanted to do. But he usually goes out anyway. Like one night we was watching TV, and Melvin said he was tired and went to bed. So then I get a phone call from a lady who wants to know if Melvin is here because her son is with him. I said, "No, he has gone to bed already." She says, "Are you sure?" I said, "I'm pretty sure." So I went downstairs and I peeked in and saw a lump in the bed but I didn't see his head. So I took a look and he was gone. He came home about 12:30, and we talked for a while. (What did you do?) Well, I told him he was wrong going against his parents like that, but he keeps sneaking out anyway. (What does your husband do about it?) Well, he don't do much. I'm the one who gets upset. My husband, he'll say something to Mel and then he'll just relax and forget about it. (Husband and wife laugh together.) There's little we can do, you know. It's hard to talk to him 'cause he just go ahead and do what he wants anyway.

These children, most between the ages of 6 and 10, were some of the most puzzling people I met on this study. Their behavior always seemed to make perfect sense to them, but it also seemed to make so much sense that they could not produce accounts for it. Although they sometimes exhibited a touch of bravado, they were only rarely defensive, and most managed to carry themselves with what can only be described as miniature adult poise. . . .

These children are a testimony to the fact that basic rules about authority are not accepted automatically, even among the young. The assumption of dependence must be cultivated before it can be used as a basis for control; in fact, that becomes quite clear when for some reason the assumption of dependence is never made. In these cases, the children often demonstrate a remarkable capacity to take care of themselves. In fact, one could argue that the pre-adolescent who does not conceive of himself as dependent on his parents also does not really conceive of himself as "a child," particularly when he loses his virginity at eight and supports himself on lunch money taken from classmates. Once the authority rule is rejected, the family as an activity system becomes an entirely new game. Legally the child is not an adult, but sociologically it is hard to argue that he is still a child.[18]

Not only is the assumption of autonomy the important issue at home, it also has important implications for the way gang boys are treated by school officials and officers of the law. Most young people adopt a posture of deference in the presence of adult authorities because this posture is a "taken-for-granted" assumption about the self. Yet to gang boys this posture is a matter of choice. They can defer or not defer, depending on their feelings about a teacher or a "cop"; and for most adult authorities, the very existence of the assumption that submissiveness is a matter of choice is either sufficient grounds for the withdrawal of "trust" or is considered a personal affront.

THE MEANING OF "DELINQUENCY" IN THE SCHOOLS

The posture of premature autonomy is carried directly into the schools and the result is the "pre-delinquent." As early as the first and second grade, his teachers find him wild, distracted, and utterly oblivious to their presumed authority. He gets out of chairs when he feels like it; begins fighting when he feels like it; and all of this is done as if the teacher were not present.

Further, once the boys begin to prove that they are "tough," there seems to be little that the schools can do to stop them. If they are suspended, they come to school anyway; and if they are transferred from one class to another, they return to the first class or to whatever teacher they happeen to like. Moreover, since the boys seem immune to sanctions, their bullying, thefts, and truancies are often blatantly displayed.

It is not until the fifth or sixth grades that organized gangs begin to form, and, in a certain sense, it is not until this age that the boys can be brought under systematic group control. Since most of my work was done with older boys, however, this discussion must be confined to them.

Although there are many differences between contemporary sociological portraits of the lower-class juvenile delinquent, the same model of his educational problem is used by most authors. Regardless of whether the delinquent is viewed as ambitious and capable,[19] ambitious and incapable,[20] or unambitious and incapable,[21] the school is sketched as a monolith of middle-class personnel against which he fares badly.

Yet the school difficulties of these boys occur only in some classes and not others, and this fact suggests that pitting middle-class schools against variations in the motivation and capacity of some lower-class boys is at best too simple and at worst incorrect as a model of the problem. Good and bad students alike are consistently able to get through half or more of their classes without friction, and it is only in particular classes with particular teachers that incidents leading to suspension flare up.

We thus need . . . to look at the classroom as a place where a range of possible activities or "constitutive orders of events" can take place. The most common set is known as "teaching and learning," but these are not the only activities that can take place. Many young people, including gang boys, tend also to see the classroom as a place to see friends, converse by written notes, read comic books, eat, sleep, or stare out the window. For example:

If I'm bored then I have to do something to make it exciting. First, second, and third ain't too bad because I get me two comic books and they last me three periods.

Further, most gang boys will "test" the limits of the classroom situation before making up their minds whether a teacher can be trusted. This is done by purposely violating a rule preferred by the teacher in such a way as to suggest that their participation in the classroom is a voluntary act and should be acknowledged as such with the proper amount of respect.

When confronted with activities other than "learning" or behavior that is clearly designed to "test," most teachers respond by insisting that their rights to teach be respected and their authority be properly maintained. They thus resort to the imperative and begin to issue commands. But this response, in turn, is almost always defined by gang boys as "getting smart." The boys view the teacher's insistence on his rights to authority as a violation of their rights to autonomy, and thus the prospect of a "character contest" arises over whose honor is to remain intact. Moreover, if the boys do not concede the contest for fear of being expelled, they often challenge the authority of the teacher again.

This challenge tends to take one of three forms: it is either done subtly with demeanor, directly with words, or forcefully with violence. . . .

.   .   .

The issue of who decides what takes place in classrooms is not the only matter of dispute that sometimes arises. For example, although the students may be willing to comply with the rule establishing the teacher as the source of preferred rules, they may also feel that there are limits to the kinds of things a teacher can legitimately make rules about. These issues are most likely to arise when teachers feel it is within their jurisdiction to pass judgment on the dress and physical appearance of their students; and if a gang boy feels that his moral character has been reconstituted by a teacher on the basis of the clothes he wears, he is likely to register his sense of injustice.[22]

A gang boy's career as a "delinquent" in the schools is thus a highly problematic affair, since the genesis and outcome of character contests are in part affected by the conduct of teachers themselves. In many instances, of course, the boys will "test" a teacher to see if a claim to autonomy will be honored. Yet if the teacher is willing to concede the fact that school is meaningless to some boys and that other activities besides "teaching and learning" will necessarily go on in class, and if he is willing to limit the scope of his jurisdiction to the activity of "teaching and learning" itself, then his authority is likely to remain intact. Whether or not he can persuade the boys to join the learning process is another matter again; but it is precisely at this point that we see the merits of defining authority after Bertrand de Juvenel as "the faculty of gaining another man's assent."[23]

THE MEANING OF "DELINQUENCY" TO THE POLICE

As Aaron Cicourel has recently suggested, the transformation of gang boys into official "delinquents" by policemen, probation officers, and judges of the juvenile court can also be looked upon as an organizational rather than a legal process, since the criteria used to contact, categorize, and dispose of boys often has little to do with breaking the law itself.[24]

In studies of how boys are contacted by the police, the distinction between policemen and juvenile officers is often made, largely because these two groups often tend to organize their work in different ways. Harvey Sacks has suggested that the task of the patrolman can best be defined as "inferring the probability of criminality from the appearances persons present in public places";[25] and, as David Matza has pointed out, this task "is similar in almost every respect to that faced by the sociologist." Both must "classify individuals" into a set of social or legal categories since "true indicators rarely exist";[26] and the indicators of suspicion mentioned most frequently by policemen and gang boys are a combination of race and neighborhood, plus an odd assortment of clothing, hair, and walking styles.[27]

Although it is difficult to imagine how patrolmen could organize their work in any other way, the indicators of suspicion they use provoke considerable outrage among the boys. As soon as a patrolman makes contact with a boy, the structure of the situation itself reveals his mistrust. The boy instantly knows that if he were not a Negro and was not sporting boots and long hair, his moral character would not have been called into question and he could walk the streets without insult, risk, or fear.

Most gang boys respond to these situational insults the way they respond to teachers who challenge their autonomy in the schools. By acquitting themselves with a straightforward nonchalance or indifference and refusing to proffer the expected gestures of respect, the boys insult the authority of the patrolman who then must either arrest, use his billy club, or withdraw from the situation as honorably as he can.

Members of Juvenile Bureaus tend to make contact with gang boys on other grounds. Unlike patrolmen, they attempt to trace particular crimes to their source in a universe of suspects rather than trying to link "suspicious people" to the universe of possible crimes.

Once suspects are contacted, however, both patrolmen and

juvenile officers proceed the same way. A variety of interrogation techniques are used, including lies about the amount
of information possessed. And the success of these techniques
is reflected in the fact that over 90 per cent of juvenile convictions in the United States are gotten because boys "confess."

Yet even these confessions do not mean much, since most
policemen, like probation officers and judges, define the "delinquent" as a boy with questionable moral character rather
than as a boy who has merely committed a crime. Thus, the
age of an offender, his family situation, his prior arrest
record, and the nature of his offense all enter into dispositions
as do the style and speed with which he manages to confess.[28]
If he confesses immediately, this act is taken as a sign that
the boy "trusts" adults, in which case it is further assumed
that his attachment to the basic authority rule is both sound
and intact. If he proves to be a "tough nut to crack," however,
he is viewed with suspicion. It is said that he is "hardened,"
does not "trust" authority, and is therefore probably "out of
control."

Piliavin and Briar also report that boys who appear fright-
ened, humble, penitent, and ashamed are also more likely
to go free.[29] And, conversely, in a study of the differential
selection of juvenile offenders for court appearances, Nathan
Goldman reports that "defiance on the part of a boy will lead
to juvenile court quicker than anything else."[30]

Given the variety of criteria that seem to enter into dispositions, the moral career of a gang boy in the eyes of the courts
and the police becomes almost as problematic as his "delinquent" career in the schools, particularly when the techniques
used by the police themselves provoke the very defiance that
ultimately sends him to jail.

OPPORTUNITIES, CONTINGENCIES, AND RISKS

There is some evidence to suggest that most gang boys
have a conception of how and when their careers as "delinquents" will end. As Short and Strodtbeck have recently re-

ported, most look forward to becoming stable and dependable husbands in well-run households, despite their reluctance to voice these expectations around one another and despite the fact that some become fathers out of wedlock along the way.[31] Similarly, although about half the boys interviewed by Short and Strodtbeck anticipate problems in securing "good paying honest jobs," their images of family life make it clear that the great majority expect to be holding down some kind of conventional occupation when they finally do become "adults."[32]

During most of the years the boys spend in gangs, however, these aspirations are neither salient nor relevant, and thus they do not think much about the future at all. They understand that as long as they are defined and define themselves as "youth," they are not the people they will someday become. And since they do not have the responsibility of maintaining a home and a job, they have little to lose by devoting their time to more expressive and entertaining pursuits.

Yet what happens to a boy at the end of a "delinquent" career is very much affected by how he deals with the various contingencies that arise during the course of career itself, particularly those associated with the way he is acted upon by policemen, probation officers, and judges of the juvenile court. For example, although the consequences of taking risks become more serious as arrest records get longer, a boy who knows that the California Youth Authority awaits him if he is caught for theft or joyriding one more time can demonstrate possession of more courage than the boys who have never been caught. Similarly, the judge who orders a boy to discontinue his association with particular friends also makes it possible for him to demonstrate even greater loyalty than before.

Thus, to the extent that boys do not drop out of gangs as the sanctions they face become more severe, they tend to constitute an increasingly select elite. In the identity system of the gang world, reputation increases with the fatefulness of the situation in which a boy is willing to take a risk, and thus the boys who have been sent to the more important prisons can flaunt this fact as evidence that they have paid and were willing to pay a more significant price for maintaining their identity on the streets.

.   .   .

In addition to the contingencies associated with a boy's situation in the eyes of the law, the progress of his moral career is made even more indeterminate by the fact that it is often difficult for him to assess the consequences of his acts until *after* they have been committed. As we have seen, this is particularly true in cases involving the courts and the police where many more rules are invoked to pass judgment on the offender than were actually involved in the offense.

Also, there is the fact that courts sometimes create their own special rules to judge the "improvement" of a boy, but when these rules are violated, there is a sense in which they have created the very criteria by which the boy is then condemned. Consider, for example, the following conversation between this researcher and a twelve-year-old boy who had just run away from his foster home. He had been living with "Uncle Eddie," his mother's brother, essentially because his older brothers were in jail, his father deserted the family some years ago, and, as a result of these actions by other members of the family, his mother was declared "unfit" and Danny was forced to go.

(Why did you stay away from school yesterday?) I felt like comin' to San Francisco to see my mother. (Didn't you go back last night?) Yeh, but my cousin Darlene said they was lookin' for me, you know, my probation officer. He came to visit me in school and couldn't find me. I got scared so I came back up here. (Where did you stay last night?) I slept in a friend of mine's car. I figured I better not go home. I don't want to get my mother in dutch. They'll call her and if she says I'm home that'll get her in trouble. . . .

(Well, what do you plan to do now?) I don't know. I figure I could keep running. I could stay with my brother up in Tahoe, but it's tough bein' on the run. What do you think I should do? (I don't know either. Let's discuss it. You're the one that has to make the decision. How do you like living down at your Uncle Eddie's?) I don't like it. They talk about me behind my back, and they say bad things about my mother. And Eddie's no good. He won't even buy me gym clothes. They told me at school I can't go to gym class unless I got the clothes, and he won't get them. He said he already bought me some and I lost 'em but he's lyin'. He never bought me no gym clothes. (Would you rather live somewhere else?) Yeh, but they won't let me come home. They say I got too many friends up there and the school won't let me back. But all my friends have left, and I could go to a different school. I know I could make it. But they won't let me. . . .

This is a good example of what can happen with probation restrictions. A boy is sent to a foster home because he comes from a broken one and then plays hookey in order to come back. The truancy is produced by the desire to see his mother, and the terms of his probation make this act an offense unless it is properly approved. . . .

Yet the fact remains that boys who remain on the streets take more serious risks than boys who leave them; and thus, in terms of the logic underlying the identity system itself, they justifiably see themselves as more committed than others to this round of life. The most serious change in their situation occurs, however, when the police finally decide to "crack down." The boys are warned to "stay off the streets or else," and after this injunction has been issued, the character of the streets is fundamentally transformed. The neighborhood, the territory, and the hangout cease being places where it is merely dangerous to be found since the probability is nearly perfect that if they remain on the streets they will go to jail.

In summary, then, by viewing the "delinquent career" as a more or less stable sequence of acts taken in risky social situations in order to claim an identity or define a self, often followed by changes in the rules that make up these situations, and followed again by new choices of the self in the new situations, it is possible to see how a gang boy could arrive at the age of 18 or 21 to find that his situation makes it costly, painful, or difficult for him to take the conventional job that he always expected to take, particularly if he has come to view the conventional world as a place full of the kinds of people who have labeled him a "delinquent."[33]

Once a gang boy gets beyond the age of 18, moreover, he has a choice to make about what identity system to enter. He could get married, get a job, and assume the status of a full-fledged "adult"; he could decide to postpone this decision in legitimate ways such as joining the Army or going to school at night; or he could spend a few more years as an elder statesman on the streets.

The decision he makes at this point in his career will depend in part on his situation. If he managed to graduate from high school, he may well decide to go on to college; but if he was expelled from high school, he may feel either bitter or reluctant about getting the high school degree. He knows that he has been administratively reborn in the eyes of the law, and thus the risks he takes by staying on the streets increase considerably, since he now may be processed by the courts as an adult. On the other hand, if his status in the gang world is still high, he may not want to trade it for a low-paying blue-collar job; and he knows he will be rejected by the Army if he has a jail record of any kind.

In short, it is at this point in his career that the "opportunities" available to him will affect his behavior, his attitudes, and the decisions he makes about his life. If there are no legitimate options open to him that would not mean a sudden decrease in status, he may well decide to stay on the streets, despite the greater consequences involved in taking risks.

If he remains on the streets, however, his perception and use of theft becomes increasingly instrumental until it finally turns into a particular version of the "hustle." These hustles still involve risks, but the risks are no longer incurred exclusively for the sake of demonstrating something about the self. The boys now need the money, and their relationship to the risky situation changes as both positive and negative outcomes become more consequential. The actual thefts themselves are also talked about less and less: as attempts are made to avoid detection, a boy's source of money becomes more and more his own business.

Along with the hustle comes a full-blown ideology: when a boy views the conventional world as a place he is expected to enter, he tends to develop a "position" on it. Jobs become "slaves"; going to school becomes "serving time"; and the assumptions about marriage and getting a conventional job are replaced by exploitative relations with women and fantasies about a big "score." These are no longer the "delinquent boys" described by Cohen.[34] They are the defensive aristocrats described by Finestone, and by Sykes and Matza. They have an answer to everything, and they always "know the score."

By this time the boys are really at the end of their "delinquent" careers. If they do not get jobs, go to jail, or get killed, they simply fade into an underground of pool rooms, pimps, and petty thefts. Most cannot avoid ending up with conventional jobs, however, largely because the "illegitimate opportunities" available simply are not that good.

EL BARRIO'S WORST BLOCK IS NOT ALL BAD

David and Sophy Burnham

A BLOCK in El Barrio—Spanish Harlem—despite all the speeches and studies and community-action programs of the last years, remains remarkably foreign to most Americans, who have never lived in the crowded, dirty world of aging, six-story tenements, or talked to the people who live there— the parents, the children, the wage-earners, the welfare-takers, the healthy and the sick. Another reason why the area is hard to understand is that most studies of this world have focused on only one of the dark aspects of its life—the lack of family stability, or the decaying housing, or the drug addicts, or unemployment or the obviously unsuccessful schools —and failed to portray the stable families, the industrious working fathers, and the teen-agers who have rejected drugs, the large numbers who grow strong and survive.

This block . . . has been more completely portrayed. The work was begun four years ago by Drs. Bernard Lander, Nathan Lander, and H. P. O'Brien, and sponsored by the University of Notre Dame. A rare picture has emerged by now of one period in the life of the block and some changes in the life-styles of its residents.

The 25 tenements facing the 630-foot street are of red brick, most of them blackened with grime. They seem to press in on the street. Two buildings have been abandoned, their windows broken, their insides gutted by fire and emptied by thieves. Between some of them are sudden open spaces where a building has been torn down and the empty lot has become filled with rubble and beer cans. In contrast are five freshly painted tenements on one side of the street which are being renovated by a local housing organization, Metro North.

Today, after the removal of a few tenements, there are 400 families of 1,750 individuals. Three out of every five residents are Puerto Rican, almost all the rest Negro. The population is far younger than that of the city as a whole; every other person is under 21.

A complete census of the block found that two of every three families are headed by men; the rest by women. Of these family heads, more than half had not finished school, more than half were unemployed, a quarter were on welfare, a third made less than $60 a week. Rent, compared with the rest of Manhattan, seems low; two-thirds of the families pay between $25 and $45 a month for a three- or four-room apartment.

Since one of the advantages of poor accommodations is low rent, the poorest people tend to remain on the block; and the poorest are also those with the least education, the least resistance to and the fewest outlets for frustration, the highest incidence of ill health, mental disturbance and unemployment. The interior of the housing on the block has often been described: brown hallways with their rotten stairs and the acrid smell of garbage; cold apartments with overflowing toilets and moist, peeling paint. Housing probably is the worst problem because it is always with you. Your son can be a junkie, or your daughter in trouble with the police, and this is a worry, gnawing at the back of your mind. But if your roof leaks, it leaks on you and all around you. You cannot get away from it.

. . . The fighting gangs are gone now, and apparently there are fewer crimes of violence, but the street—almost without shops, seemingly deserted on a cold winter day—is a marketplace for drugs. A bookie hangs out here. A numbers racketeer. Two pushers. Youths watch for fags to service for $5, money that immediately will be converted into a bag of heroin. Girls walk the streets. You can find almost anything here, and the activities permeate the lives of everyone, whether they participate and approve or not.

The fact is that the majority of the people on the block do not participate even peripherally in the life of crime, beyond a regular bet on the numbers. Crime is often a matter of definition. In some cases, it is simply an accommodation to a situation. And on this block, if there is considerable crime, particularly of a sort that is not found in well-off areas (numbers, pushers, fences), there is also a surprisingly conservative, even middle-class, morality.

Of the 50 teen-age members of the old fighting gang that was centered on the block, for instance, three are now in rackets, eight or ten are addicts; but three are members of the police force, one is a lieutenant in the Marines, and the remaining 30 or 35 have also "gone straight." It seems to be a matter of growing up.

Look at Angelina, the 19-year-old mother of an illegitimate child, who admitted she smoked pot when she was 14, shoplifted, roamed the streets. She doesn't do that anymore.

"It's not lady—it's not for a woman. That's men's stuff. Boy's stuff."

The block is composed of 1,750 individuals as different as characters in a good novel. There is the short, heavy woman, a social worker, with direct brown eyes and a finely arched nose, strong, proud, self-sufficient. She has lived on the block with her husband and four children for 40 years. She sent one son through college. And there is the woman whose two daughters are lesbian—and it is a sad commentary on the neighborhood that the third will probably be one, too. (There seems to be a lot of lesbianism on the block. Many girls are drawn to it, either from fear of the hit-and-run tactics of the boys, or else because they grew up in state institutions where homosexuality is common. Lesbianism does not prevent accidents, though; and what does a mother feel when she discovers that her 14-year-old daughter is a lesbian—and later watches the 14-year-old belly swell with pregnancy anyway? "I thought you liked girls! And a boy, who you don't even know where he lives.")

A large number of people on the block believe that ability is more important than pull or "who you know." Many of the 25 per cent on welfare are ashamed of receiving it, though others accommodate themselves to it quite cynically. There is Johnny, a Negro, whose wife is on welfare despite her paying job. Sometimes he lives with her, sometimes with his girl friend on another block, and sometimes he even gives his wife some of the $80 a week he makes as a full-time social worker. There is the addict whose wife and four children live on welfare on another block. They have an apartment for $75 a month, and he told her to stay on welfare because even though he has a job he can't afford both the rent and his habit.

Perhaps drugs have the most to do with the evil reputation of the block. One-twentieth of all the deaths from overdoses in Manhattan in 1967 (20 out of 400) occurred on this block, and despite continued and frequent arrests, the block has maintained its reputation as a place to get heroin. Cars with Jersey plates cruise down the street, looking for a connection. (Yet only a small proportion of the block's population, less than 2 per cent, uses heroin.)

There is a lot of talk on the block about drugs—OD's (overdoses), copping (procuring drugs) and skin-popping and mainlining (intramuscular and intravenous injection). Every now and then the addicts go to a hospital for a cure or to reduce the amount of heroin they need. An addict named Ralph has tried to kick the habit 11 times, and each time, the first day out, as soon as he can, he mainlines.

Yet heroin gets different holds on different people. Some addicts lead quite normal lives. There is the man on the block who has been using heroin every day for 10 years, skin-popping only, never putting it in his veins. There is another who mainlines only on weekends, and holds a regular job during the week.

On the block, there is a distinction between an addict and a junkie. An addict has pride. A junkie will stoop to anything to support his habit. "He'll hustle his own sister. That's disgusting. I can't see it. I feel that if you have a habit, support it. . . . Be a man about it. . . . If you got to steal, go steal. It's a job like any other job. You make faster money, and you deprive people of other things, but it's a job. . . . They require certain skills and stealing is one of them."

One young man, speaking of his addict brothers, recalls with pride: "They did a lot of stealing, but not from our house. . . . They respect my mother and respect my father. If they did anything, they did it outside. The door was open to them 24 hours a day."

The block is not afraid of the addicts. Addicts are usually not violent. "They just support their habit by stealing. They're only like a rat. If you corner them, they have to jump you. Because they are—the point is—if they would go to your house, and you will be there, they won't enter. They're just as scared as anybody."

Not all addicts on the block steal to support their habits. At least a third of them, according to Lander's study, have regular jobs or are supported by parents or a working husband or wife.

So the addicts survive. They scrounge and get by, and for the most part live unmolested on the fringes of the block. Moreover, it seems eventually some of them do stop.

While Lander found that during the four-year period of his study one-third of the kids began taking heroin, he also discovered that about one-third of those with a drug history —22 out of 60 addicts and former addicts—had quit. It seems they reached their late 20's and early 30's and simply stopped. On the average they had been off drugs for three years or more. All but three stopped without the assistance of the various government programs.

Unlike the addiction-prevention agencies, which appear to

have reached almost none of the people on the block, welfare and schools touch many. Of the quarter of the families on welfare, some get off the rolls quickly, others remain on welfare for years.

"Yes, welfare helps, because it's a salary, just like being a husband to some women," said Juan, a young man who lives on the block. "But to others, it's a hold-back, the chain that's holding him back."

The schools are not wholly admired either. "Yeah," said one young man, looking back on his education, "we used to go to the classroom and the airplanes flying all over the room, and then in a hour you have finish another class and there's a different program. You weren't in one place long enough to learn anything."

If the welfare system and the schools often fail at the task of developing citizens capable of standing on their own feet, it seems clear that the system of criminal justice—the police, courts and prisons—is often equally irrelevant to the problem of crime. Many on the block, especially the young people, admit that they commit illegal acts on a fairly regular basis. For the teen-agers, for example, the weekly shoplifting trip down to Macy's or up to Incredible Alexander's in the Bronx is a regular Saturday entertainment, like going to a movie.

"Why do you steal?"

"To get what we wanted. Pocketbooks and clothes."

They go in groups of twos or threes, the girls in their cliques, the boys in theirs. One girl will stand guard watching for the store detectives, while her friends stand at a rack of chain belts, trying them on, choosing the one they want. At the all-clear, they rip off the price tag and move out of the store. Sometimes they are spotted by the detectives and they hit the door running, and race across the street, dodging among the cars, to collapse laughing a few blocks away.

They rarely are caught, partly because they are very adept, partly because the stores find it cheaper to accept a certain amount of shiplifting than to hire enough clerks to wait on each customer. One store detective estimated that his staff catches one of five of the shoplifters, about half of whom are middle-class. When the slum kids are caught, he said, "the

Puerto Ricans break down and cry; the Negroes are cool, tough."

Often the youngsters don't bother with the long trip downtown. They pocket an item from stores in the neighborhood as they have undoubtedly seen adults do. Sometimes, more rarely, the kids will steal on order, the casual comment by some adult that he could really use a radio becoming the signal for a profit-making transaction.

The kids on the block experiment with drugs (one addict said he first tasted heroin when he was 11), "scheme" (pet) the girls, sneak into the subways, break into cars, hang around and get bored, rubbing up against the police as they roam the streets. No backyard or open field gives them the buffer against the law which is available to the suburban young. Despite this constant confrontation, however, a check of police and F.B.I. records shows that surprisingly few persons on the block have ever been arrested—or given, if under 16, a Youth Division card. Only one out of 11 on the block has any kind of police record. (Checks on similar blocks in Washington, D.C., and Chicago showed much more police activity than in New York.)

As of 1964, about one in four of those between 11 and 20 (128 out of 488) had been picked up by the police. Most of the charges were trivial. About a third of them were for truancy, running under subway turnstiles, disorderly conduct and fighting. About one in 10 was for either assault or burglary.

The charges brought against adults were more serious. There were seven for robbery, three for shoplifting, two for purse-snatching, and 16 for petty larceny. The single largest category of crime charges against the adults on the block involved drugs—crimes which seldom involve unwilling victims.

If surprisingly small numbers are arrested on the block, an even smaller proportion ever get to court or prison. According to police records, only 11 per cent of the boys between 11 and 20, and only 30 per cent of the adults who were arrested ever went on to court. These figures raise the questions whether the larger police force many call for would actually reduce crime and whether efforts would not be better directed to the schools, which at least have direct contact with almost everyone living in the area. Particularly so since what contact the block has with the law hardly seems to contribute to a higher sense of morality. There is an almost unanimous lack of respect for the police there, a widespread belief that they are corrupt and brutal.

"One of my friends got killed by a cop," a pretty young Puerto Rican girl remembered. "The cop was drinking and they say he came out of a bar on 103d Street, and the kid was running and some lady was yelling, and he got shook up and he shot him in the back and got him killed, and he died."

"Had your friend done anything?"

"I don't know. You really don't know what happened 'cause the cop told his story and that's all the story. It was still wrong 'cause he coulda shot him in the leg or something, but he shot to kill."

She added: " 'Cause you're a Puerto Rican or Negro, they just take you in the car and beat you up and then take you to the precinct and everything."

Tonio was beaten up that way and returned home with his face swollen as evidence of the treatment. Also Peter, who tried to escape from Elmira prison. "They beat him on the body. They did not beat him on the head, 'cause they probably would have killed him. But they beat him with rubber nightsticks."

A young man was asked whether the police accept bribes.

"Oh sure, they do that all the time."

"Have you ever seen it yourself?"

"Giving them money? Oh sure."

"Who would it be?"

"Bookies. All over. Everything."

A runner for the numbers racket was even more definite. "They, you know, they come around the first of every month. There is the cop which you call the captain's man and he comes around and he picks up for the captain and then the cop on duty he gets paid, too."

"Aren't there any honest cops?"

"Yeah. You get an honest cop on Fifth Avenue someplace. You can't have honest guys around a block like this."

It is estimated that the residents of this one short block bet $270,000 a year on the numbers game (50 cents per person, six days a week). If this figure is multiplied by the 130,000 people in the local police precinct, it appears that each year about $20-million is being gambled on numbers in that small corner of Harlem. The size of this operation makes believable the rumors that some of the $10,000-a-year plainclothesmen charged with stopping gambling receive $1,000-a-month payoffs.

It is easy to see crime and evil when you look at a block. It is harder to see the good, since the good people are often "good" merely in a negative sense—that is, refrain from performing certain acts. Yet the good people on this block are often good positively and overtly—even though what they do is still overlooked. They have found $12-million to rehabilitate their housing, started programs for the addicts, stopped the old fighting gangs (there are two shopping bags full of guns and other weapons at the bottom of the East River, collected 10 years ago from willing gang members). They have organized social clubs to keep the children occupied, manned the anti-poverty agencies, and in a hundred quiet ways are trying to change their block.

DEVIANT BEHAVIOR AS AN UNANTICIPATED CONSEQUENCE OF PUBLIC HOUSING

Gerald Suttles

THE CONSEQUENCES mentioned in the title of this article are not quite "latent functions" in the Mertonian sense.[1] While they do not seem to have been anticipated by project planners and promoters, most of these consequences

This paper was written especially for this volume.

are well known to those who live in the public housing projects. Since this is not a highly vocal population, the present commentary may help to fill a void. It is based on three years of observation in a neighborhood of Chicago.

CORPORATE HOUSING AND FAMILY IMPRESSION MANAGEMENT

For most American families, the residence is at one and the same time the most apparent and the most permanent embodiment of the family reputation. If a home is painted regularly, we may feel confident in attributing to the occupants some measure of responsibility and self-respect. If the color scheme is subdued and traditional, it is provisionally assumed that the inhabitants ascribe to parallel political views and moral obligations. Should they adopt bizarre and infrequently used colors, outsiders may feel them somewhat avant garde or risqué. Similarly, the choice of a new modern lamp in a window may be taken to establish the family's concern and familiarity with current fashions and fads.

Quite aside from the particulars of this symbolism, however, it is apparent that on the basis of a very few known characteristics each family will be given responsibility for possessing a vast number of other ones. It is as if each dwelling were carrying on a mute dialogue with all those surrounding it. The care and attention devoted to a home are the first and most effective steps that can be taken to introduce one family to another. It is by the overt embellishments and arrangements of the dwelling unit that neighbors often first discover among themselves those commonalities of interest that ultimately bind them together as a community.

Physical appearances, of course, can only serve to set the early stages of contacts between families and, as with all appearances, they can be deceiving. But here, no less than in other social relations, an introduction of some form is a very necessary step. Moreover, there seems to be a widespread consensus on just how these external appearances connote the more general beliefs, morals, and practices of the inhabitants. Since both resident and onlooker usually have a certain familiarity with this symbolism, there is probably a tendency to create a consistent image that the family can sustain on at least public occasions. Thus, appearances may not be so misleading after all.

As one of the first means by which families establish communications with one another, the dwelling unit often achieves an importance that is not granted later attempts at impression management. Like the first introduction, the first impressions created by a family's residence often become the precedents that guide the subsequent course of their relationship with other families. Once a particular image of the family has been suggested, it may become a binding commitment that the family members cannot lightly abandon. If they do not "live up" to this image, they are likely to be labelled hypocrites, pretenders, or phonies. Consequently, even where a family reputation is first established inadvertently, it may still become a valued possession that absorbs much of its members' energies.

Additionally, one most important point arises from the custom of judging family members jointly rather than individually. For example, even small children frequently are defined on the basis of a reputation already achieved by their parents. Whatever the other consequences of this practice, it certainly tends to draw all family members together in a common conspiracy against all those internal and external forces which jeopardize a public image which has been meticulously and painfully constructed. The common fate of all the family members in this matter not only promotes considerable family cohesion, but gives each member a vested interest in regulating the behavior of the others. Thus, it is as if an "invisible hand" had turned private advantage into public virtue.

It is fairly obvious that any large multiple family housing unit places a number of constraints upon what, in single family residence areas, is a much used channel of communication. In a very real sense, some of the most important pieces of equipment for neighborhood communication have been destroyed for the residents of these edifices. Perhaps a reasonable analogy would be if all business firms in an area were forced to locate in identical buildings and advertising were entirely prohibited. In corporate housing, uniformity of design simply rules out most of those subtle hints that a family can convey by a new paint job, a front lawn, an odd ball door knocker, or an old floor mat. In order to keep a large building looking the way architects and rental agents think it should, the occupants must forego many embellishments according to their own inclinations. As a result, the external trappings of a project building cannot and do not say anything on behalf of the individual residents, but, instead, commemorate the skills, and tastes of architects, engineers, and city planners. Of course, occupants of corporate housing can select their curtains, put a lamp of their own choosing in the window, or even display a few Halloween or Christmas markings. But here again many of their efforts are defeated by the very size of large buildings. Once you get above the fourth or fifth story, these little insignia are lost on the outside world. For outsiders, there is no reason to think that persons living above these altitudes have any concern for the world beneath them. Even the architects seem to agree with this observation since their failure to give variety to anything more than the first two or three stories indicates that whatever goes on above this level is either unimportant or entirely the same from window to window.

The problems of impression management under such conditions of standardization and size in a housing project differ from those in large privately operated apartment houses, because residents of projects are popularly defined as wards of the city or state. In their status as dependents or recipients, they not only cannot claim individual credit for their personal contribution to the appearance of their living quarters, but they also cannot gain favorable reputation from the reputation of the total edifice. Even where considerable effort is made to beautify a project, it still will not be taken to reflect the good taste of the residents; they did not select this residence as a voluntary act of conspicuous consumption, as does someone renting in a prestigious privately operated apartment house. Sometimes this view of project dwellers as wards of the state goes so far as to discredit even those attempts at impression management which are, in fact, the results of individual effort. One woman —a nonproject dweller—whom I was attempting to convince that all women living in projects were not bad housekeepers, simply responded: "It makes no difference. The City Housing Administration gives them everything anyway."

If this definition of project residents were limited to persons who live outside the projects, its effects upon family impression management might not be so disasterous. Project dwellers could still establish among themselves an isolated status system within which they would be recognized as more or less respectable family units. As a general rule, however, physical appearances which could function in this manner are not available to the residents of public housing, because the right to project housing is jeopardized by evidence of a family's rise in status. Although they are encouraged to pull themselves up by their bootstraps and move ahead in the world, project residents must keep their efforts at self-help unknown until they feel secure to make a major residential move. Thus, in most respects they are not in command of those external appearances that notify their neighbors that they have set themselves aside from their past inadequacies and become social climbers. Although the virtues of private initiative and social betterment are unquestionably a fine thing, most persons have difficulty pursuing them for long without an appreciative audience.

This does not mean that project residents are utterly isolated and without friends. They meet each other in the laundry rooms, in the stairwells and, frequently, they sit in the hallways and converse. Sometimes they relax on the benches outside the buildings or in the vacant yards around them. However, these encounters are usually unanticipated and often occur when each party has his guard down and presents a side of himself that does not enhance his repute according to public standards. As a result many relationships are founded in the back regions of their lives. If, as I have maintained, first impressions are important in governing the subsequent course of the relationship, once a person has been exposed as less than the epitome of respectability and good taste, it is rather hopeless to then try to erect what would be taken as only pretensions.

Aside from the importance of first impressions, however, it might also be noted that these acquaintances do not typically occur between persons acting as representatives of families. Instead, they usually take place between individuals who are momentarily dissociated from their families and under no obligation to uphold the particular imagery of their respective kinship units. If two persons meet on the streets and find in each other a common realm of interests making it possible for them to share a relationship of trust, there is no necessity for them to extend these obligations to their families. Having established their relationship outside and independent of their family, they are free agents who speak only for themselves. Thus, their relationship remains isolated and unconstrained by family ties. On the other hand, where persons meet on their front steps, in family gatherings or other circumstances where there is an understanding that they are likely to confront each other's families, then they tend to present an image of themselves that will not be discredited when such a confrontation occurs. Actually, in providing for such a large measure of anonymity, public housing also provides a ready temptation for those already eager to dissociate themselves from their families. Particularly among teenagers whose parents might be regarded as "country" or "square," there is a strong tendency to escape the household lest it "cramp their style." But much the same thing may happen with adults who have learned that a double life only doubles their pleasure.

THE PROJECTS AND SOCIAL CONTROL

Within most American cities there seem to be certain inherent difficulties of social control in rather large and congested populations of poor people. At current rates of exchange, the poor have very little to transfer to one another. In contrast to more affluent people, they enjoy the dubious privilege of being able to offend their neighbors without incurring the rancor of anyone important. At most, they might hesitate lest they provoke physical retaliation. But it is just at this point we say that "social control has broken down."[2] The projects not only concentrate a rather poor population, but dramatize or highlight their poverty. In most other residential communities there is at least some ambiguity about a stranger's potential power and store of benefits. While powerful and affluent people may be rare, the conditions of residency do not totally eliminate them. This is especially the case when we include such types as local politicians, quasi-legitimate businessmen and persons who have important "connections."[3]

In project neighborhoods, however, the conditions of residency provide public testimony to the universal unimportance of fellow residents. If someone has economic resources, "connections" or "clout" there is no reason for him being in public housing. The usual assumption, then, is that strangers have little to offer or withdraw. Occasionally private disclosures may prove the contrary. Beforehand, however, there is little reason to desist from a studied indifference or even more offensive postures. Complementing these grounds for disregarding each other's role as a potential benefactor, there are others which encourage project dwellers to regard each other as potential predators. It is common to take material deprivations as an omen of opportunism, ignorance, irrationality, and resentment.[4] All slum residents must live with this oppressive view of their neighbors. Only project dwellers, however, have it on the best of evidence that everyone around them is subject to such deprivations.

Uniformity and Social Control

In most animal communities each organism is just sufficiently different from his neighbors to make life impossible without their sharing with one another. By this standard, a unisexual community is more integrated than a bisexual one because at least two organisms become essential to one another. Even a female black widow spider, for example, cannot practice indiscriminate cannibalism. Among a hunting and gathering people, acknowledged skills can turn almost every person into an essential contributor to the welfare of the remainder. Indeed, the ideal community seems to be one where each personality is so different and incomplete that its survival relies on the contributions of all its neighbors.[5] In such a community each member is so essential to the others that he cannot be attacked without harming one's self.

Housing projects, on the other hand, seem to be aimed in the opposite direction. As a rule the only objects their residents can exchange are those they already have. Their quarters are roughly the same and hardly worth displaying to one another. The necessity to maintain the uniform appearance of the projects also constrains whatever difference project dwellers might be able to introduce. Ordinarily, each resident is eligible for the same welfare benefits, the same protections, the same exemptions, and the same privileges. As a matter of course all receive about the same per capita income. Each of these uniformities is guaranteed by legal arrangements that are based on our notions of the justice of impartiality, equality, and uniformity.[6] What may be more important, however, are the restrictions imposed by the mere physical and legal arrangements of the projects. Only by the greatest stretch of imagination can one feature them as a facility for commercial enterprises. Current zoning restrictions confirm their usage as residences. Thus, it is impossible for project dwellers to confront each other as grocers, landlords, mailmen, tenants, lawyers, ministers, customers, policemen, and parishoners. Either these persons are eliminated by their excessive income or the lack of local facilities. Even those who occupy these roles are not especially likely to serve their fellow residents.

Alongside this consideration is another which almost guarantees that project dwellers will not confront each in these roles. The projects amass a large population and a considerable market for consumer goods. Alongside many projects there has developed a large shopping center composed of well-known chain stores. Naturally the owners and managers are not project dwellers. Also, in the best of American traditions they resist any attempt to have them give preferential treatment to local people. The most obvious result is the restriction this places on the number of times project dwellers face one another in their commercial exchanges. This, of course, is a common situation in most slum area which are serviced largely by outsiders. In the traditional slum, however, zoning restrictions were somewhat more flexible and could be influenced by political considerations. Thus, there often developed a larger or smaller number of local entrepreneurs whose establishments followed an unsightly but profitable career. In their role as local profiteers they could hardly neglect the chance to make friends and preserve order.

A more extended outcome is the removal of the rungs on a social ladder that reaches from petty entrepreneur to respectability. Many of the enterprises of slum residents are of doubtful character and something of an eyesore. They are nonetheless important as a stage of capital formation from which one can advance to hold such moral and esthetic standards. Indeed, if we look back on our coporate career as a capitalist country we will find the early stages abhorrent to our current esthetic and moral beliefs.[7] There is little reason to believe that contemporary entrepreneurs who start with equally small capital accumulations must not also relax somewhat their esthetic and moral ideals. Housing projects and the adjacent shopping center assure that esthetics and morality persist.

The Problem of Numbers

Since most of them are erected on valuable real estate, projects tend to be high structures that house a very large number of people. Sometimes near seven hundred people are included in the same building. Often more than twenty families use the same hallway and many more the same elevators, stairs, laundries, and so on. With such a wealth of potential associates, it is difficult to choose anyone in particular. If a resident nods to one resident on his floor, there is no reason not to nod to them all. But that would only make his neck sore. Sociability, then, forces upon one a far more horrendous task than is manageable. In less congested neighborhoods there is a fine gradation between adjacent and fronting neighbors and a firm rule for the order in which persons are included or excluded as associates. In the case of independent dwelling units our routine *path-*

ways need not include more than the four other units which fix upon each household. While the inhabitants of these households need not provide congenial associates, they at least establish a rule of priority.

In housing projects, the routine range of necessary movement includes an entire hallway, the elevator and a "lobby." These facilities are shared by such a number of persons that a relationship with all of them is near unmanageable. To invite sociability then is to lay oneself open to numerous and unselected exchanges. As with most persons who live in large apartment buildings, those in the projects have learned to treat each other's presence in the same hallway as a mere physical obstruction.

The size of most projects carries another implication. Because of their vertical plan, most of the residents are removed from the surveillance provided by outsiders; policemen do not routinely go above the first floor and there are no pedestrian, shoppers, or businessmen to come to one's aid. Project dwellers are well aware of how vulnerable they are and the lack of available persons to whom they may appeal for aid. Naturally this tends to make them cautious about approaching one another. In addition, however, it forces them to the conclusion that they had best be self-sufficient in all respects including that of having such coercive force at hand that they can stand off any predator. As reasonable men, they tend to take the "law into their own hands" since they are no longer able to depend on its immanent presence. In practice, this may entail carrying a weapon, threatening vengeance or giving evidence of one's "clout."

As might be expected these measures only generalize the threat of coercion and violence. In this sense, they only encourage a self-fulfilling myth wherein each man's presumed weapons become the provocation to another's use of them.

PROJECT DWELLERS AS A
SPECIAL LEGAL CATEGORY

According to a common understanding "a man's home is his castle." This saying has several connotations, but one of the more prominent is the assumption that each household is a private realm where, except for the most extraordinary reasons, the communications of each domestic unit cannot be divulged or the authority of each head of household superceded. As evidence of our value for such securities, one might cite Amendments 3 and 4 of the United States Constitution. In housing projects these notions about the sanctity of a man's dwelling are hard to sustain. First, housing projects tend to segregate out a special strata of people and to subject them to a separate set of legal requirements that do not apply to others. All that needs be done is to restrict these rules to the contract a resident signs.[8] A few examples have already been mentioned; the obligation not to engage in commercial trade, the economic exclusion of those in public office, enforced asceticism, and the restriction of unique embellishments for each abode. One can also regulate the purchase of television sets, the use of telephones, the ownership of pets, the length of time relatives can be "put up" and the decibel level at which people can socialize. The singular advantage of the projects is that it is possible to pass such rulings without affecting anyone else other than the residents themelves.

When the police receive a complaint about someone's behavior, they usually proceed to his home, possibly produce a warrant, and make an investigation. In the meantime, nearby residents usually look on as bystanders. Occasionally, they may warn their children to stay away from the offender's household. When the offender happens to live in a project, however, more strenuous precautions are necessary. First, all the doorways must be blocked for there are many passageways an offender may use within such a labyrinth. All those entering or leaving must be questioned. In the meantime, residents are unable to tell their children exactly *how* to avoid the offender. In the end, the offender's territory or routine range of movement cannot be isolated from their own. They cannot say "don't go *there*" because "there" is a lobby, elevator, stairwell, or hallway that all of them must use. All they can say is "don't have anything to do with him." Such a warning is futile as long as one cannot specify the place and time of the offender's appearance.

In this regard, project dwellers are interdependent with

one another at exactly the time that the rightful agents of social control are attempting to enforce public rulings. All of them are offended by the interrogations, blocked doorways, and suspicious stance that policemen are compelled to adopt out of mere practicality. As a result, the residents' plight is more nearly that of the offender than that of the policeman. The policemen seem to recognize the shared condition of both residents and offender and proceed with caution.[9] Minor complaints are ignored; major ones draw them out in full force so that they can contend with what they assume to be a collusion on the part of all residents. A more subtle practice is to plant "undercover" agents in each project so as to head off such collusive reactions. Among the residents, in turn, this has the effect of arousing the "myth" that there is a "fink on every floor." Thus, the project dwellers are either successful in obstructing the enforcement of public rulings or their confidence in one another is undermined by the success of those who invade their castle.

PROLETARIAN COSMOPOLITANISM

"A man's home is his castle" also implies that it is a location where his ancestors have lived, where he exercises ultimate authority, and for which he must accept final responsibility. With the localization of so many of his insignia, a householder is closely tied to the small plot of ground that surrounds what he occupies. Most of the signs of his personal identity and voluntary behavior are evident in that region. Thus, it is often among neighbors that we can set aside our required roles and put on display our personal identity. However with a growing population and increased anonymity together with a lack of control over the impressions he betrays or the privacies he hides, a person's abode and neighborhood become more a burden than a stage for engineering one's presentation of self. To find an appreciative audience each performer must search for a larger marketplace.

For project dwellers the most obvious implication is that they will seek out an audience where their residence is immaterial, where intimacy does not force its way into their occupational or financial background and where their current performances cannot be contrasted against future or past ones. The most promising opportunity in this direction is for project dwellers to sever themselves from local ties and to enter the cool world of nightly and weekend cosmopolitanism described in Finestone's, "Cats, Kicks and Color."[10] In these social gatherings so attractive to project dwellers, the earmarks of eligibility are only those which the individual can carry on his immediate person. Good clothes, an ingratiating manner, familiarity with an exotic vocabulary, and other fads are their stock in trade. Life is carried out in discrete parts, where they "make the scene," while the more "permanent" features of their character, such as their family, neighborhood, and residence, become only historical accidents. Their residences then are places for sleeping—a pad —and nothing more. External references are important only by their dullness when contrasted with present "kicks." Where others "talk shop" and organize their lives about the continuous dictates of the occupational and domestic worlds, they center their's on the recreations that occur after the workday. Social relations remain casual and impermanent and agreements are binding for only the specific occasion.

Within these cosmopolitan gatherings, it is important that all participants endorse an ethic of tolerance which permits each to pursue a number of courses except those suggesting the "square" living in his project cubicle. In due course, great emphasis will be placed on experimenting with behavioral patterns that might be regarded as "unnatural" or "abnormal" in more provincial circles. With such an ethic of tolerance, however, none of these experiments can end in a permanent discovery of what is "right" and compelling. The content of life becomes a "fad" while its performance is evaluated only by its "style."

Looking back over the old traditional slum, one is reminded of its seclusivism, the residents' attachment to their locality, and their collusions to protect each other from public exposure. Groups took their name from a local area and, in the case of teenagers, fought for small turfs or territories. Practically everyone had his special station, sometimes on the streets, or on the front stoop, or in a local store or nearby tavern. Churches, playgrounds, and shops were often restricted to a single ethnic group and, with residential segregation, became neighborhood establishments. In these circumstances, a resident was so thoroughly contained among his neighbors that social controls were very strong indeed. To an outsider such controls might even seem oppressive or unduly severe.[11]

By contrast with the cosmopolitanism outline above, the old urban slum may be thought rather virtuous. But this evaluation of the people who participate in either way of life can only muddle our understanding of them. Basically the decline of provincialism among project dwellers results from the dearth of local exchanges and the constant availability of nonlocal exchanges. Thus, the shift from provincialism to cosmopolitanism is only a change of scenes where each enacts his self-presentation while exchanging benefits and services with his audience. Both the provincial stage of the old urban slum and that of the cool world of cosmopolitanism provide a definite order within which one can demonstrate personal talents, skills, tastes, and concern for other people. Housing projects are remarkable for their lack of such communicative devices or opportunity for local exchange. By comparison, establishments for casual and cosmopolitan gatherings provide a situation where there are many shared signs to be displayed and differences to be exchanged. Thus, what we have is a people gravitating from one scene where they are solitary consumers to another where they can share something.

What is transacted of course, varies a great deal between each way of life. But that is hardly the choice of those who gravitate toward either type of conduct. Generally, the people only seem to be like algae which drift together in quiet water to form colonies. The old urban slum drew people together into multiple exchanges, which encouraged role specialization. This made their exchanges profitable and fairly permanent. In the modern housing project there is little room for multiple exchanges, specialization, or even a recognition of the degree to which these may exist. It is natural, then, that project dwellers drift past one another until they find an exchange system where their goods gain enduring value by continual exchange and display.

STRUCTURAL DEVIANCE AND NORMATIVE CONFORMITY: THE "HUSTLE" AND THE GANG

Michael Lewis

INTRODUCTION

THERE are two basic sociological interpretations of slum crime and delinquency. The first posits the presence of cultural emphases or themes in the slum (or among lower-class groups) which, because they deviate from mainstream American (or middle-class) cultural expectations, lead those who behave in terms of them into conflict with the law and with law enforcers. The second interpretation holds that slum crime and delinquency are largely the products of blocked access to desired conventional (or mainstream) careers and rewards. One variant of this position posits that gang delinquency is the product of a kind of contra-culture which slum youths adopt after they have been disappointed in their pursuit of conventional success; that it is behavior calculated to smite those who are perceived as denying access to the means for such success while at the same time destroying the material or property representations of the conventional value system. Another variant suggests that criminal behavior is often an innovation in which those who have internalized conventional success expectations and find the institutionalized means to such success inaccessible create alternative and deviant routes to the rewards all of us essentially desire.

This paper was written especially for this volume.

In spite of the substantive differences between these two positions they do have one very important quality in common. They are both *criminogenic* interpretations. Whatever their differences, both positions take for granted that the evoked behavior is *intrinsically deviant;* that given the conventional standards of "right and wrong" in contemporary society these behaviors are "wrong" because they *violate* the institutionalized expectations for the "right." Implicit in both interpretations is the view that behavioral norms and conceptions of legality are inextricably wed; that behavior which is criminal (or delinquent) must, of necessity, be behavior which violates common conceptions of what is generally accepted and valued in our society. In other words, to say that certain behavior violates the law is also to say that it violates our broader normative sense of the kinds of things people ought to do.

It is the intention of this paper to present an interpretation of two major forms of slum crime and delinquency—"the hustle" and "gang behavior"—which is unequivocally dissimilar from either of the positions sketched above in that it does not view such behaviors as *intrinsically deviant.* In the argument presented below I eschew the necessary connection between illegality (or criminality) and normative deviance. I shall posit that while much of the behavior I am discussing is illegal it is also within the range of that which is normatively valued in the cultural mainstream of contemporary society.

THE HUSTLER

The common conception of the hustler holds him to be a small-time, petty criminal who "lives by his wits." He is the "fence," the "pimp," the "numbers runner," the "crap shooter," or perhaps even the small-scale purveyor of "grass" (marijuana) or "horse" (heroin). Superficially the hustler seems to fit very well into Robert Merton's characterization of *innovative anomie.* The *innovator,* says Merton, is the individual who, having internalized a common conception of success and finding legitimate means to its realization blocked, undertakes deviant practices as substitute means to his desired goal.[1] The hustler seems to be doing just that. In the first place he usually comes from the "bottom of the heap." He is characteristically a member of a socially stigmatized and disinherited group—a familiar figure, for example, in the black ghettos of American cities.[2] Typically, his formal education is limited while he pursues material rewards which are usually inaccessible to the majority of those who are similarly stigmatized but who do not hustle. The pursuit of such rewards which are symbolic of conventional success seems to integrate the hustler into the mainstream— at least as far as ends or goals are concerned. At the same time, however, the nature of his "hustle," numbers running, procuring, etc., seems to be a deviant means to conventional success which the conditions of his identity force him to adopt in lieu of conventional access modes such as legitimate business, entrepreneurial, or otherwise. If, because of who is, he cannot sell stocks and bonds, he *can* "make it" by taking bets on the numbers.

Some of the facts which lead to such an interpretation are obviously incontrovertible. It is beyond question, for example, that Negroes as members of a stigmatized group have characteristically been denied conventional access to material rewards. It is also true, subcultural arguments notwithstanding, that there is no appreciable difference between white and black when it comes to material aspirations. Moreover, it may even be granted without fear of serious challenge that the hustle represents an adaptation to exclusion from what we commonly perceive as standard modes of access to material rewards. However, there is some question as to the "deviant" nature of the innovation or the "hustle."

If we follow Merton's argument we are forced to characterize the behavior of the hustler as essentially deviant, because it is illegal and often evokes a moralistic repugnance from us. Such an approach equates the nature of the behavior with the way it is commonly *labeled* in society at large. In a very real sense such an approach leaves the behavior in question unanalyzed. Its use tells us little about the essence of the "deviant" behavior or its *social meaning* for the behaver. The position taken here is (1) that from the hustler's perspective his means behavior is in conformity with much of the means behavior employed in "legitimate or conventional" access modes to material reward (the integrating goal), and (2) that the sociologist who looks carefully at the hustler's behavior must concur that while it is often prohibited by law it is only infrequently deviant in terms of social meaning for the actors involved—the "hustler" and, indeed, the "hustled." To support this contention let us examine the following depiction based upon studies in two contemporary black urban ghettos.

Whatever the hustle, it invariably involves a high degree of *rational planning* and the exercise of mental agility. Not only does the hustler have to "outwit the law," but he must also be several jumps ahead of his clientele. For example, there are some who hustle "their bread" by selling goods they purchase from junkies who no doubt have stolen them. Trafficking in contraband, the hustler has to escape public attention in order to stay in business. Beyond this he must also engage in a market analysis of considerable sophistication. He has to take on goods which are likely to have a fast turnover on the market to which he has access. This means that the hustler has to assess accurately local taste and consumer demand. Like the legitimate buyer for a retail outlet, if he makes an incorrect assessment he will be stuck with the goods, which besides representing an economic loss also represents an increased possibility of detection (on the assumption that these are contraband). Beyond maintaining a market or consumer analysis, the hustler who is "fencing" must also work out acceptable profit margins in his "retailing" operation. He knows that in order to make a sale he must offer his goods at prices below those asked on the legitimate market. He offers no guarantees and provides no service; thus, if he did not undersell his legit competitors he would soon lose his clientele. If he must undersell or underprice his goods while at the same time be far enough ahead to make his efforts worthwhile, he must pass on, as it were, the disparity between his retail price and that of his legitimate competition to his suppliers. Thus, he must find suppliers who not only can provide him with goods for fast turnover but who also are in desperate need of quick cash so that they are willing to sell to a middle man even though this means accepting a very tangible economic loss. It would indeed be difficult to find in a legitimate economic enterprise endeavors which exceed this hustle in the exercise of sophistication and rationality.

Other examples of hustlers commonly found in black ghettos also illustrate this emphasis on rational planning and market analysis. Numbers running and policy, common forms of gambling in these areas, are small bettor games which enable low income players to continue playing even when they lose consistently. The numbers and policy both promise the possibility of a very big payoff for a small investment—although the odds are overwhelmingly against it—and in areas where money is short and releases from the desultory routines of daily life are few, each of these games fits a need. If the player is lucky he can "win big." At the very least, each time he plays he can partake of the *excitement* which inheres in the *possibility* that he might win. Those who run such games know their clientele. The numbers runner, for example, is a master psychologist in his environment, knowing very well the meaning of his game in the lives of those who play. It would be an overstatement to say that this awareness consciously led to the emergence of the numbers (or policy) as a characteristic hustle in the ghetto; yet it is clear that hustlers who "turn their bread" in this game know their market and sell to the needs which abound therein, the needs for money and for the possibility of the unexpected. They are full of stories about big winners and, like any good legitimate salesman, they keep their clientele interested by keeping alive those myths of possibility which draw them in. There is little difference between them and the "legitimate" myth makers, the advertising copy writers, or the used car salesmen.

Besides the planning rationality or the market awareness typically a part of the hustle, there are two other themes which run through this behavior and define its social meaning. They are (1) an emphasis upon achievement and the demonstration of personal skill, and (2) an emphasis upon dependability and integrity—or, in other words, honesty.

There is probably no social milieu which is more achievement oriented and in which demonstrations of personal skill are more admired than the hustler's world. The hustler is always "scuffling" or working at his "hustle." In part this is so because only infrequently does he get far enough ahead financially to ease off for a while. Also, many hustlers such as runners, pimps, pushers, and bootleggers (those who sell liquor without a liquor license) have a regular clientele who require that the hustler and his product be available on a regular basis. Whatever his hustle, the individual who "brings it off with style" excites the admiration of his fellows. The pimp who can keep a long string of prostitutes "sweet for him" is usually perceived as an expert in the psychology of women and in the context of his operations he probably is just that. Certainly he is adept at manipulating his women to the point that they are willing to go along, although each knows that she is just one of a number of his women. The bootlegger whose after-hours place is always well stocked and available for drinking and gambling and is free of "The Man's" (police) interference will attract a permanent following who will extoll his shrewd business head even while he is taking their change.

The hustling world has its Paul Bunyan myths of great achievers. Passed on from one generation of hustlers to the next, these are tales of men—some still on the scene—who by prodigious effort and consummate skill at their hustle managed to accrue great wealth. In our research we came across the story of one Jackson Wheeler. It seems that Wheeler was a gambler in the black ghetto of a middle-sized city. Not only did he run the most successful policy wheel in town, but he was also (so the story goes) the bankroll behind "the house" in most of the permanent gambling enterprises located in the ghetto. Wheeler was very popular because he was perceived (even by some of the latter-day militants) as a man for his race, for although he took a great deal from the ghetto population he also spent a lot of his money in the ghetto community. The myth has it that

Wheeler became so successful that he forgot his place: he went out and challenged the white holders of economic power in the community. We are told that Wheeler covertly bought a whole city block in the heart of the business district. This proved to be his downfall. When the white business powers became aware of this Wheeler was no longer able to operate freely within the ghetto. He lost his real estate holdings and because "the heat was on" never regained the success of his earlier years, although at the time of his death he still had a policy wheel. There are several interesting points in this myth, which include its Sisyphus-like moral: do not commit the hybris of aspiring to success in the white man's arena. What is most striking, both by the way the story is told and in its content, is the admiration for Wheeler's daring and acumen. He lost, but not before he gave them all a run for their money.

At first surmise it would seem that any concept of honesty as applied to the hustler involves a self-contradiction. The hustler operates outside the law and would appear to be, by definition, lacking in honesty. In fact this is a simplistic notion which really obfuscates a more complex and truly fascinating reality. While it is undeniably true that some hustlers involve themselves in activities such as theft or one of the variety of con-games which clearly involve the victimization of the "sucker" by the hustler, most hustles involve the maintenance of a relationship between the hustler and the client which presupposes reliability and integrity. Curious as it may at first seem, the hustler seems to have a *professional* relationship with the "suckers" (if, indeed, the term is appropriate) characterized by an implicit code of ethics. The clientele link themselves with the hustler on a voluntary basis, coming to him for a service or for goods which they know he can provide. If the hustler fails to provide or otherwise measure up to expectations he will lose his clientele, his reputation in the hustle will be damaged, and he will be unable to attract new customers. Moreover, because the service provided or the goods purchased often involve a violation of the law and/or in some cases—as in a visit to a prostitute—a violation of conventional mores on the part of the customer, the hustler, if he is to maintain his reputation, must keep his relationship with his clients confidential. If he should expose a client for any reason, or even threaten to do so, he would soon lose his clientele; whatever the short-run gain, in the not-too-long-run he would be out of the business. The numbers runner has to pay off in full measure when someone hits his number. The bootlegger does not dilute his whiskey; he runs an orderly establishment so as not to attract unwanted attention to his customers and himself. The pimp keeps his girls in line; he does not try to use the "John's" peccadillos against him.

There are always those who violate the ethics of the hustle, but it would be a mistake not to recognize that these ethics do exist and that they are central to the hustler's style. Without the tacit understandings between hustler and client which govern the behavior of the former there would be no *trust.* Paradoxically, it is trust or faith in the hustler's honesty which is absolutely necessary to the client who is about to violate the law or the conventional standards of his community. Its subrosa nature makes every transaction with a hustler something of a risk for the client. It is only the hustler's reputation which allays the anxiety and at least to some extent routinizes the transaction. A dishonest hustler gives the *profession* a bad name and drives the customers away.

If you accept as accurate the above depiction of the hustler's world, it must follow that the behaviors involved are not simply deviant means to an institutionalized or legitimate goal. The three themes which permeate the hustler's behavior—*rationality, the emphasis upon achievement by individual skill,* and *honesty*—are norms which we ascribe to economic activity in the "square world" of the American middle class. Thus, the hustler, even when he is in violation of the law, typically goes about his business in a manner which attests to his substantial integration into the normative mainstream of contemporary society. We can accept Merton's notion that such behavior is deviant in that it violates legal specifications about what *is* and what *is not* a legitimate way of pursuing success goals. Structurally, the hustler *is* an innovator, a deviant; but it would be an error to equate this *structural deviance* (violation of the law) with the presence of deviant social meanings in the behavior. In terms of its social meaning for those who participate, hustling is more *imitative* than *innovative*.

Merton writes of the imperfect socialization of the innovator. He accounts for the abandonment of institutionalized means while aspirations for conventional success are maintained by suggesting that the innovator is, by virtue of his position in society, someone whose connection with legitimate means behavior is tenuous. Thus, when the will to success is overpowering and the conventional access ways are blocked, the individual easily casts off the restrictions imposed by the institutionalized prescriptions and proscriptions regarding means behavior.[3] As far as the hustler is concerned, however, our depiction of the meanings in his behavior allows for an opposite formulation in explanation of his *illegal or structurally deviant endeavors*.

If the social meanings in the hustler's behavior indicate that he is normatively integrated with the mainstream even while his behavior is illegal then it would seem, paradoxically, that such behavior is a function of normative integration at the means level in situations which only permit of its behavioral expression in ways which are more likely than not to be outside the law. If an individual is socialized to appreciate the importance of rational planning and control in economic endeavors, if he is socialized to the importance of building a personal reputation based upon skill, recognizable achievement, and integrity in his economic dealings with others, then depending upon his social location he will be on his way to becoming either a legitimate businessman, a professional, or a hustler. If he happens to have been born into the white upper middle class we can expect one of the former; if he happens to have been born into the black lower class (or some similar group) we can expect the latter.

It is indisputable that a lower-class Negro who is socialized to the norms of rational planning and reputation based upon achievement, demonstrable skill, and integrity is confronted with a legitimate opportunity structure which is less than encouraging. Imbued with a desire for material reward earned by these normative means, the lower-class Negro simply does not find positions open to him in the legitimate structure which permit such achievement. Given the technological sophistication of the legitimate economy, jobs which pay well and allow their incumbents to engage in rational planning, which allow them to develop a reputation based upon demonstrable competence and personal integrity, require a high degree of formal training and certification usually necessitating prolonged periods of preparation in the educational system. For a host of reasons—some economic, some having to do with social conditions in his immediate environment, and some having to do with the quality of education available in the schools he has access to—the lower-class Negro finds it difficult, and in some cases impossible, to obtain the training and certification necessary to qualify for positions in the legitimate economy where he could realize his conventional normative needs with reference to both *ends* and *means*. The greater his commitment to the conventional norms of rationality, achievement, and demonstrable responsibility and reliability in dealing with a public together with a desire for greater than average material reward, the more his situation—his social location—stymies his desire to enter the legitimate economy. For those whose commitment to these norms (both of means and ends) is less intense—whose aspirations are not as high—there are increasingly opportunities opening in the legitimate economy. But for those whose conventional normative commitment is high and who consequently would have to enter the economy nearer the top of the occupational pyramid, there are few opportunities for which their situation allows them to qualify. It is the very conventionality of this latter group which paradoxically leads them into one or another of the typical hustles which, although illegal or structurally deviant, allows them to realize their normative needs. The more *perfect* the normative socialization to conventional expectations in combination with situational impediments to the realization of this conventionality in the legitimate economy, the greater the probability of structural deviance.

Hustling, in the final analysis, is often a structurally deviant affirmation not only of the desirability of conventional success such as wealth, but also of the conventional social or normative meanings of behavior in pursuit of success. Hustling is indeed illegal; its transactions fall beyond the limits of mainstream definitions of what is acceptable, yet in terms of the social meanings attendant to the hustler's behavior, it is so often normatively consonant with those transactions which occur daily in the legitimate economy. To the extent that this is so, the criminality of the hustler is not an alien quality subject to change by imprisonment, counseling, psychotherapy, or vocational rehabilitation. In fact, the only way in which such approaches would have any "success" would be if they could lessen the intensity of his commitment to the complex of desired material rewards achieved in positions which allow the exercise of rationality in planning, the demonstration of personal achievement, and the demonstration of an honest quasi-professional relationship with clientele. If such approaches were effective they possibly could turn the hustler into an individual who is more amenable to accepting a place in the legitimate economy for which his social situation is not likely to be an impediment. Even if this could be successful, however, it would present an ethical dilemma for it would involve getting the hustler to forsake those same personal commitments which those who are asking him to "reform" hold dearly. In would, in fact, mean that in the absence of a change in social situation, commitment to the norms we have described can be regarded as the legitimate possession of only those who are situationally advantaged to the extent that their identity does not disqualify them from access to mainstream opportunities.

For those who are reform minded the lesson in all of this is quite clear. Reform must consist of obviating situational impediments to high-level participation in the legitimate economy, or, in lieu of that, it must consist of redefining at least some hustles as legal and therefore not structurally deviant. In any case, for the normatively conventional hustler it is not likely that reform can be successful in the long run if efforts are made to change him—and in a very real sense it may be unethical to try to do so. As epilogue the following words of a young hustler:

". . . I can't even get a job . . . I tried this summer but I didn't get nothing. I got a record so what kind of job can I get? I be better off up here hustlin than cleaning someone's latrine."

THE JUVENILE GANG

Like hustling, gang delinquency has also been characteristic of slum-ghetto areas in American cities. (Quite often some hustling is a part of the gang's activities.) During the last two decades juvenile gangs have attracted public attention to a considerable degree—more so than the hustlers—because of the sensational nature of their illegal activities. In New York City, for example, during the 1950s and early 1960s a number of homicides were linked directly to juvenile gangs. In Chicago the decade of the 1960s has seen the emergence of large-scale gang federations such as the Blackstone Rangers which have been associated, at least in the mass media, with a series of law violations ranging from homicide to alleged misuse of federal anti-poverty funds. In the public mind juvenile gangs have been identified as a major menace to person and property in the city. Consequently, there are few if any cities which have not committed at least some public resources (although often not enough) to efforts aimed at their pacification. Special police units, youth board street workers, and social workers can all be found in the high delinquency areas of any city while sociologists and psychologists have been busy in attempts to unravel the "why's" and "how's" of the juvenile gang and its opposition to conventional society. Out of this melange of activity there have emerged a number of explanations of the gang phenomenon. I shall here try to deal critically with two of the more important sociological formulations.

Walter Miller's view of the genesis of gang delinquency represents an extreme form of the subcultural argument.[4] For Miller, gang delinquency is not a reaction to *anything* like blocked access to status or material rewards; it is rather the natural outgrowth of a behavioral realization of the normative content of lower-class culture. Delinquent gangs in this view run afoul of the law because they are collectivities oriented toward the realization of norms in behavior which, because they are lower class, violate dominant middle-class expectations. Miller writes:

A large body of systematically interrelated attitudes, practices, behaviors, and values characteristic of lower class culture are designed to support and maintain the basic features of the lower class way of life. In areas where these differ from features of middle class culture, action oriented to the achievement and maintenance of the lower class system may violate norms of middle class culture and be perceived as deliberately non-conforming.

He continues that

. . . lower class culture is a distinctive tradition many centuries old with an integrity of its own.[5]

The lower-class culture generating gang delinquency in the aforementioned manner is, according to Miller, constituted of a rank order of focal concerns inclusive of (1) Trouble, (2) Toughness, (3) Smartness, (4) Excitement, (5) Fate, and (6) Autonomy. These are themes which generate commitment in some instances and avoidance in others. The gang is the collectivity in which lower-class adolescents are perceived as working out their behavioral relationships to these themes or concerns.[6]

Our criticism of this formulation is two-fold. First, on the basis of my research I would reject the notion that there is a "lower-class" culture so distinct from a dominant "middle-class" culture that behavior calculated to realize the normative content of the former automatically violates law which is based on the latter. My second criticism is based in part on the first. I find that certain normative qualities typical of middle-class existence and certain idealizations of "Americanisms" are the underlying themes of gang organization and activity. Thus, contrary to Miller and in conjunction with the argument developed with regard to the hustler, I perceive the gang as a mechanism for the realization of mainstream norms in situations which impede most "legitimate" expressions of them. The gang in this view is not delinquent in response to deviant norms; but it is delinquent to the extent that its members are socialized to mainstream norms while at the same time they find themselves impeded from expressing their commitments in the manner of the middle class. This position will be developed further through our materials on juvenile gangs. Before doing so, the most cogent alternative to the Miller position now in the literature will be presented and examined critically.

In a manner similar to Merton's formulation, Albert Cohen argues that in an open-class society such as that characteristic of present-day America, all individuals irrespective of their class identities are exposed to, and to some degree internalize, the dominant normative qualities of that society.[7] Thus, says Cohen, in American society "it is difficult to find a 'working class' milieu in which 'middle class' standards are not important."[8] As this is the case, working-class (lower-class for our purposes) youth are confronted with a mighty dilemma. On the one hand they cannot escape measuring themselves against middle-class standards. The mass media, the schools, and even their peers who seem to be "getting ahead" all attest to the importance of middle-class life styles in this society. On the other hand, because of their working-class status, their socialization has rendered them deficient in attributes which would allow them to compete successfully for opportunities and rewards generally accessible to the middle class.

Some adolescents in this situation, suggests Cohen, resolve their dilemma by pushing hard to achieve middle-class status and despite situational impediments do manage to succeed. Others do not resolve the dilemma at all, but, in effect, choose to compromise by living their lives according to the familiar terms of the working-class milieu while keeping open the option of social mobility. Still others resolve the dilemma by partaking of the delinquent subculture of the gang. The delinquent subculture in Cohen's view consists of a grand repudiation of everything middle class. It is in every sense a *contra-culture* in which middle-class values and standards are inverted. Because the middle-class standards are perceived as unattainable, their value or importance is denied, indeed even ridiculed, by an orientation to their opposites. In the acts of denial the delinquent establishes for himself a status which he can regard as superior to that which those who accept middle-class standards aspire. Thus, the delinquent gang is a collectivity which in effect gives legitimacy to the individual's *reaction-formation* (Cohen himself regards this term as applicable) against the middle-class normative universe. For as long as the lower- or working-class adolescent accepts that universe as important he must live with the realization of his own status inadequacy. When in the company of peers confronted with the same problems he denies the desirability of middle-class morality, he obliterates that realization and creates in its stead a sense—ersatz though it may be—of his own status superiority.[9]

Although Cohen's formulation is superior to Miller's from the perspective of this essay, there are some important questions which should be raised about its overall adequacy as an analytic treatment of gang delinquency. On the basis of my research I agree with Cohen's assertions that working- or lower-class youth are exposed to mainstream norms, and that the delinquent gang represents an attempt to deal with situationally based impediments to their realization in the manner of the middle class. However, I find it difficult to accept the notion that the delinquent gang represents a collective reaction-formation in denial of middle-class morality.

In the first place it is difficult to conceive of a collectivity whose only basis for existence is a psychological defense mechanism "writ large."[10] In order for any collectivity to persist it must be possessed of positive functional attractions from the perspective of its membership. Even recognizing, as Cohen does, that motivation for membership in the gang may vary from one member to the next does not clearly depict the attractions of the collectivity *as a collectivity* for the lower-class adolescent. What can he derive from membership in the gang which meets his needs for the behavioral realization of the norms to which he subscribes? What does the collectivity "do" for its members which they themselves would be unable to accomplish as solitary individuals? Again it is not enough to argue as Cohen does that the gang is the reference group sustaining the individual's reaction formation against middle-class morality. It is clear from clinical histories that "reference groups" are not always necessary for maintaining psychological defenses. Moreover, assuming the necessity of the reference group thesis, it is certainly conceivable that other forms of association among lower-class individuals might serve as functional equivalents. If either or both of these assertions are accepted, then one cannot, with assurance, assign sole cause to the reference group function. The gang must be the product of other social and psychological factors.

Second, in his description of gang characteristics Cohen highlights only those which seem to fit his contra-cultural thesis. It may indeed be true that juvenile gangs engage in property destruction and it may be true that gang members can be found who are malicious and "short-run hedonists,"[11] but it is certainly nothing short of arbitrary to assert that these characteristics (along with *group autonomy,* etc.) to the exclusion of others, define the behavioral universe of the gang. As we shall see below there are other qualities of the delinquent gang which do not fit the contra-cultural thesis quite so well. In this vein it is important to note that Cohen virtually ignores the social organization of the gang. Little attention is paid to differential roles or status within the gang and the rules governing behavior within the gang. A focus upon these extremely important sociological characteristics, I submit, would lead to conclusions less supportive of the contra-cultural thesis. Indeed, by placing the contra-cultural characteristics in the context of the social organization of the gang we reach the conclusion that the gang is more mainstream than deviant. The gang as I have suggested above is a collectivity which is normatively consonant with the "mainstream" while at the same time it may very well be engaged in illegal or structurally deviant activities. Like the hustle, it is conventional in social meaning for those who constitute it; like the hustle, it is an outgrowth of the inability to realize conventional norms in the conventional opportunity structure by adolescents of lower-class and/or caste origins.

The following material is offered in support both of our criticism of the Miller and Cohen formulations as well as the alternative formulation I have proposed.

It is important to distinguish between two different kinds of groups, both of which are usually classified together as juvenile gangs. The first is an amorphously-structured peer group of adolescents who "run together" and more often than not seem to get in trouble together. Such "gangs" seem to come close to fitting Cohen's description. They seem to be aimless congeries of youngsters who drift into delinquency out of quixotic maliciousness or meanness. While these "gangs" are no doubt an ubiquitous phenomenon in the slum ghettos of American cities, and while they are obviously responsible for much of what is generally termed juvenile delinquency, they are ultimately no more than adolescent peer groups which for a variety of seemingly idiosyncratic reasons (unless one wishes to account for their delinquent behavior as either Miller or Cohen would) "raise hell" from time to time. An understanding of their behavior might easily be found in the psychology of adolescence or the social psychology of essentially expressive groups.

More interesting sociologically and more to the point of the argument I am pursuing are those *organized gangs* which are also very much a part of the slum-ghetto scene. The organization of the *organized gang* is taken seriously by its members and so ought to be viewed similarly by sociologists. Such gangs display the kind of formal organization we usually associate with large-scale collectivities characteristic of the nondelinquent or "straight" world of middle-class adults. The organized gang invariably has a president, at least one vice president and sometimes a treasurer, and a war minister. In some instances where the gang is really a federation of a number of smaller gangs (as is the case of some of the large gangs in New York City and is apparently true of some of the larger Chicago gangs), there is a hierarchical structure of control and authority with a governing council of representatives from the constituent subunits.[12] Such offices are no sham caricatures of the way the game is played in the straight world. They are functional characteristics of

the group and if they are not always filled by democratic procedures—and in many cases they are—those who do occupy
them are more often than not possessed of demonstrable
skills which seem to qualify them for their responsibilities. A
case in point is Lotus Fenton (a pseudonym), president of the
major organized gang in the ghetto of a middle-sized city.
Lotus is 19-years-old and a high school graduate. Short and
stocky, he has a well-earned reputation as a real fighter, although as he himself wryly noted, since he earned his "rep"
he normally does not have to do much fighting. Lotus is also
regarded as brainy and judicious, capable of exercising
Solomon-like wisdom in smoothing over disputes among his
constituents. He keeps things cool. Beyond this he has the
respect of his fellows and even older men in the community
for the courage he has shown in resisting pressures from the
police to inform them of local "violation of law." Myth or not,
Lotus, we are told, marched into police headquarters and
asked if they were looking for him. When told that he had
better play ball and inform or they would really be after him,
he refused and walked out.

The organized gang is remarkable for the emphasis placed
upon rules which may govern anything from the exercise of
aggression as a gang activity to the personal demeanor or
comportment of members. A gang fight is not entered into
lightly. Before an organized gang gets itself involved in active
hostilities with another group there is a certain amount of
deliberation by the gang, and particularly by its leadership,
sometimes to the point of arranging a prebattle meeting of
the war minister and the president with representatives of
the opposition to set the ground rules under which the violent
confrontation may take place. Gang fighting is not synony-
mous with the seemingly purposeless and random violence
sometimes perpetrated by gang members as individuals. In
order for it to occur, a case, or rationale, has to be made; a
grievance has to be elaborated to the point where the only
functional recourse is redress by means of violent confrontation. Even after the decision to fight has been made, the
violence is controlled and planned. Assignments are made,
fighting roles are taken, and as in a military organization,

each member has a particular responsibility for which he is held accountable.

There is no question but that rules of personal deportment are imposed upon gang members—even if they are not always obeyed. Often such rules belie the supposed malicious hostility to middle-class expectations. In one such instance the gang leaders said that they would expel from membership any member who was behaving badly, i.e., "making a mess of himself," drinking, "running around wild," and who did not respond to their counsel to desist. They would do this because such a member would not be worthy of their continued fellowship and because the activities of such a misguided fellow would bring down community criticism on the gang so long as he was associated with it. Respectability, usually assumed to be a middle-class normative characteristic, was clearly being expressed by lower-class gang adolescents in this case.

Some gangs recruit among almost all youngsters who live within their territory; some, having age-graded divisions, begin their recruitment in grade school; others are as exclusive in their membership as the most snobbish college fraternity. In such cases prospective members have to "measure up" by providing evidence of their courage, fighting skills, personal integrity, and in at least one case known to the author, evidence of their clean record. In this latter case the gang leaders maintain that they screen out the troublemakers—those who get into trouble on their own—because such individuals are likely to be known to the police, a fact which would invariably lead to police scrutiny of the gang if these individuals were admitted to membership.

In all that has been noted thus far, it would seem clear that the organized gang is a far cry from the rebellious congeries of individuals implied in Cohen's treatment and also in Miller's lower-class street corner group, depicted as pursuing distinctive normative concerns into certain conflict with middle-class morality and legality. The gangs of which I write are organizationally sophisticated in a manner not unlike middle-class collectivities. They emphasize universalistic task rationality in their allocation of roles, the necessity for rational planning, and obedience to rules of collective action and individual demeanor.

Of course, it may be countered in defense of either the Miller or the Cohen theses that while the organization of these gangs resembles the organization of middle-class collectivities the actions of such groups clearly deviate from middle-class expectations. After all, it can not be denied that violence and theft, for example, are clearly deviant from the middle-class point of view. Such an assertion may be answered in the following manner. What is illegal or structurally deviant in gang activities is not necessarily normatively deviant when seen in the context of the gang's organization and its (the gang's) social meaning for its members. Indeed, in such a context illegal or structurally deviant acts, even those as severe as homicide, may be seen as imitative of behaviors regarded as legitimate in the "mainstream."

A major concern of the organized juvenile gang is its sovereignty over a "turf" or territory. In this the gang acts as a kind of local shadow government monitoring the comings and goings of individuals in its age category and often exerting social control over members and nonmemebrs as well. There are, for example, reported incidents in which gang members, with considerable effect, have both "encouraged" or "discouraged" school attendance among adolescents living on their turf. This collective concern for sovereignty can hardly be designated as normatively deviant in terms of the American mainstream, except in the sense that the gang has no legal right to exercise it. The attempt to exercise sovereignty is legally deviant because the gang has no recognized mandate from the state to do so, but the aspiration to organized authority over a constituency is as American as apple pie. Thus, the concern for territorial sovereignty is itself imitative of a common-place theme in middle-class-dominated American life.

As a general matter, the concept of sovereignty has two major implications. It implies first that rules, norms, and protections against harm are applicable to all who fall under or owe allegiance to the sovereign authority, and second that none of these is extended to those who are beyond its pale.

The notion of sovereignty, in effect, distinguishes between an in-group for whom a series of moral imperatives exists and out-groups whose treatment by members of the in-group is not necessarily governed by such imperatives. Thus, a moral code may govern the relations of statesmen to their constituents (a code often honored in the breach) but it is *interest* which governs the relations of these same statesmen in the *real-politik* world of confrontation and competition between sovereignties. An individual may live by a code which abhors violence and respects the right to life for those who share his allegiance to a given sovereignty but at the same time he feels free in the exercise of violence in war or in espionage against those who do not share that allegiance and whose existence may be designated as inimical to the interests of that sovereignty.

Juvenile gangs usually attempt to establish their sovereignty according to the following dimensions. They first try to establish unchallenged authority over a "turf" or physical territory which has fairly specific boundaries. Those who live within these boundaries are considered by gang members to be subject to their "authority." Second, they establish age limits on their sovereignty, usually only an upper limit. This limit may not be explicitly recognized and it may even be revised upward or downward depending upon the power of the gang, but it does, nevertheless, exist. Thus, the gang concerns itself with its sovereignty over individuals up to a certain age living within a specified physical area.

I would venture that a considerable amount of the illegal or structurally deviant gang activities (except for hustling) victimizes only those who in one way or another are beyond the boundaries of the gang's sovereignty and are thus not protected by the usual in-group moral codes. Much of the violence, for example, which seems characteristic of the gang occurs when the gang is either seeking to extend its sovereignty or, conversely, is seeking to protect it from incursions by other gangs or outsiders. And what seems to be wanton property damage and nonutilitarian theft is not an indication of a generalized repudiation of the middle-class valuation of property. Much of this destructive activity is aimed at one or another of the out-groups—adults or other adolescents outside the turf—and is a purposive act of aggression against those whose interests are defined as inimical to those of the gang. In-group property is respected while out-group property can be destroyed with impunity and without eschewing its value. If the above depiction is accurate, we may again conclude that rather than being normatively deviant these structurally deviant behaviors are imitative in their social meanings of elements in the American mainstream. The suspension of morality in the service of interest is not a typically middle-class characteristic. (Alas, it is typically American as it pertains to out-groups; it may even be a universal characteristic.) And while what occurs does not imitate middle-class behavior neither does it represent a wholesale rejection of it.

In order to understand what has just been described, one has to have some sense of what the organized gang does for its constituents and why it seems to be a collectivity associated with lower-class slum-ghetto areas in American cities. It would seem abundantly clear that the organized gang is a setting in which conventional normative content is realized, although in a manner which quite often violates law, just as was shown for the hustle. Where in the conventional opportunity structure can these ghetto adolescents so readily gain recognition for their leadership ability and their interpersonal competence? Where in the conventional opportunity structure can these ghetto adolescents experience organizational participation in which they have as visible a chance of rising to the top by their own merits? Where can they exercise highly valued rationality? And in which conventional contexts can they participate in controlling their own destinies by determining what is right and what is wrong and who their enemies are? All of these are conventional aspirations which, given the stigmatization and functional incapacity for mainstream achievement, can only be realized by many slum-ghetto youth in a context at once imitative of but divorced from the mainstream. The organized gang provides just such a context. Its rules and regulations are real enough; it rewards achievement, control, rationality, and courage; it makes social control accessible to those who are otherwise powerless by scaling things down to a point where sovereignty is a realistic concern. The gang, it may be said, is the "imitation of life." Not a reaction-formation writ large but an imitation of American reality writ small. The gang's violence, its aggressiveness, is legally or structurally deviant because the gang is a sovereignty without a charter. But it is not normatively deviant.

CONCLUSION

In this paper I have argued against explanations of structurally deviant behaviors which imply their normative deviance. Quite to the contrary, in the cases which I have analyzed, the hustle and the organized juvenile gang, I have concluded that the existence of illegal behavior or behavior which is structurally deviant is paradoxically the function of intense commitment to normative qualities which are well within the conventional range in American society in situations (the slum ghettos) which make their behavioral realization in the legitimate opportunity structure all but impossible. If this is indeed so, then there are several implications which those who are interested in reform and in the reduction of crime must confront.

As long as situational impediments remain, approaches which attempt to change the offender's behavior are likely to fail. It does no good to tell a highly successful hustler about the gratifications of being a lathe operator; he is deriving conventional rewards from his hustle which he could never derive at the lathe. Moreover he would probably cling to the hustle even if he earned as much money at the lathe, for the hustle offers him an opportunity to achieve some of the gratifications many middle-class people value in their work. Likewise, it does no good to tell a gang leader to give up his role. Only if he were willing to give up some of the conventional satisfactions which so many middle-class people take for granted would he be willing to do so.

If the impeding situation does not change, as long as there is normative conventionality in the slum ghetto there will be structural deviance. (How much easier it would be if their commitments were deviant; we would argue that ours are better and that they should change, but *their* commitments are *our* commitments; *their* values are *our* values.) Since we cannot deprive these individuals of their commitments, we must either give legal sanction to at least some of their presently regarded deviant behaviors or we must change some of the requirements for entrance at relatively high levels into the "legitimate opportunity structure." Maybe a successful numbers banker would make an equally good stockbroker. He certainly has the same normative commitments as the stockbroker and in spite of limited formal education his success attests to his cerebral acuity. Perhaps this hustler would become a stockbroker; he certainly would refuse to become a lathe operator. Maybe gang leaders ought indeed be placed in situations of trust; maybe the gang's concern with sovereignty could be put to good use in developing the reconstruction of the slum ghetto. Since the gangs already have a constituency and since they function to serve conventional aspirations, why not build conventional organizations for them from the ground up in such areas?

It should be clear that if it is not deviant norms which must be changed, the existing criminality and delinquency is ultimately a function of a situation. If this is so, then all the "therapy" of probation officers, social workers, psychologists, vocational rehabilitators, etc., will be too little or no avail. If this is so, it is not the criminal who must change, but the situation which turns his conventionality toward illegal expression. If this is so, social reform is needed in place of the various and sundry individual "therapies" which are imposed upon the violator of law.

VIOLENCE AND THE CITY

Daniel Glaser

IT IS DIFFICULT to know the dimensions of criminal violence in American cities because statistics on crime are collected primarily by the police, yet most violence is not reported to the police. This has been proven when the general public has been polled on their experiences as crime victims; most persons who report suffering a serious assault or a rape indicate that they consider this experience too personal or too humiliating to inform the police about it, or they simply do not tell the police as they do not expect the police to do anything about it.[1] Increases in police statistics on the frequency of violent crime in our cities could well represent only increases in the fraction of these offenses that are reported to the police and recorded by them, rather than an increase in the actual amount of violence. Periodic carefully conducted polls, asking people if they had in a recent period (e.g., the last six months) suffered an assault or other crime of violence would greatly increase our knowledge of violence trends, even though such measurement methods also are far from perfect.

Homicide statistics, however, have long been collected independently by two types of agencies, the police and the public health units of local, state, and national governments. Health department statistics on homicide come from physicians' reports on the causes of death. They are collected nationally in the Vital Statistics Reports of the U.S. Public Health Service. The fact that the F.B.I.'s homicide rates from police departments and the Vital Statistics rates from health

Based on a statement on "Individual Violence in the United States" prepared at the request of the National Commission on the Causes and Prevention of Violence, Washington, D.C., for its hearings in September, 1968.

departments have been very similar for the past 25 years suggests that both are fairly complete and accurate.

The most striking feature of our homicide rates is their decline. Between the 1930s and the 1950s our homicide rate was cut in half, and we have not gone back nearly to the levels of the 1930s.[2] In areas where police statistics have been compiled in a fairly consistent manner for over a century, as in Boston and New Haven, it is evident that the homicide rate of these cities was much higher in the nineteenth century than in the 1930s.[3] However, there has been some increase of homicides in the past decade, from a low of 4.5 per 100,000 in the 1950s to 6.1 per 100,000 persons in 1967.[4] There are five main causes for this recent increase.

The first is that our population now has an unusually large proportion of people in age groups highest in violence rates, especially men in their twenties. It is estimated that one-third of the increase in violence rates in the 1960s was due to the impact on our population's age distribution of the boom in babies born right after World War II.

Secondly, there has been an increase in the proportion of our population living in a "subculture of violence." This refers to the prevalence of customs and expectations in a group that make the ready use of violence to settle interpersonal differences not only expected, but considered honorable, manly, and proper. It has been vividly described in innumerable accounts of the escalation of petty arguments into deadly battles in communities where violence is most concentrated. Homicide statistics indicate where such subcultures are most intense:

a. In Latin American countries, notably Colombia and Mexico, the homicide rate is six times that of the United States. The obligation to meet rebuff by violence, and to seek violent revenge when one's honor is affronted, are part of a traditional set of values there known as "machismo" or manliness. We see portrayals on our television screen of something similar in our frontier culture. At present, in the United States as a whole, the extent and intensity of the subculture of violence seems appreciably less than in these Latin American societies. However, violence is also much greater in the

United States than in the countries of Northwestern Europe, such as Britain and Scandinavia, if we can judge by differences in homicide rates.

b. Our southeastern and South Central states have long had about twice the homicide rate of the rest of the country, even though these states are lower than other regions in rates of nonviolent crime, such as theft and fraud. The tradition of settling quarrels by violence seems greater there than elsewhere, and lethal weapons are more prevalent. Another distinctive feature of homicide in the South is its higher concentration in rural areas, as opposed to large cities; in the rest of the country it is relatively more concentrated in the central cities of metropolitan areas. Yet in a national poll conducted for the President's Crime Commission there were less frequent reports from the general populace in the South of suffering aggravated assaults than there were in the North Central and western states. This difference, which contrasts with the homicide rates, was almost entirely due to assault rates being high in central cities outside the South and relatively low in southern cities.[5]

c. We have always had our highest violence rates in those sections of our major cities which have been the segregated settlements of povertous migrants from areas with intense subcultures of violence. In the 1920s it was the Sicilian and other southern Italian groups. In the 1950s and 1960s it has been the areas of settlement of poor migrants from our rural South and from Latin American countries. It is notable that in southern cities, especially the older southern large cities like Atlanta, Charleston, and New Orleans, there has not been as high a degree of spatial segregation of the Negro residents as there has been in the North, where they have been newer migrants who are more concentrated in the slums, barred by prejudice from moving out of these areas as other migrant groups did when they became more prosperous. Indeed, it has been demonstrated by Professor Thomas Pettigrew of Harvard that one can predict the Negro homicide rate of northern states by the white homicide rate of the states from which the Negro population came.[6]

Thus we have had a southern rural and Latin American

subculture of violence transplanted to the slum areas of our northern and western cities. But the violence in our cities is not so much from these migrants as from their descendants. The transported subcultures of violence have been concentrated and intensified in city ghettoes by prolonged isolation of those reared there, under conditions of weak social control due to unemployment (especially of youth), poverty, poor public services, and weak social institutions.

d. On the whole, in most countries of the world, the youthful, the unskilled, and the least educated components of the population have had the highest rates of violence. The murder rate of standard metropolitan areas in the United States is very negatively correlated ($-.62$) with the median family incomes of the areas.[7] Opinion polls in the United States indicate that low education is especially associated with the belief that one should not allow insults to one's honor to go unpunished. More educated persons learn to settle their differences verbally or to ignore them.[8]

A third factor has been an increase in the alienation and discontent of youth, especially those already associated with subcultures of violence. Studies of rebellious behavior in youth, particularly in the high school age range, indicate that rebellion is especially associated with a failure to see a connection between conforming behavior and future status. Professor Arthur Stinchcombe of the University of California at Berkeley has demonstrated, with rather dramatic statistics, that it is the youth who are pressured to do well in school but do not, and the youth who do not expect to benefit from their schooling, who are most often hostile, sullen, malicious, and delinquent. These are disproportionately, but by no means exclusively, the youth from poorer families.[9] However, in the slum ghettoes of our urban centers, especially in the North and West, we have had a concentration of out-of-school and out-of-work youth, and their work failure plus other handicaps have demoralized those still in school. Therefore, there is much alienation from the dominant society's norms among them, and this is readily manifested as violence.

A fourth significant feature of subcultures of violence is that their traditions not only determine the readiness with which violence will be employed, but also the form in which violence will occur, augmented by such opportunity factors as the availability of traditional weapons. Thus in Texas most killing is by shooting, whereas in New York it is mostly by stabbing, cutting, and clubbing. This reflects both the emphasis on gunplay in the Texas subculture, and the ready availability of guns there, whereas a strict law against unlicensed possession of guns in New York State reduces their availability in that state. After the violent riots in Detroit, Newark, and elsewhere in the late 1960s, there was a sharp increase in the sale and the theft of small arms. Both in the ethnic ghettoes and especially in the areas around them, according to widespread reports, we approached closer than ever to a fully armed society. It is no wonder that with these conditions the proportion of homicides committed by guns increased by approximately one-sixth in 1967 over 1966.[10] The readier availability of guns would increase the proportion of assaults that are deadly even if the assault rate remained constant.

A final factor is the relative breakdown of our criminal justice system. Indeed, it might well be described as a non-system, with each of its three main components—the police, the courts, and corrections—operating without much concern for the consequences of their activities on the other components. The police are expected to intervene in a volume of criminal behavior so much greater than the courts could process to conviction by prescribed procedures, that police tend to evaluate their work solely by their arrest rates, and not by the consequences of the arrests. The courts cannot keep up with the volume of business given them without a combination of excessive delays and extensive failures to process to conviction on the charges indicated in the arrest report. It is well established that whenever the police are pressured to act in offenses for which there is little prospect of securing a conviction, they are inclined merely to harass, to reduce the presumed potentiality of offenses or of complaints, rather than to seek convictions. Once they are not oriented to obtaining convictions, their concern for due process decreases, and they are thus less regulated by the law of criminal procedure. This was observed years ago in the American Bar Foundation study of police handling of gambling and other vices for which convictions were unlikely.[11] I think we have good reason to infer from reports in recent years that court regulation of police behavior in dealing with violence has decreased. I also am suggesting that as a consequence of this decreased court regulation of police conduct there has been an escalation in both the ready use of violence and its provocation by counter-violence in police-community relations in many city neighborhoods with high violence subcultures.

The solutions to these problems are not easy. One can only recommend measures that should reduce violence in the long run, rather than provide instant solutions. The following are major suggestions for this purpose.

1. We should institutionalize victim survey research. An independent agency should conduct scientific inquiries with representative samples of the population to determine: (a) the extent to which the persons polled have been victims of violence in a recent period; (b) whether they contacted the police when violence occurred; (c) if they did not contact the police, why not; (d) if they did contact the police, what was the consequence; and (e) what are their attitudes and concerns regarding the use of violence. This will provide estimates of violence rates independent of the violence which comes to the attention of the police, and it will help pinpoint areas and trends of police success and failure in coping with violence.

2. One should support all measures which contribute to the transformation of subcultures of violence into customs of resolving differences by nonviolent means. This would be fostered by more educational and employment opportunity, and by increasing the extent to which youth can see prospects of a direct and somewhat immediate relationship between their educational efforts and their employment rewards. The culture of violence will be especially transformed if the ghettoes where it is concentrated can become permeable and ultimately dispersed, since it is a sociological law that social isolation promotes cultural differentiation.

3. The escalation of minor affrays into mass violence, and

of temporary altercations into careers of violence, will be reduced if police, courts, and corrections officers can consistently react to violence by effective due process, rather than by counter-violence alone, which is often equally lawless.

4. The severity of personal and social damage from violence will be reduced by diminishing the ready availability of lethal weapons through effective measures of gun registration and control.

Part IV

Urban Social Control

Introduction

R O B E R T Derbyshire and Jane Jacobs both show, though
in vastly different ways, that the informal relationships of the
city street—more than coercive measures by the police—determine the safeness of the streets. Indeed, time studies show
that most of a policeman's activity in a large city consists of
trying to settle domestic arguments, directing traffic, counseling those who are lost or distraught, and other supportive
services rather than control.[1] The police are the citizen's most
readily available resource, at all times, for almost any type of
emergency.

While police acquire new functions in the city, courts
acquire new procedures. Instead of the adversary contest
envisioned by the statutes, the metropolitan courtroom is
primarily a place for negotiation. Adversary gestures there
often are sham recitals, since the outcome of the proceedings
is agreed upon by all parties in advance, in accordance with
local custom rather than statutory prescription. As Blumberg
shows, the judge in such a metropolitan court becomes primarily a bureaucrat. The few who are most bureaucratic get
most of the court's work done, and the manner in which it is
completed often has little relationship to jurisprudential or
correctional principles. In most cities this can readily be
verified by a late morning visit to the crowded rooms of the
lower-level criminal courts, a memorable experience for most
undergraduates.

Perhaps the most overlooked social institution in our large
cities is the jail. Yet jail scandals which periodically shock
the public reflect the normal state of the jail, Glaser contends. The conditions exposed as scandals are inherent in the
physical and social structural arrangements of the jail.

THE SOCIAL CONTROL ROLE
OF THE POLICE IN
CHANGING URBAN COMMUNITIES

Robert L. Derbyshire

PUBLIC criticism of police and their tactics is a favorite American pastime. The validity of most police criticism is analogous to reprimanding a physician for not saving the life of one whose heart has been punctured by a bullet. In the case of the physician, there are biological and physiological forces determining the patient's expiration, over which the physician has little or no control. Similarly, policemen are exposed, in their battle against deviancy, to cultural, social, and psychological forces over which they have little or no control. Generally, these social forces are the political structure of the community, including the efficiency and reliability of elected and appointed officials; the patterns of coercion, leadership, and responsibility of and between police officials and political leaders; the capabilities, training and experience of policemen; the attitudes and behavior of citizens toward the police; and the particular conditions or set of circumstances under which these forces interact.

The urban condition is complex. Reciprocal relations between community and police present myriad problems. Police systems operate at an efficiency level commensurate with their ability and training, their status and salary and the community's attitude toward its own responsibility for social control. . . .

Abbreviated with permission of the author and publisher from *Excerpta criminologica* (The Netherlands), Vol. 6, No. 3 (May–June, 1966), pp. 315–321.

SOCIAL CONTROL

Social control among Homo sapiens is based upon custom. The system of social control consists of those mechanisms and techniques used to regulate the behavior of persons to meet societal goals and needs. All cultures provide adequate control over behavior. Controls are initiated either formally or informally. Informal controls usually start in the family and consist of orders, rebukes, criticisms, reprimands, ridicule, blame, gossip, praise, rewards, etc. How an individual responds to informal and formal social control in the community frequently depends upon the consistency and certainty of these controls in his family experience while growing up. Most frequently, informal controls are used by primary groups. Primary affiliations require emotional reciprocity, therefore they are more subject to informal control.

Formal controls are those sanctions instituted by the body politic and its agencies. Since emotional attachment is seldom a part of secondary associations, laws, sanctions, and punishments are explicitly stated and theoretically apply to everyone no matter what his position in the social structure. Schools, hospitals, welfare agencies, and the police are examples of secondary socializing agencies who use formal social control methods.

Theoretically, a continuum of social control exists from unregulated to institutionalized behavior. Unregulated behavior is unknown to contemporary man. Even within one's most intimate thoughts and isolated conditions, pressures from the social system both inhibit and stimulate behavior. Fantasies, hallucinations and delusions of persons whose behavior appears most unregulated (e.g. the psychotic), are determined by socio-cultural experiences.[1]

. . .

Social control systems operate most effectively and efficiently, the police notwithstanding, where there is constant and unified, both overt and covert, cultural and social support from all social control agencies. This support must be unambiguously stated in the value systems of families, community and the greater society of which the individual is a functional part.

.   .   .

MOBILITY AND NORM CONFLICTS

Lack of social cohesion and integration is a major problem in areas of high mobility. Cohesion and integration are major social control devices. Secondary socializing agencies are most effective when cohesion and integration have existed, but for some reason have suddenly broken down. Evidence supports the fact that the police, social workers, courts and other secondary socializing agencies do their most effective work with persons who temporarily lack integration with the prevailing society, while they help the least, those individuals who have rarely or never experienced cohesive and integrated community life.

One of the penalties American society pays for its major value of progress is instability. Progress means change, and change encourages cynicism toward the traditional and sacred. High cultural values are placed on the new, young and different. These are tied in with youthful attitudes, that to be adventuresome and daring is "good," while stability and conformity is for "squares." Where else is it more appropriate or easy to display these attitudes than during a riot?

Norm and social role conflicts are rampant in the inner city. Next door to a law abiding citizen who maintains conventional sexual and moral behavior, may live a sexually promiscuous person who has little respect for law, officials, property or others. Tremendous variations exist in religious beliefs, family system and means of achieving and satisfying human relationships.

The increased impersonality of city life fosters individual freedom. This individualism is a peculiar type. Most inner city or slum persons pay lip service to their own individuality while simultaneously conforming to the expected behavior of those persons or segments of their associations applying the most pressure at any particular time. With these persons frequently there is a lack of intimacy, yet a need to conform to perceived wishes; this type of man has been termed by David Riesman as "other directed."[2]

Primary socializing agencies are the immediate family, relatives by blood and marriage, age and sex peers, neighbors and others who aid persons, usually on a long term, face-to-face basis, with intimate contact, to learn culturally approved ways of controlling one's behavior. On the basis of present knowledge, it appears that social control is most effective when it is practiced at this level.

Secondary socializing agencies are those whose specific purpose is to aid in socialization or to re-socialize individuals whose primary agencies have for some reason become ineffective. The presently established secondary agents of social control are most effective as re-integrators and are less effective as substitutes for primary agents of social control.

URBAN POLICE

The police, particularly for the inner city urban community, is the most important agency of social control. Historically police systems have been primarily concerned with coercive control. Coercive control which emanates from law and government agencies is accomplished by force or threat of force.

Power and authority are vested in the symbols of the uniform and badge and, if that is not enough, the spontoon, side arm and handcuffs take on functional elements of legal authority. Pillars of the middle class community feel safe with the knowledge that this type of control protects their neighborhoods, while lower class persons more frequently view the coercive powers of the police as a threat. There is every reason to believe that the coercive powers of the police are most effective with persons who have internalized controls over their behavior. In other words, coercive control is most effective with those who need it the least.

Much of the requirements and education for police work places emphasis upon physical strength and stamina, marksmanship, selfprotection, knowledge of certain laws, police tactics, investigation and interrogation procedures, and other methods of coercive control. Traditionally this has been necessary for adequate control but more recently it is not sufficient for effective control. The policeman's role has been primarily concerned with crime detection, control and prevention. These behavior patterns have been sufficient and effective for small communities where social relations among members have been intimate and long term, and where homogeneity of values, and behavior patterns prevailed. Under more intimate rural conditions, crime detection and control functions of police systems are more frequently aided by citizens.

COERCIVE CONTROL: "THE COP"

Coercive control is a necessary function for all police systems, but more important, particularly in urban centers, is the need for persuasive control functions of the police. Middle class youth who have the advantage of intact homes and adequate supervision seldom see a policeman except possibly directing traffic. Middle class citizens learn in school that "we should obey the laws" and "the policeman is our friend," but direct contact with him is seldom encountered. Little firsthand knowledge of behavior patterns associated with the police role exists in middle class culture.

On the other hand, in the inner city many youngsters observe the police more frequently than their own fathers or other important relatives. These same children lack much of the informal social controls taught by and expected of the middle class. Young persons in lower class communities see policemen breaking up family fights, taking drunks and derelicts off the street, raiding a prostitute's flat or a gambling house, picking up some of the local boys for interrogation, knocking on the door because a disturbance had been reported, breaking up a game of pitching coins or shooting dice on the street, checking locked doors of merchant neighbors, evicting slum residents, asking questions pertaining to rat control, transporting patients to mental hospitals, beating others and being beaten, taking bribes and arresting bribers, and numerous other behaviors associated with most police systems. It is within this context that the growing lower class child forms his impressions and develops attitudes toward the police. These attitudes are then transferred toward the larger adult world and its system of social control. Within this environment he gains his most purposive information about law, rights, duties, privileges, loyalties and many other items necessary for adulthood. Many of these, are developed from impressions received from the policeman, one of the few representatives of the social control system with whom he has had direct contact.

In the lower class community the function of the police is integrated into the child's knowledge before he knows the role of teachers. More important for the policeman in inner city crime control is the role of persuasive control. Lower class youngsters need a stable, steady, friendly person with whom to identify, to help them understand that controlling their behavior is most effective and appropriate when it is controlled because one wants to do what significant persons in his life wish him to do and not because he is afraid of force if he doesn't control his behavior.

The inner city situation for policemen is analogous to that for teachers, that is, seldom does one volunteer to assume the responsibilities for these areas, because the problems are multiple. Therefore, more frequently lower quality police officers and teachers are assigned to areas that are in dire need of the highest quality professional.

PERSUASIVE CONTROL: THE POLICEMAN

Effective persuasive control emanates from a particular type of policeman who has the personality, motivation, interest, time, training and the fortitude to work closely with slum families and other human beings. He should be specifically and adequately trained for this role and commensurately rewarded. An emulative image must be presented consistently so that children, adolescents, young and old adults alike will look to him for guidance in areas other than crime control.

One of the major reasons for members of urban communities standing passively by, while policemen are being
beaten is due to a total disinterest in, and disrespect for
laws which have little meaning to them, and a lack of
identification with persons who enforce these laws, for whom
they have little respect. Any lack of respect is not totally due
to the law, its enforcing agency or the lower class dweller.
Responsibility for this behavior can be identified as the result
of the interaction of these variables and a social system that
permits inequities and irregularities in law, stimulates poverty
and inhibits initiative and motivation of the poor, and
relegates low social and economic status to the police while
concomitantly giving them more extraneous nonpolice duties
than adequately can be performed.

RECOMMENDATIONS

Cities and states must pay adequate salaries, extend fringe
benefits and provide professional pride and status to the degree
that police departments can hire the type of men and women
necessary to fulfill the role of future policemen. This new
role should place greater emphasis upon crime prevention.
Excellent persuasive control is good crime prevention. Certainly, knowledge of riot control and police tactics is essential
to stopping riots and criminal activity after they start; this
is a necessary coercive function of the policeman's social
role. But, more important than stopping a crime is its prevention.

A number of suggestions for more effective social control
over urban conflict during a period of rapid social change
are: (1) More important than placing Negro policemen in
Negro communities is to rid the police hiring procedures of
discrimination. Hiring a man on the basis of his ability to
meet specific criteria does more to increase the social status
and image of the police in all Negro areas than "tokenism"
as it has been practised in the past. (2) The most highly
educated and motivated, and those persons whose character
is beyond reproach should be placed in inner city areas. These
persons should seek out and identify indigenous leadership.

Also, they should learn to communicate effectively with persons in the community. Knowledge of potential ignitors of tension and conflict is a necessary part of the police role. After identification of such persons, the policeman's duty is to seek a change in attitudes, to call in appropriate resocializing aid when necessary or at least to see that those persons who are potential agitators are immobilized during periods of high tension. In an area where stability is seldom evident, the policeman should be emotionally stable and a pattern of social stability must exist, in that turn-over of men on these assignments must be minimized. Inner city dwellers need some source of a stable predictable relationship, this the police can provide. (3) Raise the social status of the police by increasing the quality of men hired and requesting improvement programs for those who are already on the force. Education programs sponsored and promoted by law enforcement agencies in collaboration with behavioral scientists in universities is indispensable. State and local officials and police organizations must stop paying lip service to the need for responsible, educated policemen. Responsible, emotionally stable, well educated policemen will make more lasting contributions to crime prevention and control, than many other measures already requested by responsible politicians. (4) The police image must be changed to such a degree that middle class mothers will say with pride, "my son the policeman." (5) Each policeman involved in learning this role must be aided to live with himself. That is, the dichotomy between persuasion and coercion is great, and frequently appears incompatible, therefore each law enforcement officer must learn to integrate both roles with as little discomfort as possible. (6) Discrimination toward Negroes and other minorities in areas of employment, housing, in fact in all areas, must cease. As long as it exists institutionally or socially, the American lower class ghettoized Negro is a potential for urban conflict. He is in this conflict-producing situation partly because he is Negro, but more, because he has the same American aspirations for achievement and success, but the social structure restricts this American's ability to obtain his goal.

Langston Hughes has related the explosive potential of the lower class urban Negro in the following poem.

What happens to a dream deferred?
Does it dry up
Like a raisin in the sun?
Or fester like a sore —
And then run?
Does it stink like rotten meat?
Or crust and sugar over —
Like a syrupy sweet?
Maybe it just sags
Like a heavy load.
Or does it explode? *

American urban policemen who involve themselves in the role of persuasive control can and will be the most influential and vital inhibitors of this explosion. If over the hot and humid summers during the next decade, urban racial conflicts become a part of the American scene, responsibility will be in the hands of persons who neglect to recognize the importance of the police as preventors of conflict, rather than just maintainers of order.

THE DEATH AND LIFE OF
GREAT AMERICAN CITIES

Jane Jacobs

T O D A Y barbarism has taken over many city streets, or
people fear it has, which comes to much the same thing in
the end. "I live in a lovely, quiet residential area," says a
friend of mine who is hunting another place to live. "The
only disturbing sound at night is the occasional scream of
someone being mugged." It does not take many incidents of
violence on a city street, or in a city district, to make people
fear the streets. And as they fear them, they use them less,
which makes the streets still more unsafe.

To be sure, there are people with hobgoblins in their heads,
and such people will never feel safe no matter what the
objective circumstances are. But this is a different matter
from the fear that besets normally prudent, tolerant and
cheerful people who show nothing more than common sense
in refusing to venture after dark—or in a few places, by day
—into streets where they may well be assaulted, unseen or
unrescued until too late.

. . .

It cannot be tagged as a problem of older parts of cities.
The problem reaches its most baffling dimensions in some
examples of rebuilt parts of cities, including supposedly the
best examples of rebuilding, such as middle-income projects.
The police precinct captain of a nationally admired project
of this kind (admired by planners and lenders) has recently

admonished residents not only about hanging around out-doors after dark but has urged them never to answer their doors without knowing the caller. Life here has much in common with life for the three little pigs or the seven little kids of the nursery thrillers. The problem of sidewalk and doorstep insecurity is as serious in cities which have made conscientious efforts at rebuilding as it is in those cities that have lagged. Nor is it illuminating to tag minority groups, or the poor, or the outcast with responsibility for city danger. There are immense variations in the degree of civilization and safety found among such groups and among the city areas where they live. Some of the safest sidewalks in New York City, for example, at any time of day or night, are those along which poor people or minority groups live. And some of the most dangerous are in streets occupied by the same kinds of people. All this can also be said of other cities.

.   .   .

The first thing to understand is that the public peace—the sidewalk and street peace—of cities is not kept primarily by the police, necessary as police are. It is kept primarily by an intricate, almost unconscious, network of voluntary controls and standards among the people themselves, and enforced by the people themselves. In some city areas—older public housing projects and streets with very high population turn-over are often conspicuous examples—the keeping of public sidewalk law and order is left almost entirely to the police and special guards. Such places are jungles. No amount of police can enforce civilization where the normal, casual enforcement of it has broken down.

The second thing to understand is that the problem of insecurity cannot be solved by spreading people out more thinly, trading the characteristics of cities for the character-istics of suburbs. If this could solve danger on the city streets, then Los Angeles should be a safe city because superficially Los Angeles is almost all suburban. It has virtually no dis-tricts compact enough to qualify as dense city areas. Yet Los Angeles cannot, any more than any other great city, evade the truth that, being a city, it *is* composed of strangers not all of whom are nice. Los Angeles' crime figures are flabbergasting. Among the seventeen standard metropolitan areas with populations over a million, Los Angeles stands so pre-eminent in crime that it is in a category by itself. And this is markedly true of crimes associated with personal attack, the crimes that make people fear the streets.

. . .

The reasons for Los Angeles' high crime rates are undoubtedly complex, and at least in part obscure. But of this we can be sure: thinning out a city does not insure safety from crime and fear of crime. This is one of the conclusions that can be drawn within individual cities too, where pseudosuburbs or superannuated suburbs are ideally suited to rape, muggings, beatings, holdups and the like.

. . .

Some city streets afford no opportunity to street barbarism. The streets of the North End of Boston are outstanding examples. They are probably as safe as any place on earth in this respect. Although most of the North End's residents are Italian or of Italian descent, the district's streets are also heavily and constantly used by people of every race and background. Some of the strangers from outside work in or close to the district; some come to shop and stroll; many, including members of minority groups who have inherited dangerous districts previously abandoned by others, make a point of cashing their paychecks in North End stores and immediately making their big weekly purchases in streets where they know they will not be parted from their money between the getting and the spending.

Frank Havey, director of the North End Union, the local settlement house, says, "I have been here in the North End twenty-eight years, and in all that time I have never heard of a single case of rape, mugging, molestation of a child or other street crime of that sort in the district. And if there had been any, I would have heard of it even if it did not reach the papers." Half a dozen times or so in the past three decades, says Havey, would-be molesters have made an attempt at luring a child or, late at night, attacking a woman. In every such case the try was thwarted by passers-by, by kibitzers from windows, or shopkeepers.

Meantime, in the Elm Hill Avenue section of Roxbury, a part of inner Boston that is suburban in superficial character, street assaults and the ever present possibility of more street assaults with no kibitzers to protect the victims, induce prudent people to stay off the sidewalks at night. Not surprisingly, for this and other reasons that are related (dispiritedness and dullness), most of Roxbury has run down. It has become a place to leave.

I do not wish to single out Roxbury or its once fine Elm Hill Avenue section especially as a vulnerable area; its disabilities, and especially its Great Blight of Dullness, are all too common in other cities too. But differences like these in public safety within the same city are worth noting. The Elm Hill Avenue section's basic troubles are not owing to a criminal or a discriminated against or a poverty-stricken population. Its troubles stem from the fact that it is physically quite unable to function safely and with related vitality as a city district.

Even within supposedly similar parts of supposedly similar places, drastic differences in public safety exist. An incident at Washington Houses, a public housing project in New York, illustrates this point. A tenants' group at this project, struggling to establish itself, held some outdoor ceremonies in mid-December 1958, and put up three Christmas trees. The chief tree, so cumbersome it was a problem to transport, erect, and trim, went into the project's inner "street," a landscaped central mall and promenade. The other two trees, each less than six feet tall and easy to carry, went on two small fringe plots at the outer corners of the project where it abuts a busy avenue and lively cross streets of the old city. The first night, the large tree and all its trimmings were stolen. The two smaller trees remained intact, lights, ornaments and all, until they were taken down at New Year's. "The place where the tree was stolen, which is *theoretically* the most safe and sheltered place in the project, is the same place that is unsafe for people too, especially children," says a social worker who had been helping the tenants' group. "People are no safer in that mall than the Christmas tree. On the other hand, the place where the other trees were safe, where the project is just one corner out of four, happens to be safe for people."

This is something everyone already knows: A well-used city street is apt to be a safe street. A deserted city street is apt to be unsafe. But how does this work, really? And what makes a city street well used or shunned? Why is the sidewalk mall in Washington Houses, which is supposed to be an attraction, shunned? Why are the sidewalks of the old city just to its west not shunned? What about streets that are busy part of the time and then empty abruptly?

A city street equipped to handle strangers, and to make a safety asset, in itself, out of the presence of strangers, as the streets of successful city neighborhoods always do, must have three main qualities:

First, there must be a clear demarcation between what is public space and what is private space. Public and private spaces cannot ooze into each other as they do typically in suburban settings or in projects.

Second, there must be eyes upon the street, eyes belonging to those we might call the natural proprietors of the street. The buildings on a street equipped to handle strangers and to insure the safety of both residents and strangers, must be oriented to the street. They cannot turn their backs or blank sides on it and leave it blind.

And third, the sidewalk must have users on it fairly continuously, both to add to the number of effective eyes on the street and to induce the people in buildings along the street to watch the sidewalks in sufficient numbers. Nobody enjoys sitting on a stoop or looking out a window at an empty street. Almost nobody does such a thing. Large numbers of people entertain themselves, off and on, by watching street activity.

In settlements that are smaller and simpler than big cities, controls on acceptable public behavior, if not on crime, seem to operate with greater or lesser success through a web of reputation, gossip, approval, disapproval and sanctions, all of which are powerful if people know each other and word travels. But a city's streets, which must control not only the behavior of the people of the city but also of visitors from suburbs and towns who want to have a big time away from the gossip and sanctions at home, have to operate by more direct, straightforward methods. It is a wonder cities have solved such an inherently difficult problem at all. And yet in many streets they do it magnificently.

It is futile to try to evade the issue of unsafe city streets by attempting to make some other features of a locality, say interior courtyards, or sheltered play spaces, safe instead. By definition again, the streets of a city must do most of the job of handling strangers for this is where strangers come and go. The streets must not only defend the city against predatory strangers, they must protect the many, many peaceable and well-meaning strangers who use them, insuring their safety too as they pass through. Moreover, no normal person can spend his life in some artificial haven, and this includes children. Everyone must use the streets.

On the surface, we seem to have here some simple aims: To try to secure streets where the public space is unequivocally public, physically unmixed with private or with nothing-at-all space, so that the area needing surveillance has clear and practicable limits; and to see that these public street spaces have eyes on them as continuously as possible.

But it is not so simple to achieve these objects, especially the latter. You can't make people use streets they have no reason to use. You can't make people watch streets they do not want to watch. Safety on the streets by surveillance and mutual policing of one another sounds grim, but in real life it is not grim. The safety of the street works best, most casually, and with least frequent taint of hostility or surpicion precisely where people are using and most enjoying the city streets voluntarily and are least conscious, normally, that they are policing.

The basic requisite for such surveillance is a substantial quantity of stores and other public places sprinkled along the sidewalks of a district; enterprises and public places that are used by evening and night must be among them especially. Stores, bars and restaurants, as the chief examples, work in several different and complex ways to abet sidewalk safety.

First, they give people—both residents and strangers— concrete reasons for using the sidewalks on which these enterprises face.

Second, they draw people along the sidewalks past places which have no attractions to public use in themselves but which become traveled and peopled as routes to somewhere else; this influence does not carry very far geographically, so enterprises must be frequent in a city district if they are to populate with walkers those other stretches of street that lack public places along the sidewalk. Moreover, there should be many different kinds of enterprises, to give people reasons for crisscrossing paths.

Third, storekeepers and other small businessmen are typically strong proponents of peace and order themselves; they hate broken windows and holdups; they hate having customers made nervous about safety. They are great street watchers and sidewalk guardians if present in sufficient numbers.

Fourth, the activity generated by people on errands, or people coming for food or drink, is itself an attraction to still other people.

This last point, that the sight of people attracts still other people, is something that city planners and city architectural designers seem to find incomprehensible. They operate on the premise that city people seek the sight of emptiness, obvious order and quiet. Nothing could be less true. People's love of watching activity and other people is constantly evident in cities everywhere. This trait reaches an almost ludicrous extreme on upper Broadway in New York, where the street is divided by a narrow central mall, right in the middle of traffic. At the cross-street intersections of this long north-south mall, benches have been placed behind big concrete buffers and on any day when the weather is even barely tolerable these benches are filled with people at block after block after block, watching the pedestrians who cross the mall in front of them, watching the traffic, watching the people on the busy sidewalks, watching each other. Eventually Broadway reaches Columbia University and Barnard College, one to the right, the other to the left. Here all is obvious order and quiet. No more stores, no more activity generated by the stores, almost no more pedestrians crossing—and no more watchers. The benches are there but they go empty in even the finest weather. I have tried them and can see why. No place could be more boring. Even the students of these institutions shun the solitude. They are doing their outdoor loitering, outdoor homework and general street watching on the steps overlooking the busiest campus crossing.

THE JUDGE AS BUREAUCRAT

Abraham Blumberg

OF THE 8,180 judges officially reported in the courts of America, 599 are on the federal bench, 5,301 are state or county judges, and 2,280 sit in city courts.[1] Many other thousands serve in police courts or as justices of the peace, although many of these have other occupations. Perhaps as many as 5 per cent of the country's approximately 285,000 lawyers are thus serving as judges at any one time.

.   .   .

Judicial biographies have generally emphasized judgeship in the "grand" tradition.[2] They are for the most part paeans of praise and adulatory studies, revealing little of the judge's actual work role. In the main they concern themselves with judges who have established careers in the higher appellate courts, far removed from the administrative fray of the lower civil and criminal courts. But much of the charismatic

Abbreviated with permission of the author and publisher from *Criminal Justice*, Chicago: Quadrangle Books, 1967, pp. 117–131, 137 as edited for this volume.

quality of the judge flows from the "grand" tradition and its accompanying mystique. There seems to be little that is intellectually exciting or grandiose in the career of a judge at the lowest level. He is so close to the publics served daily by the bench and bar that, while he may retain the charismatic flavor of the office, his reputation becomes tarnished and somewhat mundane. He bears the brunt of criticism and dissatisfaction with the legal system, and especially with the administration of the criminal law. In the prestige hierarchy of judges and lawyers, those in the criminal courts are in the lower levels, however important their work is. The civil courts, which oversee the orderly transfer of wealth in our society by their appointment of receivers, executors, administrators, trustees, guardians, and other caretakers of property, are considered far more important areas of practice —and sources of remuneration. This "prestige gap" is an important source of the profound feelings of marginality that plague judges and lawyers alike in the criminal court.

Few of the judges serving in the trial courts have been memorialized, so we know little of real value about the real "infantry-men" of the entire legal system. For it is they who ultimately stage manage and direct the drama that occurs in the lower courts. With the defense lawyer in the criminal court, they make the system of criminal justice work. Without the judge's active involvement, in pursuit of rational values in disposing of the maximum number of pleas, the entire system of criminal justice would founder.

Despite the fact that the upper-level judge serves as the role model in literature, there are at least three levels of the judicial career line. The Lower Level is available and followed by most lawyers who become judges. Quite simply, this level has the most positions to offer, and they are manipulated as patronage plums at the clubhouse level of local politics. The judicial career aspirant at this level has usually attended a proprietary or part-time law school of dubious quality, whose major emphasis is on preparing its graduates for the state bar examination. A marginal member of his profession, he may trade upon his ethnicity and translate his rather strong personal mobility aspirations into a cluster of contacts in his local political club, as well as a variety of memberships in fraternal, benevolent, and religious organizations. A lawyer at this stage of his career can look forward to a long apprenticeship—possibly most of his adult life—performing a wide range of legal and other services in return for the occasional legal business which may bring a meaningful fee. The number of judicial candidates far exceeds the available posts, so most aspirants are doomed to disappointment. Clubhouse lawyer regulars often find that they have dedicated most of a lifetime of law practice to the club, only to find judicial or other rewards snatched from them by nepotism or other higher claims.

The law practice of the upwardly mobile clubhouse ethnic often reflects the status limitations and concerns of his clients. "Italian," "Irish," "Puerto Rican," and "Jewish" lawyers find that their client appeal is not based on their intrinsic skills but rather on their presumed ethnic characteristics. Lawyers learn early in their career to exploit ethnic loyalties in securing practice as well as in their political life. Their law practice at this level is largely of the negligence, landlord-tenant, criminal work variety, and most court appearances, if any, occur in the lower-level courts where their clubhouse brethren sit as judges. Thus the clubhouse becomes an important career nexus not only for the judicial or political aspirant but as a source of "contacts" so necessary to a busy law practice.

Wallace Sayre and Herbert Kaufman indicated recently that the "going rate" for judgeships in New York City was the equivalent of two years' salary contributed to the political party.[3] Although most Metropolitan Court judges have a lower-level career line, their incumbency has been free of the usual taint of rumors so prevalent elsewhere about paying for a seat on the bench. Nevertheless, their ascendancy to the bench was preceded by many years of clubhouse activity, including heavy contributions of time and money to party activities. These contributions continue, because strong clubhouse ties are needed for re-election or promotion. The situation generates commitments and obligations to "politically visible" lawyers in Metropolitan Court, who in turn feel entitled to some sort of quid pro quo for their long years of service to the club. If they cannot receive payment in cash, they will accept payment "in kind"—judicial favors dispensed at critical junctures in the criminal lawyer's practice.

The lower-level judicial career, then, has a built-in socialization process. It assures the early acceptance of clubhouse norms and expectancies with regard to the character of future conduct on the bench, should one be designated to run for the office. Those who are not picked will often seek posts as law assistants and law secretaries, which they regard as a favorable career compromise. These positions are considered critical in the power structure, because they conduct a good deal of the "judge's business" at the lower level and act as his intermediary.

The lower-level judicial career pattern described here is likely to be found in many civil courts of first instance as well as the criminal courts. Municipal court justices, magistrates, justices of the peace, county court judges, and the like are typical judicial careers of this stratum.

. . .

There are of course many judges whose particular career line may not fit any of the foregoing patterns. But it is clear that the "grand tradition" judge, the aloof, brooding, charismatic figure in the Old Testament tradition, is hardly a real figure. The reality is the working judge who must be politician, administrator, bureaucrat, and lawyer in order to cope with a crushing calendar of cases. A Metropolitan Court judge might well ask, "Did John Marshall or Oliver Wendell Holmes ever have to clear a calendar like mine?" The Metropolitan Court judge who sits in a court of original jurisdiction, in his role as trial judge, arbiter, sentencer, and awarder, cannot avoid the legal, interpersonal, and emotional dynamics of the small group of court regulars and those hangers-on who are inevitably present in a criminal court. By way of contrast, the middle-level or upper-level appellate judge is far removed from the original dispute and is therefore relatively unconcerned with the interpersonal dynamics of a given case and the various parties connected with it. His major sources of contact with a particular issue are lifeless briefs and a trial record.

Metropolitan Court judges, although they are among the

highest paid in the world and wield considerable power in their limited domain, nevertheless feel somewhat marginal. They consider their activity to be peripheral to that of their civil court colleagues, and often they wistfully contrast the social importance of their work to that of the civil courts. They understand, however, that the bench and bar view them and the practitioners in their court as part of the least desirable aspect of law practice. The great intellectual challenges, and the arena in which the movers and shakers of our society operate, are thought to be in the civil courts. . . .

SOCIO-DEMOGRAPHIC VARIABLES IN RECRUITMENT

By the time he has been elected to the bench, the mean age of a Metropolitan Court judge is fifty-one years. Retirement is mandatory at seventy. In the more than two hundred years of its existence, Metropolitan Court has never had a woman judge.

Of the nine justices who regularly sit in Metropolitan Court, only one is a graduate of a "national" law school; the others are graduates of part-time, proprietary, or "factory" types of schools.[4] Three of the nine justices completed their baccalaureate work before going to law school. In so far as their legal education was concerned, its course content did little to prepare them for their actual functions on the bench. Virtually all courses in most law schools are of the "bread and butter" variety, directed toward the candidate passing the bar examination of the particular state. Only rarely do they concern themselves with the serious issues of law administration, and virtually never do they deal with the social and economic implications of law and legal decision-making. As a result, there is no formal, systematic body of knowledge in legal education which can form the minimum requisite for a judicial career. Metropolitan Court judges—and most criminal court judges—are therefore, for the most part, poorly equipped to deal with the role challenges, dilemmas, and problems which they confront on the bench. A thorough knowledge of the criminal law is only rudimentary knowledge in the context of the onerous demands made by the criminal court bench.

Because he is ill-equipped to be a sophisticated decision-maker in a job that requires decision-making daily and routinely, and at the same time requires him to be an administrator, manager, and overseer, the judge must lean heavily on the services of others. As a consequence, Metropolitan Court justices, when they are initially appointed, are "broken in" by court clerks and other civil service functionaries who socialize them toward the "practical" goals and requirements of the court organization. This socialization is in fact actively sought by the judges in order to make their own work lives easier and to assuage their personal insecurities. As a matter of organizational and personal practicality, regardless of their individual predilections, they learn to accept and internalize the routineering and ritualism of their socializers.

.　　.　　.

There is a continuing popular belief that the field of politics is an important exception to class rigidities and distinctions in America, that it still offers greater chances for social mobility than any other activity. But the experience of Metropolitan Court judges would belie this part of the American Dream. Seven of the judges are drawn from middle- and upper middle-class backgrounds. The fathers of the justices were at least as successful as their sons, although perhaps they did not have as high prestige. Only one justice, Judge X, is the son of a former city official, who is reputed to have acquired the family fortune in the course of his civic duties. Justice A, the other judge of considerable means, derived his wealth from his father's successful mercantile venture.

JUDICIAL DECISION-MAKING AND ANOMIE

Observers have used several frames of reference to try to explain the basis for judicial decision-making, the most fundamental aspect of the judge's job. These range from exploring the judge's personality[5] to applying small group theory, game theory, and a scale analysis of judicial voting behavior.[6] Indeed, the disciplined effort to identify the decision process with mathematical precision has been dubiously labeled "jurimetrics."[7]

One of the more significant variables in judicial decision-making is the level of the court. Upper-level judges are more scrupulously concerned with the niceties of legalism, for they do not face the voluminous case pressure and daily administrative tensions of the lower courts. Their distance from the persons involved in the case and the point of origin of the issues allows them to be sage-like, rather than bureaucratic and instrumental.

Similarly, political pressures—visible and invisible—will manifest themselves. Even though there may be no pressures on specific cases, the judge may not wish to offend those who have contributed to his past or may control his future when he comes up for reappointment or renomination. Only federal judges and some higher appellate state justices are appointed for life and are thus presumably above political pressures, but even they may be interested in being promoted. Inasmuch as most judgeships are often political rewards, there is likely to be an assumption of repayment by the judge for the reward. It may be in the form of judicial sympathy for the interests of the sponsors or former associates of the judge when litigation involving such interests comes before him. The judges of Metropolitan Court, being elected for a term of years and not for life, must always maintain a keen sensitivity to the desires, requirements, and interests of their political sponsors. In fact, the "easy" decision is the one that is politically inspired.

Of course, a judge's social biography will affect his decisions. Even the kind of law school he attended, or the nature of his practice before his judicial career, are elements in judicial decision-making. A judge who has come from a corporate or a commercial civil practice may have an entirely different decision pattern than one who has devoted much of his prior practice to criminal law and negligence. And class factors will have been a strong influence in determining the kind of practice the judge had. Indeed, sometimes a judge may react against his past as a criminal lawyer by being extremely harsh and punitive with the kinds of criminals he used to defend. This is the case with at least one well-known judge in the Metropolitan Court system.

The non-rational aspect of judicial decision-making may be best summed up by the confessional statement of one of America's leading contributors to jurisprudence, Chancellor James Kent. He indicated well over a century ago, in explaining how he reached a decision, that ". . . I might once in a while be embarrassed by a technical rule, but I almost always found principles suited to my view of the case . . ."[8]

Legal literature for the most part deals with the problems of judicial decision-making at the appellate level. At the level of Metropolitan Court the matter is much more complex because of the incredibly greater number of decisions that must be made, the greater variety of publics that must be served by the judge, and his greater anxiety because the legal rules themselves do not furnish adequate guidelines for his behavior. For example, if the Metropolitan Court judges were to permit themselves to be bound by statutory provisions for sentencing procedures, they would meet head on many groups in and out of the court who have vested interests in mitigating sentences and other rules. The judicial ambivalence toward rules is also apparent in connection with institutionalized evasions of the Canons of Judicial Ethics, especially Canon 14 requiring that "a judge should not be swayed by partisan demands," and Canon 28 forbidding his participation in politics except in connection with his own election. He cannot really adhere to these rules because every day he must respond to political commitments. Clubhouse lawyers are part of a constant procession of visitors to the judge's chambers, where there is frequent negotiation over plea and sentence.

Metropolitan Court judges rationalize their more obvious violations of the canons in terms of "community service" and "concern with social problems." They are caught in a bind which, by the nature of their office, compels them to behave with bureaucratic concern for production, efficient administration, and dispassionate enforcement of rules—and at the same time to be instruments of their political benefactors' particularistic designs and concerns.

Another aspect of the anomic character of the judge's conduct is reflected in the reluctance to place an individual on probation if he has been convicted after a jury trial. The justices in Metropolitan Court from time to time publicly affirm the importance of the jury trial as a central element of justice and due process. But privately, in their decision-making process, they will as a rule deny a probation disposition to a jury-convicted offender. In fact, the judges, the district attorney, and the probation report will, upon sentence of such an individual, explicitly note that "the defendant has caused the state to go to the expense of a trial." In 1962 the Metropolitan Court probation division investigated 3,643 out of 4,363 cases processed that year. Of the number investigated, 1,125 were placed on probation; all but three of these had pleaded guilty *before* trial.

. . . The Metropolitan Court judges make an even more active effort than is usual in a bureaucracy to diffuse responsibility and authority. They simply are reluctant to carry the entire burden, and unlike the appellate courts, there are ample intermediaries and groups who can be invoked to share in the responsibilities which are ultimately those of the judge. Reluctant to shoulder the decision-making burden, and ambivalent toward formal rules and criteria which may interfere with his informal relations with political bene-factors, lawyers, and other court personnel, the judge tailors each decision to suit his own needs. Thus for different decisions the judge will involve different court personnel, to diffuse responsibility and at the same time alleviate his own formal obligations.

. . . Metropolitan Court judges are largely content to "pass the buck" to the district attorney who will frame the nature of the lesser plea to be accepted. Traditional judicial formulations would require the judge to act as an instrument of the whole community in reviewing the propriety of an accepted lesser plea. But here too Metropolitan Court judges have abdicated and prefer to ratify the plea negotiated by the district attorney, the defense counsel, and sometimes even the police. While the judge may have the right to reject a given plea, he rarely does so.

Although Metropolitan Court procedures are highly rational, it is not surprising to see the frequent number of spontaneous, last-minute, private conferences at the judge's bench in which minor details of a lesser plea are ironed out. Too often a judge has not been privy to the details of a negotiated plea. There is a fairly typical scene in which a judge has to muster all the authority of his office to smooth out a badly staged "cop-out ceremony." The judge must redirect the scene for the record, so that the plea will stand and the court can proceed to other matters.

. . .

It is, however, in the area of sentencing that judges show their greatest ambivalence and inconsistency. Some men may glory in being a criminal court judge, but others are entirely ambivalent about the responsibilities of sentencing their fellow men to prison or death. The latter description for the most part fits the Metropolitan Court judges. They have therefore arranged for elaborate probation and psychiatric reports which they can "lean on" in deciding an otherwise difficult case. Where there are strong political considerations, or where there is a mandatory penalty with little exercise of discretion possible, judicial decision-making is circumscribed. But often the judge is confronted with a situation that offers too few or too weak criteria for decision. He will then deliberately involve probation and psychiatric reports or a district attorney's recommendations to diffuse responsibility or to mitigate his own anxieties. And what *appears* to be a group decision is also more palatable in organizational life to client, workers, and the publics concerned. The bureaucratic admonition of "cover yourself" applies as well to the judge as to any other individual in the organizational world. The group decision functions not only to conceal individual mediocrity but can also be pointed to as evidence of profound efforts to individualize, and at the same time make the administration of justice more uniform and equitable.

.   .   .

SOME NOTES ON URBAN JAILS

Daniel Glaser

PERHAPS no institutions for dealing with criminals are more neglected by both criminologists and the public than urban jails. Yet these facilities probably house a much larger proportion of our population, at one time or another, than any other type of residence for persons who commit deviant behavior.

JAIL POPULATIONS

The typical American jail is a county institution. Its management is one of several responsibilities assigned to an elected official, the sheriff. In urban counties he delegates this burden to a jail superintendent or warden, who has traditionally been a political patronage appointee. Most other staff appointments for jails also are granted as rewards for services in the precinct and ward offices of the party in power. However, this system of recruitment has partially been replaced by civil service in the past few decades. Also, in a few large cities jails have long been operated by the municipal government.

Most jail staff are relatively unskilled guards. High school graduation generally is advocated as a minimum education requirement for them, but most guards are high school or

This paper was written especially for this volume.

even elementary school dropouts. The total guard force numbers, on the average, only one-ninth the number of inmates in the jail, but the guards operate on several shifts. Thus at any one time the guards on duty are likely to be outnumbered by the inmates by a ratio between fifteen and fifty or more to one.[1]

Jail inmates consist mainly of persons awaiting trial who could not afford to gain release by paying their bail, or persons serving short sentences, of whom about one-third are there because they cannot pay their fines. One day's confinement is commonly equated with $5 off the fine, but the rates vary greatly in different areas. At any rate, it is clear that poverty puts men in jail independently of criminality.

Also resident in city jails are some men sentenced to long prison terms, and even a few men sentenced to death. They are in jail awaiting transportation to a penitentiary, or they have been brought back to appear in court in appeals of their convictions, or as witnesses in trials. A few metropolitan jails actually conduct executions and have a "Death Row." Because of these several types of highly desperate inmates, and because the pretrial prisoners include persons facing serious charges who expect severe sentences, jails are operated with great concern for custodial security. This is the case despite the fact that most of the jail's inmates are considered relatively nondangerous petty offenders. Indeed, by far the most frequent basis for admission to jail is public drunkenness.

Jails usually house both sexes, but in separate sections, and their inmates are of a wide range in age. However, some large cities now have separate detention centers for women, and most also operate detention homes for juveniles, variously defined as persons under 16-, 17-, or 18-years-of age. The homes for juveniles usually are supervised by the probation offices of the juvenile courts. They often are considerably different in architecture and social climate from the typical city jail, but some differ from jails only in name. Another jail-like facility in most cities is the "lock-up" at each police station. However, these hold inmates only until they can be brought before a judge or transferred to the jail, a period of hours as a rule, or at most a few days.

JAIL ACTIVITY AND INACTIVITY

As implied in the foregoing, most jails are designed and managed so that a relatively small number of staff can insure the secure confinement of a comparatively large number of inmates. This low-cost control usually is achieved by a few basic measures. The first is to confine most of the men—those deemed least dangerous—not in separate cells, but in a few large cages. These are commonly called "bullpens," "tanks," or "dayrooms," depending partly on whether they are used for confinement around the clock, or just in the daytime in conjunction with adjacent cells or dormitories crowded with multiple-bunk beds. Augmenting this custodial economy is the practice of passing food and clothing or other supplies in or out of these cages through small openings instead of by opening the doors. They also have lavatories unscreened in a corner of these cages. Such arrangements and practices make it unnecessary to move the men to a dining hall, washroom, supply rooms, etc., as occurs in state or federal prisons. A consequence of these physical arrangements is a great reliance on inmates to control other inmates in the cages. Under this system of management, most inmates are idle most of the time. Some of the short-term sentenced prisoners are quartered in a separate section and assigned housekeeping and maintenance tasks; a few are even given outside groundskeeping jobs, and increasingly there are school programs of a few hours per day for the younger prisoners. The inmates given jobs in the jail generally have a short workday, perform their tasks at a slow pace, and receive no monetary compensation. The rest of the inmates only do the negligible amount of work involved in helping to keep moderately clean the space in which they are confined.

The classification and segregation of different types of prisoners which does occur consists mainly of separating the sentenced from the unsentenced, in addition to separating the sexes, placing a few of the greatest security risks of each group into single cells, and having separate cages for those on work crews. Thus, first offenders and recidivists, as well as persons of many ages, are likely to be confined together.

Usually jails in large cities are overcrowded; as they have low priority in government budgetting, there is considerable lag between the growth of a metropolitan area and the expansion of its jailing capacity. Most United States jails are over 25-years-old, and 35 percent are over 50-years-old.[2] However, the crowdedness of jails declined considerably in some areas during the late 1960s first from an increased use of "release on recognizance" (release without bail) pending trial, and secondly, through a shift from jail to mental health commitments for public drunkenness. Jail guards keep the men in cages and cells under surveillance through the bars, but there generally is only one guard present for several of these grilled rooms, and they also have some supply checking, telephone answering, and other duties besides trying to achieve the impossible objective of observing every inmate all of the time. Furthermore, many guards are relatively indifferent to what goes on inside the cages, as long as it does not generate mass disturbances or lead to public scandals. As a consequence, control over inmate behavior can usually be achieved by other inmates more immediately, directly, and completely in jails than in other types of confinement institutions, such as penitentiaries or state hospitals.

The division of power among inmates is a function of a variety of factors, notably physical strength, aggressiveness, manipulative skills, and especially, organization. A few inmates with these qualities in a jail unit can lead or suppress others so as to control the unit. Therefore, each separated component of the jail, such as a residential unit or a work crew, has its dominant clique most of the time. New inmates are sized up and pressured to conformity with the expectations of the clique. If the new member is weak and has resources scarce in the jail, such as cigarettes, these are likely to be commandeered by the clique, and he will be pressured to have his family deposit funds in his jail commissary account so that more can be purchased. If, as frequently is the case, the clique leaders in this one-sex world are oriented to homosexuality (at least while in jail), the weaklings will be forced to provide sexual services.

Each newly admitted inmate has to negotiate to establish his status and his *modus vivendi* in his unit's social world. In this bargaining and jockeying for advantages he uses such personal resources as his persuasive powers, aggressiveness, fighting skill, money, or attractiveness as a homosexual partner. Negotiations are recurrent, as the status structure is unstable. Sometimes conflict flares within the leadership clique, and often rival cliques or factions emerge to vie with the "Old Guard." They frequently are organized by racial, age, or home neighborhood differences (e.g., a "West Side clique").

An important factor in the inmate social struggle is the jail staff, since they can influence an inmate's dominance or resources in dealing with other inmates, and their control is enhanced if they have the cooperation of already dominant inmates. Accordingly, roles of authority and responsibility in inmate work crews are often unofficially delegated to those inmates whose performance in such roles is most dependable. The distribution of food, bedding, and other supplies and the supervision of housekeeping in the inmate quarters may also be assigned to an inmate "barn boss," as the guards tend to transmit orders through the inmate whom they recognize as effective in getting things done. This occurs even when assignment of such authority to inmates is prohibited, for it is the easiest way for the guards to maintain control and get their work done. The guard staff has almost total disciplinary power, and will remove to special punishment cells those inmates whose behavior they find most objectionable. These are especially likely to be any inmates who become defiant, or whom they suspect of plotting escape or mass disorder. However, to maintain stability in a unit which manifests no problems for them, the guards are inclined to overlook much misbehavior that they manage to see performed by dominant inmates, and jail conditions are such that most misbehavior can be hidden from the guards anyhow. This, of course, facilitates abuse of inmates by other inmates. To avoid extreme scandals, and especially to avoid any prospect of a jailbreak, jail officials use both threat and promise to encourage inmate informing on other inmates with respect to behavior that would create a serious threat of scandal, escape, or mass disorder. The control of both formal and informal and negative or positive sanctions by the guards motivates inmates to try to ingratiate themselves with the guards, despite counter-pressures by inmates to discourage and punish informing.

Because of these conditions which facilitate abuses by dominant inmates, strikingly similar jail scandals have recurred intermittently for many decades.[3] However, what the scandals expose is endemic at most jails most of the time. This is particularly true of robbery, extortion, homosexual rape, and other violence of inmate against inmate. Also, with guard qualifications, pay, and job security so low, there is continual prospect that a few affluent prisoners will be able to pay some guards for special privileges or the chance to smuggle in contraband. The fact that most jail inmates are of low status and that outsiders of influence seldom are familiar with the jail's inner life probably explains the public's indifference and ignorance with respect to the usual condition of its jails.

The major costs to society from jail conditions probably stem not from the clear violations of moral norms that the inmates suffer there, but rather, from the prolonged idleness of the inmates in highly diverse groups cut off from much communication with outsiders. In this inactivity and crowdedness day after day, those inmates most committed to crime "brainwash" the inexperienced to convert initial feelings of guilt or shame into smug rationalizations for crime. Also, jail prisoners become extremely habituated to "killing time," especially during pretrial confinement. Thus, deficiencies of ability to support themselves in legitimate employment, which may have contributed to their criminality, are enhanced at their release. While reformatories and prisons are often called "schools for crime," it is a far more fitting label for the typical urban jails.

JAIL REFORMS

Unfortunately, journalists and civic leaders often take a purely moral stance in expressing outrage at jail conditions. This is unconstructive because it casts blame and calls for action only against officials who happen to be in power when scandals are exposed, instead of addressing the conditions which make such scandals persist despite recurrent change-overs to reform-oriented new administrators. Nevertheless, other sources of pressure and innovation have promoted some important changes in jail conditions at scattered times and places. Standards for jail architecture, staff recruitment, and provision of psychological, educational, and other services to jail inmates have slowly risen in large part because the federal government inspects and evaluates most large city jails in connection with the rental of jail space for persons awaiting trial in federal courts. A few states also have their own jail inspection staffs which enforce minimum standard regulations. However, much more far-reaching changes have been demonstrated as possible, although none has been widely enough accepted to diminish radically the use of jails primarily as storage bins for humans.

The number of pretrial prisoners has been sharply reduced in New York City, and to a lesser extent elsewhere, following several innovative and successful experiments directed by the Vera Institute for Justice. In their most influential project they proved that if more attention is paid to investigating the residential and job stability of the accused when considering pretrial release, instead of simply fixing bail mechanically according to the offense, release without bail does not reduce the rate of appearance of the accused in court at the time they are scheduled for trial.[4] Nevertheless, because of their own inertia, and their preference for bureaucratic mechanical procedures, most courts still set bail by the offense rather than by the character of the offender. This is a boon to many professional criminals, whose separate thefts or burglaries generally are minor, as it permits them to commit new crimes while out on bail, so that they can pay their lawyers to defend them on the old charges. The cost of the unnecessary jailings of the impoverished accused who would show up in court if released without bail probably is much more than the cost of the extra investigative staff necessary for the probation office to administer properly their granting of "release on recognizance," and high bail for those not safely released without bail.

A large proportion of arrests are unnecessary, the Vera Institute proved, by demonstrating that for an appreciable number of petty offenders now arrested the police could simply issue summonses to appear in court, making unnecessary their confinement in police lock-ups and jails pending a hearing on bail. Finally, even for many who have not enough of an employment record or other evidence of stability to warrant outright release without bail, the Vera Institute has demonstrated that it is possible to release them on condition that they cooperate in a vocational training, counseling, and job placement program. This pretrial rehabilitative service has made many men good probation risks by the time they are tried who would have been poor risks when arrested, and would be made even worse risks by differential association with other offenders in idleness in the jail's cages for unsentenced prisoners.

For those who are found guilty and would normally be sentenced to jail terms, a variety of substitutes for jail confinement has developed. For drunks picked up by the police, the newest procedures in many cities involve not even arresting or bothering with trial and sentencing, but simply transporting them to a medical care center. They are free to depart, but almost all stay until sober, and some cooperate in long-term treatment for alcoholism. For sentenced shorttermers there are a variety of county farms and workhouses providing somewhat less crowdedness and more employment than occurs in jails. Much more dramatic, however, are arrangements which permit jail terms to be served only at night or on weekends, or installment payment of fines, so that employment in the free community and support of dependents is not interrupted by jailing. Finally, probation has been proven to be quite successful, when well administered, for many offenders who would traditionally have been given jail terms.

The economic savings—let alone the human savings—made possible by the alternatives to pretrial and short-sentence jailing described here could defray all or part of the cost of additional services to reduce the criminogenic character of life in jail. This would involve construction and staffing to permit more separate housing, classification, and supervision for different types of offenders. It would also permit greater education, vocational training, and counseling services, in addition to renumerated employment. These could be available to both pretrial and sentenced prisoners. Also important would be more extensive family visiting in many cases, and a social work staff to help resolve the inmate's family and other problems in the outside world, and to arrange housing and employment for him at release. Such measures, to be effective, would certainly require the abolition of political considerations in the recruitment of jail staff. Above all, it would require an end to the public neglect and indifference which characterizes our jails today.

Part V

The City of the Future:
Predictions
and Prescriptions

Introduction

T H E   C I T Y of the future will be an urban region, much more decentralized than today's metropolitan areas, Bollens and Schmandt advise. Both the wealth and the political power of urban society will be more diffused, they suggest, and one can infer that its social problems will also become less concentrated in slum areas. Indeed, they anticipate that today's slums will disappear, but our standards of what constitutes a slum probably will rise, so that slums will be identified in the future that would not be considered slums by today's standards.

Prisons of the future, Glaser suggests, will consist of many small urban institutions, instead of the huge rural storage facilities for predominantly urban offenders which now comprise our state and federal prisons. Their social structure and procedures will differ markedly from those of today's prisons. Small trends towards such a change began in the 1960s.

Prescriptions for all aspects of crime control and prevention were generated from the work of over three hundred social scientists in 1967 by the President's Commission on Law Enforcement and the Administration of Justice. Most of these are applicable primarily to urban areas; they thus form an apt conclusion to our study of crime in the city.

THE SHAPE OF THE FUTURE

John C. Bollens and Henry J. Schmandt

A s T H E second half of the twentieth century moves on, the metropolis becomes an ever more predominant feature of contemporary society. The urbanizing trend which has produced vast settlements of human beings and reduced the agricultural population to a shadow of its former self shows no signs of abating. Cities continue to break out of their old bounds and invade the "open country" in their quest for *lebensraum*. Ring upon ring of suburbs continue to be added to what were once single and relatively compact communities. Census figures on population, density, and territorial area—we need not repeat them here—present a picture of massive change and astonishing growth. The "exploding metropolis" is more than a figure of speech.

THE EXISTING SYSTEM

. . . Most aspects of the metropolitan system, including its social organization, land use patterns, and functional distribution of economic activities, have undergone substantial modification during the past half century. Of the key elements, only the governmental pattern has been able to avoid major alteration. Adjustments have been made in the traditional arrangements, new expedients such as special districts have been employed, and considerable school district con-

Abridgment of "The Shape of the Future," pp. 577, 579, 580–587. 590–598 from *The Metropolis: Its People, Politics, and Economic Life.* Copyright © 1965 by John C. Bollens and Henry J. Schmandt. Reprinted by permission of Harper & Row, Publishers.

solidation has taken place, but basically the system remains as it was before large-scale urbanization. Lack of serious crisis in the existing governmental structure and the strong forces for continuing the present pattern of balkanization are important factors contributing to this result.

. . .

As political scientist Norton Long reminds us, metropolitan areas are going concerns and hence can be expected to react vigorously to attempts at major alteration. For if the existing system of local government could be easily changed, "it would be intolerably unstable." And if no powerful interests were vested in the status quo, "the existing order would have so little allegiance, it could scarcely run, much less endure."[1] . . . In the case of Miami, area-wide restructuring was aided by the lack of any strong organizational interest in keeping the old governmental pattern. In virtually all other metropolitan areas the forces with large stakes in the status quo were too powerful to overcome.

Previous chapters have called attention to some of the elements hostile to governmental reorganization: the established bureaucracy, the favored tax position of various units, central city-suburban antagonisms, political differences among sections of the area, and the general lack of community bonds. Another strong factor favoring the retention of the present system, according to Robert Wood, is the opportunity a governmentally fragmented structure affords for social segregation. Modern suburbs may use their political boundaries "to differentiate the character of their residents from their neighbors," and their governmental powers—zoning, residential covenants, taxation, selective industrial development—"to promote conscious segregation." From the variety of classes, occupations, income levels, races, and creeds in the metropolis, "a municipality may isolate the particular variant it prefers and concentrate on one type of the metropolitan man."[2] In this way socially homogeneous subcommunities with protective armor can be maintained within the larger complex. And as in the case of other vested interests, any attempt to reconstitute the governmental system so as to destroy or minimize this power of segregation can expect to meet bitter resistance from the affected suburban enclaves.

EMERGING TRENDS

Each metropolitan community faces important policy decisions in seeking to determine its future. It cannot avoid questions of how it shall organize governmentally, how it shall develop economically and physically, and how it shall deal with social issues. Nor can it disregard the processes by which it evolves over a period of time or the day-to-day interaction that takes place within its territorial confines. It must, in short, be conditioned to accept change and to make the decisions that will guide this change in the direction most conducive to the furthering of community values and goals.

In making an assessment of the future, individuals concerned with the governmental organization of the metropolis must keep in mind certain emerging trends. Three of the more significant are: (1) the rise of the megalopolis; (2) the movement of community decision-making powers to higher echelons of public authority; and (3) the increasing emphasis on cooperative devices as an alternative to formal restructuring of the governmental pattern.

The Megalopolis

More than 2000 years ago, a group of Greek settlers founded a new community in the Peloponnesus which they called *Megalopolis,* to express their hope that it would become the largest of the Hellenic city-states. In subsequent centuries, the word's dictionary definition as a "very large city" was largely forgotten. Recently, however, it has reappeared in the vocabulary as a result of the writings of geographer Jean Gottman, who used the term to designate the cluster of metropolitan areas in the northeastern part of the United States. Gottman's description of this section of the nation portrays its amazing character:

An almost continuous system of deeply interwoven urban and suburban areas, with a total population of about 37 million people in 1960, has been erected along the Northeastern Atlantic seaboard. It straddles state boundaries, stretches across wide estuaries and bays, and encompasses many regional differences. . . . Crowded within its limits is an extremely distinguished population. It is, *on the average,* the richest, best educated, best housed, and best serviced group of similar size (i.e., in the 25-to-40-million-people range) in the world. . . . It is true that many of its sections have seen pretty rural landscapes replaced by ugly industrial agglomerations or drab and monstrous residential developments; it is true that in many parts of Megalopolis the air is not clean any more, the noise is disturbing day and night, the water is not as pure as one would wish, and transportation at times becomes a nightmare.[2]

Along similar lines, political scientist Charlton Chute had earlier employed the term "urban region" to designate an area in which two or more SMSA's adjoin each other. Identifying nineteen such regions in 1955, Chute argued that the historic concept of a metropolitan area as a core city surrounded by suburbs is no longer adequate for analytical purposes. It is now necessary, he stated, to take into account the interrelationships between neighboring SMSA's and to study clusters of such areas as closely as we do clusters of cities and other urban groups.[3]

The trend toward megalopolis or urban regions has several clear implications for local government. First, as urbanized agglomerations expand in population and territorial size, integration of local units as an answer to the problem of government in such areas loses all meaning. It would be ridiculous, for example, to talk in terms of forming one municipality or other type of local government out of the congeries of units extending almost continuously from Boston to the District of Columbia, or out of the group bordering the southern end of the Great Lakes. Such a solution may still be desirable in the case of the smaller and spatially separated SMSA's. But even if a consolidated government were feasible for those in this category on the basis of their present size, what happens as urban growth continues? Is the territorial jurisdiction of the government also expanded repeatedly to keep pace with this growth? If so, at what point does the area become too large for governance by a single unit? Or at what point do the qualities that are customarily associated with local government disappear?

Second, the emergence of megalopolitan areas also casts doubts on the adequacy of the two-tier arrangement as the ultimate solution to metropolitan problems. This approach, as commonly understood, is based on the purported distinction between local and area-wide functions. But how is area-wide to be defined when a cluster of metropolises is involved? One function like flood control or air pollution may be of common concern to the entire group of metropolitan areas; another, such as sewage disposal or water supply, may lie within the competency of the various parts of the megalopolis; and still others, such as refuse disposal and public health services, may be adequately handled by individual metropolises within the complex. The phenomenon here is not unlike that within a single SMSA where certain problems of the central city and suburbs spill over into adjacent units; the difference is that in this case, the spillover occurs between one metropolis and another, thus necessitating even broader areal treatment than is normally contemplated.

Third, the persistent expansion of urban settlements raises an interesting question as to the future of local government. If we consider the comprehensive urban county and other types of metropolitan agencies as essentially local in character, what is the case when an area becomes so large as to require either some form of regional government or the assumption of critical urban functions by the state? In the first instance, does the possible need for a unit of larger areal scope than the individual SMSA imply the need for a tripartite division of powers: local, metropolitan-wide, and regional-wide, with the last administered by a third tier of government that would transcend state as well as municipal and county lines? . . .

The Upward Shift of Power

Metropolitan areas develop and take their particular form as the result of countless decisions by both public and private agencies. . . . A decision by local public officials to encourage industrial growth can have real meaning only if economic factors are favorable to such expansion. Or a decision to undertake a major program of public works can be realistic only if the existing or potential resources of the community are sufficient to warrant such expenditures and the voters are willing to support them.

When government acts, moreover, it must do so within an environmental framework shaped by the cumulative past policies and actions of public agencies and private organizations. Local authorities, for example, may consider it desirable to relegate the central business district to a lesser role, but earlier investment decisions relative to buildings, transporation arteries, and public utilities may compel them to take the opposite tack and promote additional investment in the area to protect what already exists. Or past policies of the planning commission and city council may have resulted in the establishment of land use patterns that severely circumscribe the extent to which future changes in the physical design and ecology of the city can be accomplished.

In addition to these limitations, the ability of individual metropolitan communities to control their own destiny has been steadily diminished by the increase in scale of the urban world. Policies which at one time were determined largely at the local level are now dependent upon the decisions of agencies outside the community. As one observer has appropriately noted, "The discrepancy in organizational scale between local government and the nature of large-scale society results in a movement of power upward, to organizational centers outside the control of the local polity. Such organizations wield power that is area-wide in scope and consequences. But the use of such power does not require either concern for the interdependence of different aspects of the metropolitan community, or the concern for the ultimate nature of the city that a local polity might implement. In consequence, existing trends are simply accelerated."[4]

. . .

The uplift shift of power is by no means confined to government; the same phenomenon is occurring in the private sector with similar effects on the metropolis. The rapid

disappearance of the family-owned enterprise (which traditionally has had a strong personal commitment to the local
community) and its displacement by the national corporation
with headquarters in one city and branches in many others
has caused drastic shifts in the spatial location of power.
Many investment decisions which at one time were made
locally are now determined at the main offices of the absentee
owners who have no emotional attachment to the affected
communities. These decisions may have important implications for the development or functioning of individual metropolitan areas, but the latter have no voice in their formulation.

.   .   .

THE FUTURE METROPOLIS

A Boston public official a few years back gave this capsule
description of his city's core area: "The average building in
downtown Boston is 75 to 100 years old. Our downtown
streets are winding cow pastures. Traffic is so chaotic that
an expressway we just built which was to have been adequate
for nearly a decade was filled to capacity on the rush hour
almost as soon as it was opened. It would cost us $2 billion
to get the city core back into shape again and then we
couldn't begin to show results for a good ten years."[5] The
Boston picture is not atypical; it might be applied, with
changes in details, to most of our large metropolitan areas
and to an increasing number of smaller urban communities.
The spread of blight, particularly in the older metropolises,
continues to outrun the clearing of slums and the upgrading
of neighborhoods despite extensive redevelopment efforts. . . .

But blight is only one aspect of the problem. . . . Walter
Gropius, the well-known architect, charges that the development of our cities is guided by zoning laws that merely "forbid
the worst." Lewis Mumford sees the metropolis as an accumulation of people accommodating themselves "to an environment without adequate natural or cultural resources:
People who do without pure air, who do without sound sleep,

who do without a cheerful garden or playing space, who do without the very sight of the sky and the sunlight, who do without free motion, spontaneous play, or a robust sexual life."[6]

. . .

Physical Design

. . .

Is the physical shape of the metropolis likely to undergo major transformation in the foreseeable future? Will the present pattern of development continue or will growth be directed into satellite cities separated from the main metropolitan centers by open space and greenbelts? Will most Americans soon be living, as some writers predict, in a dozen or so vast "super" or "strip" cities, which are really not cities but great sprawling complexes covering hundreds and even thousands of square miles? No one, of course, can answer these questions with assurance. Events such as a nuclear war or new technological breakthroughs in transportation and communication could result in drastic alterations in the present urban pattern. So also might a change in the life styles or values of the average American family. But discounting the unexpected, we see no indications on the immediate horizon of a major shift from current trends. Changes, some of substantial significance, will undoubtedly occur, but most of them will likely be adjustments in existing arrangements rather than a radical departure from them.

. . .

Social Pattern

Observers of the contemporary metropolitan scene have often expressed fear that the central city will become increasingly the home of low-income workers and non-whites while the suburbs will continue to attract the middle- and upper-income whites. Some, however, are quick to point out that a simple social dichotomy between the core city and its periphery does not now exist and is unlikely to do so in the future. The suburban portion of the metropolis, contrary to the common stereotype, does not constitute a socially homogeneous settlement but a mosaic of sub-communities segregated by income and classes. There are working-class suburbs as well as fenced-off islands of the well-to-do; industrial as well as residential satellites; blighted as well as carefully maintained and manicured fringe-area villages. This pattern could mean, as Coleman Woodbury suggests, that "socially and psychologically, both the metropolitan and suburban bodies politic will remain split up into groups and classes unable to communicate effectively, mutually suspicious, incapable of defining their common interests or of cooperating to realize them."[7]

As in the case of its physical design, there is little reason to believe that the social structure of the metropolis will undergo major modification in the near future. The pattern will likely continue to evolve along present lines with the central city shouldering a disproportionate share of responsibility for the economically and culturally deprived segments of the populace, and the suburbs continuing to attract a large proportion of white families in the lower-middle to upper-income range. However, the revolution in race relations now taking place will inevitably lead to a substantial increase in non-white penetration across the core city border. Construction of expressways and circumferential highways will further accelerate suburban dispersion by reducing the time-space ratio and making new and farther-out sections of the metropolis accessible to settlement. Decentralization of activities throughout the area will continue, with cultural facilities, such as little theatres and music halls, making their appearance at various points in the suburban complex along with the commercial and industrial enterprises.

In looking ahead, a number of emerging developments pertinent to the social structure of metropolitan communities deserve notice. Although their potentiality for change is still to be determined, they cannot be ignored in speculations about the future. First, the continuous upward movement of urban dwellers in socioeconomic rank will give a higher proportion of the metropolitan population greater freedom of choice in housing, life style, and place of residence. This in turn may serve to dilute the homogeneity of suburban communities by reducing the extent of economic segregation of the present system. The increasing freedom from racial barriers will further enhance the possibility of greater social diversity in suburbia.

Second, the steady rise in income levels for all segments of the urban community will add to the number of citizens with a stake in the social order. This fact, once the racial issue is settled, should lead to a greater degree of internal order and less social tension. It could also lessen central city-suburban hostility and pave the way for a more effective organization of the governmental system to meet the problems of metropolitan living.

Third, extensive urban renewal programs will provide quality housing in the metropolitan core and make this section a safer and more attractive place to live. As a result, the central city will be in a better position to stem the exodus of leadership talent to suburbia and to achieve a more balanced social pattern. This latter development seems a remote possibility at present with the wave of migrants from the rural hinterlands inundating the central community. However, the number of these migrants will diminish in the future as the surplus population of the rural areas is drained off. This fact, coupled with economic betterment of the urban populace in general, makes the prognosis somewhat more hopeful than present events appear to warrant.

The social structure of the metropolis, in brief, exhibits both encouraging and disturbing trends. The growing affluence of the total society, the rising level of education, and the upward mobility of an increasing proportion of urban residents constitute elements of strength in the system. At the same time, the slow progress in eliminating racial discrimination, the relatively feeble efforts to upgrade the disadvantaged and culturally deprived members of the community, and the spectre of technological unemployment serve warning on the future.

Economic Structure

The economic structure of the metropolis has undergone substantial modification in the present century. Continued growth in size has been accompanied by increasing specialization and industrial diversification. It has also been accompanied by major changes in the location of commercial and industrial enterprises. At one time, not too many decades ago, economic activities were overwhelmingly concentrated in the core city. Today, the situation is strikingly different. Decentralization which began early in this century has created an entirely new pattern. Retail trade has followed the population movement outward. Suburban industrial parks have developed along the new circumferential highways and at other strategic points on the periphery. Office buildings have appeared in large suburban communities, and warehouse and distribution centers have become common sights along the outlying arteries.

The forces which are generating the spatial diffusion of homes, factories, and shopping centers are not likely to diminish in the future. Manufacturing and wholesaling enterprises will continue to respond to obsolescence and changing technological requirements by looking for new quarters. The outward movement of people will continue to be accompanied by the outward movement of jobs, stores, and service establishments. . . .

Despite these trends, the central city is likely to remain a viable economic unit. The tremendous amount of fixed capital, public and private, invested in existing facilities makes it highly improbable that this section of the metropolis will be abandoned to the vagaries of fate. Although it may not capture as high a proportion of the area's economic activity as it has in the past, redevelopment of its physical plant and changes in its functional role should reverse the downward trend. The central business district will become more reliant for its economic existence upon office activity; cleared areas will provide room for certain types of commercial and light industrial enterprises; new housing construction, much of it in the form of middle- and upper-income apartments, will provide a ready clientele for the shops, restaurants, and theatres; and the assumption of a greater portion of the city's welfare costs by higher echelons of government will lessen the tax strain on the local economy.

Governmental System

. . . To the extent that any action at all is taking place in the matter of governmental reorganization, the devices receiving most attention are the transfer of area-wide functions to the county, creation of special districts, and voluntary cooperation. It appears likely that the SMSA's which lie within single counties will make greater use of the county government as the area-wide instrumentality. Special districts will remain popular for functions, such as water supply, sewage disposal, and air pollution, that require administrative areas larger than the county. Intergovernmental agreements of significant scope will be increasingly employed in efforts to ward off more drastic solutions. Finally, state and federal agencies will play expanding roles in the governance of metropolitan areas.

. . . The principle of local federalism is logically sound and acceptable to most Americans; the difficulty—aside from that mentioned previously when clusters of metropolitan areas are involved—lies in a lack of consensus as to how it should be implemented and what the functional division should be. These are issues, moreover, that will not be settled by any grand design or total plan. Given our long-demonstrated penchant for making marginal rather than major adjustments in the local governmental system, problems of this nature will be resolved only by the gradual accumulation of lesser changes made in response to immediate and concrete problems.

. . . . .

THE GOOD METROPOLIS

Urban man is so immersed in his personal pursuits and day-to-day problems that, like the Muckraker in *The Pilgrim's*

Progress, he does not raise his head to see the broader vision of the good community. The full potential of the modern metropolis escapes his thought as the difficulties and maladies which plague urban living capture his attention. Traffic congestion and overcrowded schools have meaning for him, as do crime and physical blight. He is unhappy about the racial problem and he grumbles occasionally at the rising costs of local government. But none of these developments seems to impair seriously the attainment of his own goals or to disturb him to the point where he is ready to take action to reconstruct the system. Perhaps, as political scientist York Willbern has expressed it:

... the great sprawling urban areas of this country fall short not so much in their achievement of the goals and ambitions of their residents, as in the degree to which they achieve or fail to achieve the speculative constructs of the intellectuals who concern themselves with the matter. The disparity is not between the metropolis as it is and the metropolis as its residents wish it; the disparity is between the existing metropolis and the City of God of the planners and the dreamers.[8]

.   .   .

The system of local government in a metropolitan area exists to assure order and supply public services. Beyond these basic tasks, it exists to nurture civic life and to foster the values of a free and democratic society. It serves this higher role to the extent that it is able to fashion an environment suitable for the expression and development of human potentialities and for the personal growth of its individual members. Government is by no means the sole or possibly even the most important instrumentality for promoting men's goals. ... The special role of the governmental system is to provide an appropriate framework within which the energy and resources of the community can be mobilized and directed at improving the quality of urban life. Pessimistic as the outlook may seem to some, the good metropolis is more than a figment of utopian fancy. Its achievement is within the capabilities and resources of modern man. The choice of the future is his to make.

THE PRISON OF THE FUTURE

Daniel Glaser

T HE P R I S O N of the future will differ drastically from today's prison, if it is rationally designed for goals which already are generally accepted. These goals are:

(1) to evoke in offenders an enduring identification of themselves with anti-criminal persons;
(2) to enhance the prospects that released prisoners will achieve satisfaction in legitimate post-release activities.

The pursuit of these two goals, in the light of today's common knowledge about criminals, would lead one far from traditional approaches to prison design and management. Already, there are signs that such movement has begun.

One of the most immediately evident differences between tomorrow's prison and that of today will be in location. The prisons of the future will be located in the communities from which most of their inmates come. This means that most prisons will be in metropolitan areas.

A home community location will have many advantages for a prison. It will simplify the staff's task of knowing both the anti-criminal and the criminal and disorderly personal influences in the community which affect their prisoners. It will permit a graduated release of inmates on a trial basis, for visiting prospective homes and seeking or even filling jobs in the community, prior to receiving complete freedom. This graduated release also will protect society, by providing a better test of the risks in releasing a man than can be had either by observing him only in a prison, remote and different from his post-release life, or by releasing him to

Reprinted from *Key Issues*, Vol. 2 (1965), 42–46.

traditional parole supervision, where his contacts with his parole agent are few and brief. Such graduated release also will permit the inmates to solve their social and economic problems piecemeal, reducing their prospect of finding themselves in desperate straits soon after they leave the prison, from having to face all their post-release problems at once. Finally, the predominantly urban location of tomorrow's prison will facilitate recruitment of superior employees, both line staff and part or full-time specialists (e.g., teachers and physicians), for there will be a larger pool of potential employees within commuting distance of the prison.

The short-sightedness of current prison labor legislation will eventually be recognized. Therefore, in addition to their new locations, prisons of the future will have many program features distinguishing them from today's prisons. Prisons will operate industries and services comparable to those in which there is post-release employment opportunity for the prisoners. Also, any inmate who engages in the activities considered optimum for his rehabilitation, including school assignments, will get some financial compensation. This will be at a variable rate, to offer incentives for increased diligence and responsibility, and thus, to provide prior to release that sense of achievement which comes from truly earning rewards. An appreciable portion of these earnings will be deposited in a savings account, for gradual use by the inmate during his parole, based on a budget developed during his confinement, but subject to later revision, with consent of the parole staff.

The prison of the future will have extensive links with community organizations. Churches, social and fraternal organizations, service clubs, hobby groups, professional or trade associations, as well as societies and persons aiding each other in the control of vices (e.g., Alcoholics Anonymous), will participate in the prison more actively than heretofore. This is in addition to the great encouragement of visiting by non-criminal relatives and friends of the inmates. Many of these outsiders will be actively involved in prison treatment programs, and in the institution's social and recreational life.

The staff of the prison of the future will not have many

of the sharp distinctions now characterizing prison employees. Whatever their job classification, they all will be treatment personnel, and all will also be concerned with maintaining whatever level of custody proves necessary. The prison staff may even include some ex-prisoners, who have demonstrated clear rehabilitation, and whose crime and reformation experience gives them unusual counseling propensities. Most of the parole supervision staff probably will have offices adjacent to, or in, the scattered urban prisons.

While there may be some formal group counseling programs, most of the treatment impact will arise from the face-to-face relations of line staff with small groups of inmates in the course of routine work, study, and play activities. The line staff will also be intimately involved in the diagnostic decisions of prison management on such matters as the custodial security required for each inmate, the optimum program for his rehabilitation, and his readiness for gradual release; the traditional central classification committee, limited to top institution officials, will be a thing of the past. Most group decisions seriously affecting the place or program of an inmate's imprisonment will be made in groups comprising the staff who know him best.

To facilitate this kind of program, the prison of the future will be small. There will be many institutions, of diverse custodial levels, within any metropolitan area. There will also be a few in rural locations for inmates of that background. Location may not be so critical for prisons to hold offenders considered so highly committed to crime or seriously disturbed as to long be dangerous. However, all inmates will be housed, for an appreciable number of months before their release, in an institution near their release destination, to procure the diagnostic and treatment benefits of community contact and graduated release.

The small institution will reduce the necessity for regimentation, and increase the extent to which most of the staff know most of the inmates on a personal basis, and know each other well. The prisons of the future, because they will be small, can be highly diverse, both in architecture and in program. For example, a graduated release establishment, or other prisons in which custodial security is not a difficult problem, may house as few as fifteen or twenty men, and can be located in large YMCA-type hotels, in sections of a low rental apartment development or in an ordinary family-type house. Where custodial security is needed, for society's protection and to prevent concern with escape from distracting inmates, custody will be achieved by having continuously connected or yard-enclosing buildings, or by having only a single edifice, so that there are few points of possible exit. Custodial emphasis can then be mainly peripheral and invisible; it will impose few restrictions on inside activities. The entire institution generally will house less than one hundred inmates, plus whatever school, work or other facilities are appropriate for the inmates housed there.

There will be less emphasis in the prison of the future on separating inmates by age than now prevails in prisons. The bulk of felony arrestees have long consisted of persons in a period of transition from childhood to adulthood. Their crimes express their prolonged difficulties, as youth, in trying to pursue independent adult roles. It is in this socialization sense, rather than in biological traits, that many offenders can be considered immature. This socialization immaturity is protracted when their social contact is primarily with persons of their own age. Older unadvanced offenders will certainly be better influences on youthful inmates than their delinquent age peers, for the most criminalized of the latter tend to set the standards of accepted behavior when they are in homogeneous age-groups. Tomorrow the most delinquent youthful inmates will be scattered and isolated from each other insofar as possible. Staff will be oriented to maximize the rewarding contact of such prisoners with those inmates least vulnerable to deleterious influence, and most likely to have a long-run anti-criminalizing effect.

In the prison of tomorrow there will be much concern with utilizing the personal relationships between staff and inmates for rehabilitative purposes. This means varying staff modes of interaction with inmates according to the individual inmate orientations towards staff. Thus, the manipulative or aggressive inmate will be met with firm but fair reactions, making violence or fraud unsuccessful, but rewarding legitimate effort. The dependent or neurotic inmate will receive acceptance and ego-support, but with encouragement of self-analysis and self-reliance. Most counseling will not be in formal programs, although these will exist; counseling will occur mainly as it is evoked by problem-revealing events in institutional life, as well as by discussions of the inmates' future plans. This means that both group and individual counseling will involve primarily the line staff, rather than clinical specialists; the latter, neither now, nor in the future, can be sufficiently numerous to be the major source of direct treatment influence on most of the nation's confined criminals.

It should be stressed that most efforts at personality influence of staff on inmates will not be considered as ends in themselves, but as means toward achievement of the two basic purposes cited in opening this paper: evoking identification of offenders with anti-criminal persons—such as staff—and increasing inmate capacity for success in maintaining satisfactory personal relationships with anti-criminal persons, in legitimate employment and other pursuits after release. The major focus in inmate-staff relationships, therefore, will be the staff's contribution to the inmate's development of a conception of himself as opposed to crime, and accepted and successful in a non-criminal life. Many types of personality may make these shifts without profound change in other aspects of their basic modes of psychological reaction.

The prison of the future will only evolve fully in the form described here, as the society of the future changes. This will be reflected in a growing interest of both government, and private groups and persons, in assisting their fellow men, not just with kindness, but with understanding. This means that research will be an integral part of the administration of the prison of the future. The research will include both routine monitoring of the effectiveness of ongoing operations, in terms of their relationship to post-release criminality, and controlled experiments for testing new measures.

If punishment is ever justified in future prison management, it will be only because of objective demonstration that for certain people, and under certain circumstances, it promotes an enduring change of behavior. In this sense, it will be a dispassionate negative reaction to proscribed behavior, administered within legal controls, and in conjunction with positive reactions to favored conduct. Of course, any restriction of freedom for inmates considered dangerous is inherently punitive. However, punishment beyond the minimum restriction essential for custodial purposes will only be imposed deliberately if its merit can be scientifically demonstrated in a given case, and it will then be subject to tight controls.

The prison of the future described here is not really so far away. We already see it foreshadowed in such enterprises as the Federal Pre-Release Guidance Centers, the Work Release programs of the North and South Carolina and Maryland prisons, and the Community Treatment Centers which the California Youth Authority has experimentally substituted for training school commitment from the Sacramento and Stockton areas. We see all of these features even more developed in new types of community institutions for treatment of mental disorders; most features of prisons once characterized mental hospitals, but the latter changed first, in many respects, with prisons following later. This sequence of change is likely to recur in the future, but as it does, the difference between a mental and a criminal commitment will be further reduced: both will be oriented to preparing their subjects for as safe and quick a release to the community as possible, yet both will continue to have custodial concerns.

The prison of the future, clearly, will be part of a society in which rationality is institutionalized, and goodness, truth, and beauty are cardinal goals. Such a society cannot be realized instantaneously. It has been evolving gradually, at least since the Enlightenment, but with many temporary delays and regressions. It will evolve more rapidly and with less interruption, the more clearly we envision it, the more adequate we comprehend the problems confronting its achievement, and the more diligently we work to procure it.

SUMMARY OF
RECOMMENDATIONS

The President's Commission on Law Enforcement

THE EXISTENCE of crime, the talk about crime, the reports of crime, and the fear of crime have eroded the basic quality of life of many Americans. A Commission study conducted in high crime areas of two large cities found that:

1. 43 percent of the respondents say they stay off the streets at night because of their fear of crime.
2. 35 percent say they do not speak to strangers any more because of their fear of crime.
3. 21 percent say they use cars and cabs at night because of their fear of crime.
4. 20 percent say they would like to move to another neighborhood because of their fear of crime.

· · ·

Under any circumstance, developing an effective response to the problem of crime in America is exceedingly difficult. And because of the changes expected in the population in the next decade, in years to come it will be more difficult. Young people commit a disproportionate share of crime and the number of young people in our society is growing at a much faster rate than the total population. Although the 15- to 17-year-old age group represents only 5.4 percent of the population, it accounts for 12.8 percent of all arrests. Fifteen and sixteen-year-olds have the highest arrest rate in the United

Reprinted from *The Challenge of Crime in a Free Society: A Report by The President's Commission on Law Enforcement and Administration of Justice*, Washington, D.C.: U.S. Government Printing Office, 1967, pp. vi–xi.

States. The problem in the years ahead is dramatically fore-told by the fact that 23 percent of the population is 10 or under.

Despite the seriousness of the problem today and the increasing challenge in the years ahead, the central conclusion of the Commission is that a significant reduction in crime is possible if the following objectives are vigorously pursued.

. . .

1. PREVENTING CRIME

The prevention of crime covers a wide range of activities: Eliminating social conditions closely associated with crime; improving the ability of the criminal justice system to detect, apprehend, judge, and reintegrate into their communities those who commit crimes; and reducing the situations in which crimes are most likely to be committed.

Every effort must be made to strengthen the family, now often shattered by the grinding pressures of urban slums.

Slum schools must be given enough resources to make them as good as schools elsewhere and to enable them to compensate for the various handicaps suffered by the slum child—to rescue him from his environment.

Present efforts to combat school segregation, and the housing segregation that underlies it, must be continued and expanded.

Employment opportunities must be enlarged and young people provided with more effective vocational training and individual job counseling. Programs to create new kinds of jobs—such as probation aides, medical assistants, and teacher helpers—seem particularly promising and should be expanded.

The problem of increasing the ability of the police to detect and apprehend criminals is complicated. In one effort to find out how this objective could be achieved, the Commission conducted an analysis of 1,905 crimes reported to the Los Angeles Police Department during a recent month. The study showed the importance of identifying the perpetrator at the scene of the crime. Eighty-six percent of the crimes with named suspects were solved, but only 12 percent of the unnamed suspect crimes were solved. Another finding of the study was that there is a relationship between the speed of response and certainly of apprehension. On the average, response to emergency calls resulting in arrests was 50 percent faster than response to emergency calls not resulting in arrest. On the basis of this finding, and a cost effectiveness study to discover the best means to reduce response time, the Commission recommends an experimental program to develop computer-aided command-and-control systems for large police departments.

To insure the maximum use of such a system, headquarters must have a direct link with every onduty police officer. Because large scale production would result in a substantial reduction of the cost of miniature two-way radios, the Commission recommends that the Federal Government assume leadership in initiating a development program for such equipment and that it consider guaranteeing the sale of the first production lot of perhaps 20,000 units.

Two other steps to reduce police response time are recommended:

1. Police callboxes, which are locked and inconspicuous in most cities, should be left open, brightly marked, and designated "public emergency callboxes."
2. The telephone company should develop a single police number for each metropolitan area, and eventually for the entire United States.

Improving the effectiveness of law enforcement, however, is much more than just improving police response time. For example a study in Washington, D.C., found that courtroom time for a felony defendant who pleads guilty probably totals less than 1 hour, while the median time from his initial appearance to his disposition is 4 months.

In an effort to discover how courts can best speed the process of criminal justice, the known facts about felony cases in Washington were placed in a computer and the operation of the system was simulated. After a number of possible solutions to the problem of delay were tested, it appeared that the addition of a second grand jury—which, with supporting personnel, would cost less than $50,000 a year—would result in a 25-percent reduction in the time required for the typical felony case to move from initial appearance to trial.

The application of such analysis—when combined with the Commission's recommended timetable laying out time-spans for each step in the criminal process—should help court systems to ascertain their procedural bottlenecks and develop ways to eliminate them.

.   .   .

2. NEW WAYS OF DEALING WITH OFFENDERS

The Commission's second objective—the development of a far broader range of alternatives for dealing with offenders —is based on the belief that, while there are some who must be completely segregated from society, there are many instances in which segregation does more harm than good. Furthermore, by concentrating the resources of the police, the courts, and correctional agencies on the smaller number of offenders who really need them, it should be possible to give all offenders more effective treatment.

A specific and important example of this principle is the Commission's recommendation that every community consider establishing a Youth Services Bureau, a community-based center to which juveniles could be referred by the police, the courts, parents, schools, and social agencies for counseling, education, work, or recreation programs and job placement.

The Youth Services Bureau—an agency to handle many troubled and troublesome young people outside the criminal system—is needed in part because society has failed to give the juvenile court the resources that would allow it to function as its founders hoped it would. In a recent survey of juvenile court judges, for example, 83 percent said no psychologist or psychiatrist was available to their courts on a regular basis and one-third said they did not have probation officers or social workers. Even where there are probation officers, the Commission found, the average officer supervises 76 probationers, more than double the recommended caseload.

The California Youth Authority for the last 5 years has been conducting a controlled experiment to determine the effectiveness of another kind of alternative treatment program for juveniles. There, after initial screening, convicted juvenile delinquents are assigned on a random basis to either an experimental group or a control group. Those in the experimental group are returned to the community and receive intensive individual counseling, group counseling, group therapy, and family counseling. Those in the control group are assigned to California's regular institutional treatment program. The findings so far: 28 percent of the experimental group have had their paroles revoked, compared with 52 percent in the control group. Furthermore, the community treatment program is less expensive than institutional treatment.

To make community-based treatment possible for both adults and juveniles, the Commission recommends the development of an entirely new kind of correctional institution: located close to population centers; maintaining close relations with schools, employers, and universities; housing as few as 50 inmates; serving as a classification center, as the center for various kinds of community programs and as a port of reentry to the community for those difficult and dangerous offenders who have required treatment in facilities with tighter custody.

Such institutions would be useful in the operation of programs—strongly recommended by the Commission—that permit selected inmates to work or study in the community during the day and return to control at night, and programs that permit long-term inmates to become adjusted to society gradually rather than being discharged directly from maximum security institutions to the streets.

Another aspect of the Commission's conviction that different offenders with different problems should be treated in different ways, is its recommendation about the handling of public drunkenness, which, in 1965, accounted for one out of every three arrests in America. The great number of these arrests—some 2 million—burdens the police, clogs the lower courts and crowds the penal institutions. The Commission therefore recommends that communities develop civil detoxification units and comprehensive aftercare programs, and that with the development of such programs, drunkenness, not accompanied by other unlawful conduct, should not be a criminal offense.

Similarly, the Commission recommends the expanded use of civil commitment for drug addicts.

3 · ELIMINATING UNFAIRNESS

The third objective is to eliminate injustices so that the system of criminal justice can win the respect and co-operation of all citizens. Our society must give the police, the courts, and correctional agencies the resources and the mandate to provide fair and dignified treatment for all.

⋅   ⋅   ⋅

Injustice will not yield to simple solutions. Overcoming it requires a wide variety of remedies including improved methods of selecting personnel, the massive infusion of additional funds, the revamping of existing procedures and the adoption of more effective internal and external controls.

The relations between the police and urban poor deserve special mention. Here the Commission recommends that every large department—especially in communities with substantial minority populations—should have community-relations machinery consisting of a headquarters planning and supervising unit and precinct units to carry out recommended programs. Effective citizen advisory committees should be established in minority group neighborhoods. All departments with substantial minority populations should make special efforts to recruit minority group officers and to deploy and promote them fairly. They should have rigorous internal investigation units to examine complaints of misconduct.

⋅   ⋅   ⋅

4. PERSONNEL

The fourth objective is that higher levels of knowledge, expertise, initiative, and integrity be achieved by police, judges, prosecutors, defense attorneys, and correctional authorities so that the system of criminal justice can improve its ability to control crime.

The Commission found one obstacle to recruiting better police officers was the standard requirement that all candidates—regardless of qualifications—begin their careers at the lowest level and normally remain at this level from 2 to 5 years before being eligible for promotion. Thus, a college graduate must enter a department at the same rank and pay and perform the same tasks as a person who enters with only a high school diploma or less.

The Commission recommends that police departments give up single entry and establish three levels at which candidates may begin their police careers. The Commission calls these three levels the "community service officer," the "police officer," and the "police agent."

This division, in addition to providing an entry place for the better educated, also would permit police departments to tap the special knowledge, skills, and understanding of those brought up in the slums.

The community service officer would be a uniformed but unarmed member of the police department. Two of his major responsibilities would be to maintain close relations with juveniles in the area where he works and to be especially alert to crime-breeding conditions that other city agencies had not dealt with. Typically, the CSO might be under 21, might not be required to meet conventional education requirements, and might work out of a store-front office. Serving as an apprentice policeman—a substitute for the police cadet— the CSO would work as a member of a team with the police officer and police agent.

The police officer would respond to calls for service, perform routine patrol, render emergency services, make preliminary investigations, and enforce traffic regulations. In order to qualify as a police officer at the present time, a candidate should possess a high school diploma and should demonstrate a capacity for college work.

The police agent would do whatever police jobs were most complicated, most sensitive, and most demanding. He might be a specialist in police community-relations or juvenile delinquency. He might be in uniform patrolling a high-crime neighborhood. He might have staff duties. To become a police agent would require at least 2 years of college work and preferably a baccalaureate degree in the liberal arts or social sciences.

·   ·   ·

While candidates could enter the police service at any one of the three levels, they also could work their way up through the different categories as they met the basic education and other requirements.

·   ·   ·

In order to improve the quality of judges, prosecutors, and defense attorneys, the Commission recommends a variety of steps: Taking the selection of judges out of partisan politics; the more regular use of seminars, conferences, and institutes to train sitting judges; the establishment of judicial commissions to excuse physically or mentally incapacitated judges from their duties without public humiliation; the general abolition of part-time district attorneys and assistant district attorneys; and a broad range of measures to develop a greatly enlarged and better trained pool of defense attorneys.

·   ·   ·

Another area with a critical need for large numbers of expert criminal justice officers is the complex one of controlling organized crime. Here, the Commission recommends that prosecutors and police in every State and city where organized crime is known to, or may, exist develop special organized crime units.

5 · RESEARCH

The fifth objective is that every segment of the system of criminal justice devote a significant part of its resources for research to insure the development of new and effective methods of controlling crime.

A small fraction of 1 percent of the criminal justice system's total budget is spent on research. This figure could be multiplied many times without approaching the 3 percent industry spends on research, much less the 15 percent the Defense Department spends. The Commission believes it should be multiplied many times.

That research is a powerful force for change in the field of criminal justice perhaps can best be documented by the history of the Vera Institute in New York City. Here the research of a small, nongovernment agency has in a very short time led to major changes in the bail procedures of approximately 100 cities, several States, and the Federal Government.

Because of the importance of research, the Commission recommends that major criminal justice agencies—such as State court and correctional systems and big-city police departments—organize operational research units as integral parts of their structures.

In addition, the criminal justice agencies should welcome the efforts of scholars and other independent experts to understand their problems and operations. These agencies cannot undertake needed research on their own; they urgently need the help of outsiders.

·   ·   ·

6. MONEY

Sixth, the police, the courts, and correctional agencies will require substantially more money if they are to control crime better.

Almost all of the specific recommendations made by the Commission will involve increased budgets. . . .

The Commission believes some of the additional resources —especially those devoted to innovative programs and to training, education, and research—should be contributed by the Federal Government.

The Federal Government already is conducting a broad range of programs—aid to elementary and secondary schools, the Neighborhood Youth Corps, Project Head Start, and others—designed to attack directly the social problems often associated with crime.

Through such agencies as the Federal Bureau of Investigation, the Office of Law Enforcement Assistance, the Bureau of Prisons, and the Office of Manpower Development and Training, the Federal Government also offers comparatively limited financial and technical assistance to the police, the courts, and corrections authorities.

.   .   .

7. RESPONSIBILITY FOR CHANGE

Seventh, individual citizens, social-service agencies, universities, religious institutions, civic and business groups, and all kinds of governmental agencies at all levels must become involved in planning and executing changes in the criminal justice system.

.   .   .

The Commission recommends that in every State and city there should be an agency, or one or more officials, with specific responsibility for planning improvements in criminal administration and encouraging their implementation.

.   .   .

The planning agencies should include both officials from the system of criminal justice and citizens from other professions. Plans to improve criminal administration will be impossible to put into effect unless those responsible for criminal administration help make them. On the other hand, crime prevention must be the task of the community as a whole.

.   .   .

Universities should increase their research on the problems of crime; private social welfare organizations and religious institutions should continue to experiment with advanced techniques of helping slum children overcome their environment; labor unions and businesses can enlarge their programs to provide prisoners with vocational training; professional and community organizations can help probation and parole workers with their work.

The responsibility of the individual citizen runs far deeper than cooperating with the police or accepting jury duty or insuring the safety of his family by installing adequate locks —important as they are. He must respect the law, refuse to cut corners, reject the cynical argument that "anything goes as long as you don't get caught."

Most important of all, he must, on his own and through the organizations he belongs to, interest himself in the problems of crime and criminal justice, seek information, express his views, use his vote wisely, get involved.

In sum, the Commission is sure that the Nation can control crime if it will.

Notes

THE NATURE OF THE SLUM

Marshall B. Clinard

1 Eric Partridge, *Origins: A Short Etymological Dictionary of Modern English* (London: Routledge & Kegan Paul, Ltd, 1958).

2 *The Oxford Universal Dictionary* (1955 ed.; New York: Oxford University Press, Inc., 1955), p. 1921. The earliest use of the word "slum" is reported as having occurred in 1812 and the introduction of "slumming" as a fashionable pursuit in 1884.

3 David R. Hunter, *The Slums: Challenge and Response* (New York: The Free Press, 1964), p. 6. The term has wide acceptance in other countries, particularly in developing areas.

4 Barnes defined the older or "ancient" London slums as housing that was close together and badly arranged. He pointed out, however, that the "modern" slum is to be "distinguished from the 'ancient' slum in that the unsanitary conditions result not from the construction or arrangement of the buildings but from the failure to maintain proper sanitary standards" Harry Barnes, *The Slums: Its Story and Solution* (London: Staples Press, Ltd., 1931), p. 5.

5 *United States Census of Housing: 1960*, Vol. 1, Part 1, United States Summary (Washington, D.C.: Department of Commerce, Bureau of the Census, 1961), p. lxiii.

6 *Ibid.*

7 David R. Hunter, *The Slums: Challenge and Response* (New York: The Free Press, 1964), p. 32.

8 William G. Grigsby, "Housing and Slum Clearance: Elusive Goals," The *Annals*, 352 (March, 1964), 107–18.

9 Quoted in Ruth Shonle Cavan, *Criminology* (2nd ed.; New York: Thomas Y. Crowell Company, 1955), p. 87.

10 Terrence Morris, *The Criminal Area: A Study in Social Ecology* (London: Routledge & Kegan Paul, Ltd, 1957).

11 Miles L. Colean, *Renewing Our Cities* (New York: The Twentieth Century Fund, 1953), p. 41.

12 Herbert J. Gans, *The Urban Villagers: Group and Class in the Life of Italian-Americans* (New York: The Free Press, 1962), p. 310.

13 Nathan Glazer, "Slum Dwellings Do Not Make a Slum," *The New York Times Magazine*, November 21, 1965, p. 57. The atmosphere of most of the areas where people live in poor housing conditions in Tokyo is not that of a slum. Furthermore, Glazer points out that it is false to assume that in the United States the physical forms of communities have inevitable social consequences.

14 See Jane Jacobs, *The Death and Life of Great American Cities* (Vintage ed.; New York: Alfred A. Knopf, Inc., 1961).

15 Michael Harrington, *The Other America: Poverty in the United States* (New York: The Macmillan Company, 1962), p. 70.

16 William F. Whyte, *Street Corner Society* (Chicago: University of Chicago Press, 1943), p. 283.

17 Charles Abrams, *Man's Struggle for Shelter in an Urbanizing World* (Cambridge, Mass.: The M.I.T. Press, 1964), p. 6.

18 E. Franklin Frazier, *The Negro in the United States* (rev. ed.; New York: The Macmillan Company, 1957), p. 636.

19 See Jacobs, *op. cit.*, pp. 55–73.

20 Chester W. Hartman, "Social Values and Housing Orientations," *Journal of Social Issues*, XIX (April, 1963), 113–31.

21 Maurice R. Davie, *Negroes in American Society* (New York: Mc-Graw-Hill Book Company, 1949), p. 220.

22 The Indian Conference of Social Work, *Report of the Seminar on Slum Clearance* (Bombay: Mouj Printing Bureau, 1957), p. 81.

23 United Nations, *Report on the World Social Situation* (New York: United Nations Publication, 1957).

24 David Hunter, *op. cit.*, p. 77.

25 Kenneth B. Clark, *Dark Ghetto: Dilemmas of Social Power* (New York: Harper & Row, Publishers, 1965), p. 31.

26 David Hunter, *op. cit.*, p. 71.

27 For a survey of the studies, see Ernest R. Mowrer, *Disorganization, Personal and Social* (Philadelphia: J. B. Lippincott Co., 1942).

28 *Final Report to Honorable Frank P. Zeidler, Mayor, City of Milwaukee* (Milwaukee: Study Committee on Social Problems in the Inner Core of the City, 1960).

29 R. B. Navin, W. B. Peattie, and F. R. Steward, *An Analysis of a Slum Area in Cleveland* (Cleveland: Metropolitan Housing Authority, 1934).

30 Calvin F. Schmid, "Urban Crime Areas: Part II," *American Sociological Review*, 25 (October, 1960), 655–78.

31 Henry Allen Bullock, "Urban Homicide in Theory and Fact," *Journal of Criminal Law, Criminology, and Police Science*, 45 (January-February, 1955), 565–75; and Marvin E. Wolfgang, *Patterns in Criminal Homicide* (Philadelphia: University of Pennsylvania Press, 1958).

32 In London, crimes of violence like criminal homicides and assaults, particularly those arising from domestic disputes and neighborhood quarrels, are largely concentrated in slum areas. See F. H. McClintock, *Crimes of Violence* (London: Macmillan and Co., Ltd., 1963).

33 See Clifford R. Shaw, *Delinquency Areas* (Chicago: University of Chicago Press, 1929); Shaw, Henry D. McKay, and James F. McDonald, *Brothers in Crime* (Chicago: University of Chicago Press, 1938), especially Chapter V, "The Community Background"; Shaw, *The Natural History of a Delinquent Career* (Chicago: University of Chicago Press, 1931), especially Chapter II, "A Delinquency Area"; Shaw, *The Jack Roller* (Chicago: University of Chicago Press, 1930); and Frederic M. Thrasher, *The Gang* (Chicago:

University of Chicago Press, 1927), especially Chapter I, "Gangland."

34 Shaw and McKay, *Juvenile Delinquency and Urban Areas* (Chicago: University of Chicago Press, 1942).

35 *Indices of Social Problems* (New York: New York City Youth Board, 1960).

36 Isidor Chein, Donald L. Gerard, Robert S. Lee, and Eva Rosenfeld, *The Road to H: Narcotics, Delinquency and Social Policy* (New York: Basic Books, Inc., 1964), p. 73.

37 Morris, *op. cit.* For discussions of delinquent neighborhoods in cities of Scotland, see John Mack, "Full-Time Miscreants, Delinquent Neighborhoods and Criminal Networks," *The British Journal of Sociology*, XV (March, 1964), 38–53.

38 See United Nations, *op. cit.*; and Marshall B. Clinard, "The Organization of Urban Community Development Services in the Prevention of Crime and Juvenile Delinquency, with Particular Reference to Less Developed Countries," *International Review of Criminal Policy*, 19 (1962), 3–16.

39 Shankar S. Srivastava, *Juvenile Vagrancy: A Socio-Ecological Study of Juvenile Vagrants in the Cities of Kanpur and Lucknow* (New York: Asia Publishing House, 1963).

40 See, for example, Whyte, *op. cit.*

41 Solomon Kobrin, "The Conflict of Values in Delinquency Areas," *American Sociological Review*, 16 (October, 1951), 653–61.

42 Robert E. L. Faris and H. Warren Dunham, *Mental Disorders in Urban Areas* (Chicago: University of Chicago Press, 1939); and Dunham, "Current Status of Ecological Research in Mental Disorders," *Social Forces*, 25 (March, 1947), 321–7. Also see H. Warren Dunham, *Community and Schizophrenia: An Epidemiological Analysis* (Detroit: Wayne State University Press, 1965).

43 August B. Hollingshead and Frederick C. Redlich, *Social Class and Mental Illness* (New York: John Wiley & Sons, Inc., 1958).

44 Leo Srole *et al.*, *Mental Health and the Metropolis: The Midtown Manhattan Study* (New York: McGraw-Hill Book Company, 1962), p. 213; and Thomas S. Langner and Stanley T. Michael, *Life Stress and Mental Health* (New York: The Free Press, 1963). Also see Frank Riessman, Jerome Cohen, and Arthur Pearl, *Mental Health of the Poor* (New York: The Free Press, 1964).

45 Quoted in Arthur Hillman, *Neighborhood Centers Today: Action Programs for a Rapidly Changing World* (New York: National Federation of Settlements and Neighborhood Centers, 1960), pp. 20–1.

46 See particularly Oscar Lewis, *The Children of Sanchez: Autobiography of a Mexican Family* (New York: Random House, Inc., 1961), especially the introduction; and Lewis, "The Culture of Poverty," *Trans-Action*, 1 (November, 1963), 17, 19. Also see Lewis, *Five Families: Mexican Case Studies in the Culture of Poverty* (Vintage ed.; New York: Alfred A. Knopf, Inc., 1959).

47 See Lewis, *The Children of Sanchez*, pp. xxv-xxvii; Walter B. Miller,

"Lower Class Culture as a Generating Milieu of Gang Delinquency," *The Journal of Social Issues*, XIV (March, 1958), 5–19; Jerome Cohen, "Social Work and the Culture of Poverty," *Social Work*, 9 (January, 1964), 3–11; Elizabeth Herzog, "Some Assumptions about the Poor," *Social Service Review*, XXXVII (December, 1963), 389–402; Joseph A. Kahl, *The American Class Structure* (New York: Holt, Rinehart & Winston, Inc., 1957), pp. 211–12; St. Clair Drake and Horace Cayton, *Black Metropolis* (New York: Harcourt, Brace & World, Inc., 1945); Whyte, *op. cit.; and Gans, op. cit.*

48 Herzog, *op. cit.*

49 Mau recently studied urban slum dwellers in Kingston, Jamaica, and he found that a considerable proportion of them had not uniformly rejected the possibility of progress and the idea of an improved and meaningful future. See James A. Mau and Walter E. Freeman, "Political Mobilization and Belief in Progress Among Slum Residents in Kingston, Jamaica," paper presented at the meetings of the American Sociological Association in Chicago, Illinois, September, 1965. Also see, Mau, "The Threatening Masses: Myth or Reality?" paper presented at the Second Caribbean Scholars' Conference, August, 1964.

50 W. B. Miller, *op. cit.* Also see Sydney M. Miller, "The American Lower Class: A Typological Approach," *Social Research*, 31 (Spring, 1964), 1–22; S. M. Miller, Frank Riessman, and Arthur A. Seagull, "Poverty and Self-Indulgence: A Critique of the Nondeferred Gratification Pattern," in Louis A. Ferman, Joyce L. Kornbluh, and Alan Haber, eds., *Poverty in America* (Ann Arbor: University of Michigan Press, 1965), pp. 285–302.

51 S. M. Miller, "The American Lower Class."

52 Gans, *op. cit.*, p. 246.

53 *Ibid.*, p. 244.

54 Harvey W. Zorbaugh, *The Gold Coast and the Slum* (Chicago: University of Chicago Press, 1929), p. 152. As Hollingshead has pointed out in one study, the upper classes view the area populated by the lowest class in these terms: "They enjoy their shacks and huts along the river or across the tracks and love their dirty, smoky, low-class dives and taverns. . . . The men are too lazy to work or do odd jobs around town. . . . This group lives for a Saturday of drinking or fighting. They are of low character and breed and have a criminal record for a pedigree." Hollingshead, *Elmtown's Youth* (New York: John Wiley & Sons, Inc., 1949), pp. 110–111.

55 See Gans, *op. cit.*, p. 170.

56 Srole *et al.*, *op. cit.*

57 Hollingshead and Redlich, *op. cit.*

58 "Power" is used here in much the same way as Floyd Hunter uses the term, "the acts of men going about the business of moving other men to act in relation to themselves or in relation to organic or inorganic things." Floyd Hunter, *Community Power Structure: A Study of Decision Makers* (Chapel Hill: University of North Carolina Press, 1953), pp. 2–3.

59 David Hunter, *op. cit.*, p. 18.

60 *Ibid.*

61 Hollingshead, *Elmtown's Youth* (New York: John Wiley & Sons, Inc., 1949), p. 111.

62 Walter Firey, *Land Use in Central Boston* (Cambridge, Mass.: Harvard University Press, 1947), p. 179.

63 Whyte, *op. cit.*, p. xv.

64 John R. Seeley, "The Slum: Its Nature, Use, and Users," *Journal of the American Institute of Planners*, XXV (February, 1959), 7–14.

65 Gans, *op. cit.* Also see Edward J. Ryan, "Personal Identity in an Urban Slum," in Leonard J. Duhl, ed., *The Urban Condition: People and Policy in the Metropolis* (New York: Basic Books, Inc., 1963), pp. 135–50.

66 W. B. Miller, *op. cit.*; and Martin Loeb, "Implications of Status Differentiation for Personal and Social Implications," *Harvard Educational Review*, XXIII (Summer, 1953), 168–74.

67 See, for example, Faris, *Social Disorganization* (New York: The Ronald Press Company, 1948), p. 203; and Svend Riemer, *The Modern City* (Englewood Cliffs, N.J.: Prentice-Hall, Inc., 1952), p. 148.

68 See, for example, Whyte, *op. cit.*; Gans, *op. cit.*; and Thrasher, *op. cit.*

69 W. B. Miller, "Implications of Lower Class Culture," *Social Service Review*, 33 (September, 1959), 219–36.

70 Whyte, "Social Organization in the Slums," *American Sociological Review*, 8 (February, 1943), 34–9.

71 W. B. Miller, "Lower Class Culture," p. 19.

72 Richard A. Cloward and Lloyd E. Ohlin, *Delinquency and Opportunity* (New York: The Free Press, 1960), pp. 203–10.

73 Harvey W. Zorbaugh, *The Gold Coast and the Slum* (Chicago: University of Chicago Press, 1929), p. 82.

74 Shaw, *The Natural History of a Delinquent Career*, p. 15.

75 Charles E. Silberman, *Crisis in Black and White* (New York: Random House, Inc., 1964), p. 321.

76 Lawrence Frank Pisani, *The Italian in America* (New York: Exposition Press, 1957), pp. 62–4.

77 Moses Rischin, *The Promised City* (Cambridge, Mass.: Harvard University Press, 1962).

78 Seeley, *op. cit.*

79 Marc Fried and Peggy Gleicher, "Some Sources of Residential Satisfaction in an Urban Slum," *Journal of the American Institute of Planners*, 27 (November, 1961), 305–15.

80 Whyte, *Street Corner Society*, p. xvi.

81 Firey, *op. cit.*, p. 179.

82 Fried and Gleicher, *op. cit.*, pp. 305–15.

83 Riemer, "The Slum and Its People," in C. E. Elias, Jr., James Gillies, and Riemer, *Metropolis: Values in Conflict* (Belmont, California: Wadsworth Publishing Co., Inc., 1964), p. 251.

84 Riemer, *The Modern City*, p. 147.

85 Donald J. Bogue, *Skid Row in American Cities* (Chicago: Community and Family Study Center, University of Chicago, 1963), Chapter 2, "Who Lives on Skid Row and Why—Views of Resource Persons," pp. 46–77.

86 Donald A. Cook, "Cultural Innovation and Disaster in the American City," in Duhl, *op. cit.*, pp. 87–93.

87 Seeley, *op. cit.*, pp. 7–14.

88 Robert K. Merton, *Social Theory and Social Structure* (rev. ed.; New York: The Free Press, 1957), p. 180; and Lewis A. Coser, "Some Functions of Deviant Behavior and Normative Flexibility," *American Journal of Sociology*, 68 (September, 1962), 178–81.

89 Ernest W. Burgess, "The Growth of the City," in Robert E. Park and Burgess, *The City* (Chicago: University of Chicago Press, 1925), and Louis Wirth, ed., *Contemporary Social Problems* (Chicago: University of Chicago Press, 1939), p. 32.

90 Zorbaugh, *op. cit.*, pp. 127–9.

91 Homer Hoyt, *The Structure and Growth of Residential Neighborhoods in American Cities* (Washington, D.C.: Federal Housing Administration, 1939), pp. 75–7; and Hoyt, "The Structure of American Cities in the Post-War Era," *American Journal of Sociology*, 48 (January, 1943), 475–81.

92 Gideon Sjoberg, *The Preindustrial City: Past and Present* (New York: The Free Press, 1960), Chapter IV. Also see Noel P. Gist, "The Ecology of Bangalore, India; An East–West Comparison," *Social Forces*, 35 (May, 1957), 356–65.

93 Sjoberg, *op. cit.*, p. 98.

94 Leo F. Schnore, "On the Spatial Structure of Cities in the Two Americas," in Philip M. Hauser and Schnore, eds., *The Study of Urbanization* (New York: John Wiley & Sons, Inc., 1965), p. 366.

95 Abrams, *The Future of Housing* (New York: Harper & Row, Publishers, 1946), p. 21. For another argument that slums are caused by the shortage of houses, see Robert Lasch, *Breaking the Building Blockade* (Chicago: University of Chicago Press, 1946).

96 Colean, *op. cit.*, p. 41.

97 J. M. Mackintosh, *Housing and Family Life* (London: Cassell & Company, Ltd., 1952), p. 16.

98 *Ibid.*, p. 113.

99 Claude Gruen, "Urban Renewal's Role in the Genesis of Tomorrow's Slums," *Land Economics*, 39 (August, 1963), 285–91.

PART II: THE DISTRIBUTION OF CITY CRIME

1 For a fuller discussion of the variety of types of crime and the problems of obtaining adequate statistics on them, as well as proposed solutions to these problems, see Daniel Glaser, "National Goals and Indicators for the Reduction of Crime and Delinquency," *Annals of the American Academy of Political and Social Science*, Vol. 371 (May, 1967), 104–126.

2 John P. Clark and Larry L. Tifft, "Polygraph and Interview Validation of Self-Reported Deviant Behavior," *American Sociological Review*, Vol. 3, No. 4 (August, 1966), 516–523

3 F. S. C. Northrop, *The Logic of the Sciences and the Humanities*, New York: Meridian Books, 1959, chap. 3.

4 *Ibid.*, chap. 4.

INDUSTRIALIZATION AND URBANIZATION IN RELATION TO CRIME AND JUVENILE DELINQUENCY

Karl O. Christiansen

1 Kingsley Davis, *Human Society* (New York, Macmillan and Co., 1949), p. 316.

2 Walter C. Reckless, *Criminal Behavior* (New York: McGraw-Hill Book Co., 1940), pp. 26–27.

3 Marshall B. Clinard, *Sociology of Deviant Behavior* (New York, Rinehart, 1958), p. 57 et seq.; "Urbanization and Crime," in *Criminology: A Book of Readings*, ed. by Clyde B. Vedder, Samuel Koenig and Robert E. Clark (New York, Dryden Press, 1953), pp. 238–246.

4 Clifford R. Shaw and others, *Delinquency Areas* (Chicago, University of Chicago Press, 1929), Clifford R. Shaw and Henry D. McKay, *Juvenile Delinquency and Urban Areas* (Chicago, University of Chicago Press, 1942).

5 Edwin H. Sutherland, *Principles of Criminology*, revised by Donald R. Cressey, 5th ed. (Philadelphia, J. B. Lippincott Company, 1955), p. 160.

6 E. H. Sutherland, *op. cit.*, p. 158.

THE DISTRIBUTION OF JUVENILE DELINQUENCY IN THE SOCIAL CLASS STRUCTURE

Albert J. Reiss, Jr. and Albert Lewis Rhodes

1 William Kvaraceus, "Juvenile Delinquency and Social Class," *Journal of Educational Sociology*, *18* (June, 1944), pp. 51–54. Robert K. Merton, *Social Theory and Social Structure*, Glencoe, Ill.: The Free Press, 1957, pp. 144–145. Albert K. Cohen, *Delinquent Boys: The Culture of the Gang*, Glencoe, Ill.: The Free Press, 1955, pp. 36–44. Walter Miller, "Lower Class Culture as a Generating Milieu of Gang Delinquency," *Journal of Social Issues*, *14* (No. 3, 1958), pp. 5–19.

2 Austin Porterfield, *Youth in Trouble*, Fort Worth, Texas: Leo Potishman Foundation, 1946; James S. Wallenstein and C. J. Wyle, "Our Law Abiding Law Breakers," *National Probation* (March-April, 1947), pp. 107–112; F. Ivan Nye, James F. Short and V. J. Olson, "Socioeconomic Status and Delinquent Behavior" in *Family Relationships and Delinquent Behavior*, New York: John Wiley & Sons, 1958, pp. 23–33.

3 Walter Reckless maintains, for example, that delinquency rates designate *categoric risks* in the population of being reported to a juvenile court. See Walter C. Reckless, *The Crime Problem*, New York: Appleton-Century-Crofts, 1950, p. 194.

4 The "Crosscut" social status structure criterion is defined as follows: The occupational distribution of each occupation group is within five per cent of the distribution for all schools. There are 10 major occupation groups: old and new professions; proprietors; managers and officials; quasi-professions; clerical and kindred workers; sales workers; craftsmen, foremen and kindred workers; protective service workers; operatives and kindred workers; laborers and service workers, except protective service.

5 This seems to be a valid inference from the Shaw-McKay and Sutherland positions, although it is never quite explicitly formulated in this way.

6 Cohen, *op. cit.*, chapter V.

7 It should be kept in mind, however, that the defined range of variation is restricted to only three classes for ascribed social status but seven classes of social status structure; some ascribed social status variation probably is lost with fewer classes.

8 To some it will seem obvious that low-status boys in high-status areas are not "representative" of low-status boys. The theories do not specify what "lower class criteria" are to be utilized in identifying low-status boys who are "delinquency prone." If class selectivity operates by residential areas, then perhaps no area has a "representative" lower class.

9 Sociometric data are available for only a cross-section of boys. These data show however, that lower class boys in middle class areas interact together in that they are most likely to choose, and to have reciprocated the choices of, lower class boys.

10 Some readers may have discerned that the deinquency rate of Crosscut: center schools is higher than might be expected, given its status composition. The higher rate here is altogether accounted for by two schools. One of these schools is the vocational high school which tends to selectively recruit boys who are "in trouble" in some other school. The other school serves a very large territorial area made up of relatively homogeneous class areas so that the social structure of each junior high school which "feeds" this high school falls either "above" or "below" the structure of the senior high context.

11 Miller, *op. cit.*

12 Richard A. Cloward and Lloyd E. Ohlin, *Delinquency and Opportunity: A Theory of Delinquent Gangs*, Glencoe, Ill.: The Free Press, 1960.

13 Cohen and Short distinguish varieties of the "parent male subculture." Most of them are viewed as lower class varieties. Albert K. Cohen and James F. Short, Jr., "Research in Delinquent Subcultures," *Journal of Social Issues*, *14* (No. 3, 1958), pp. 20–37.

14 Cohen's theory accounts for the origin of delinquent subcultures. It is not altogether clear how one would operationally identify gangs which participate in the parent delinquent subculture or one of its varieties.

SOCIO-ECONOMIC CLASS AND AREA AS CORRELATES OF ILLEGAL BEHAVIOR AMONG JUVENILES

John P. Clark and Eugene P. Wenninger

1 An outstanding example of this type of research design is Sheldon and Eleanor Glueck, *Unraveling Juvenile Delinquency*, New York: The Commonwealth Fund, 1950.

2 See Marshall B. Clinard, *Sociology of Deviant Behavior*, New York: Rinehart, 1958, p. 124, for his assessment of the validity of the study by Sheldon and Eleanor Glueck, *Unraveling Juvenile Delinquency*.

3 Most outstanding are those by Austin L. Porterfield, *Youth in Trouble*, Fort Worth, Texas: Leo Potishman Foundation, 1946; F. Ivan Nye and James F. Short, "Scaling Delinquent Behavior," *American Sociological Review*, 22 (June 1957), p. 326–331; and Robert A. Dentler and Lawrence J. Monroe, "Early Adolescent Theft," *American Sociological Review*, 26 (October, 1961), 733–743; Fred J. Murphy, Mary M. Shirley, and Helen L. Witmer, "The Incidence of Hidden Delinquency," *American Journal of Orthopsychiatry*, 16 (October, 1946), pp. 686–696.

4 James F. Short, "Differential Association and Delinquency," *Social Problems*, 4 (January, 1957), pp. 233–239; F. Ivan Nye, *Family Relationships and Delinquent Behavior*, New York: John Wiley, 1958; James E. Short and F. Ivan Nye, "Reported Behavior as a Criterion of Deviant Behavior," *Social Problems*, 5 (Winter, 1957–1958), pp. 207–213; F. Ivan Nye, James F. Short, and Virgil J. Olson, "Socio-Economic Status and Delinquent Behavior," *American Journal of Sociology*, 63 (January, 1958), pp. 381–389.

5 Dentler and Monroe, *op. cit.*

6 Richard A. Cloward and Lloyd E. Ohlin, *Delinquency and Opportunity: A Theory of Delinquent Gangs*, New York: The Free Press of Glencoe, 1961.

7 Albert K. Cohen, *Delinquent Boys: The Culture of the Gang*, Glencoe, Ill.: Free Press, 1955.

8 Walter B. Miller, "Lower Class Culture as a Generating Milieu of Gang Delinquency," *Journal of Social Issues*, 14 (No. 3, 1958), pp. 5–19.

9 *Ibid.* The matter of class differences in "focal concerns" or values will be explored in subsequent articles.

10 Cohen, *op. cit.*, Cloward and Ohlin, *op. cit.*, and Robert K. Merton, *Social Theory and Social Structure*, Glencoe, Ill.: Free Press, 1957, pp. 146–149.

11 In this report "type of community" is used to refer in a general way to a geographic and social unit having certain distinctive demographic qualities, such as occupational structure, race, social class, and size. Designations such as "rural farm," or "Negro lower class urban,"ʹ or "middle class suburbia," have long been utilized to describe such persistent physical-social characteristics.

12 Nye, Short, and Olson, *op. cit.*, p. 383.

13 Albert J. Reiss and Albert L. Rhodes, "The Distribution of Juvenile Delinquency in the Social Class Structure," *American Sociological Review,* 26 (October, 1961), pp. 720–732.

14 Albert J. Reiss, Jr., Otis Dudley Duncan, Paul K. Hatt, and Cecil C. North, *Occupations and Social Status,* New York: The Free Press of Glencoe, 1961, especially pp. 109–161 prepared by Otis D. Duncan.

15 *U.S. Census of Population: 1960.* Final Report PC (1)–15C, p. 15–296.

16 *Ibid.,* pp. 15–335.

17 *Ibid.,* pp. 15–305.

18 *Ibid.,* pp. 15–344.

19 Rates of illegal behavior were found to increase until age 14–15 and then to decrease.

20 Ordinarily, not receiving 100 per cent admission to the first few offenses listed would have raised doubt as to the validity of those questionnaires on which these extremely common offenses were not admitted. In the Nye-Short study such questionnaires were discarded. However, since the respondents were asked in this study to admit their offenses during the past year only, it was thought that less than 100 per cent admission would be highly possible when one considers the entire age range. Undoubtedly some of the respondents who did not admit these minor offenses were falsifying their questionnaires.

21 Significance of differences were calculated between pairs of communities across *all* 38 offenses by using the Wilcoxon Matched-Pairs Signed-Ranks test (described in Sidney Siegel, *Non-Parametric Statistics,* New York: McGraw-Hill Book Company, Inc., 1956, pp. 75–83). The results of this procedure were:

    1–2—P .35   1–3—P .00006
    2–3—P .0034   1–4—P .0006
    3–4—P .90   2–4—P .016

22 Dentler and Monroe, *op. cit.*, p. 734.

23 Reiss and Rhodes, *op. cit.*, p. 729. The concept of "status areas" is used here as it was used by Reiss and Rhodes to designate residential areas of a definite social class composition.

24 Because of small numbers in social classes within certain communities, categories were collapsed or ignored for comparison purposes as shown below. Refer to Table 1 for designation of categories. The Wilcoxon Matched-Pairs Signed-Ranks test was used.

Rural farm	category 1 versus 2, 3, 4	insignificant
Lower urban	category 1 versus 2, 3, 4	insignificant
	category 1 versus 5	insignificant
	categories 2, 3, 4 versus 5	insignificant
Industrial city	category 1 versus 2	significant
	category 2 versus 3, 4	significant
	category 1 versus 3, 4	insignificant
Upper urban	category 3 versus 4	insignificant

25 Reiss and Rhodes, *op. cit.*, p. 729.

METROPOLITAN CRIME RATES AND RELATIVE DEPRIVATION
Paul Eberts and Kent P. Schwirian

1 Samuel Stouffer, Edward Suchman, Leland DeVinney, Shirley Star, and Robin Williams, *The American Soldier,* Vol. I; and Samuel Stouffer, A. A. Lunsdaine, Marion Lunsdaine, Robin Williams, Brewster Smith, Irving Janis, Shirley Star, and Leonard Cottrell, *The American Soldier,* Vol. II (Princeton: Princeton University Press, 1949).
2 The SMSA's were ranked from high to low on population size. The category "large" represents roughly the upper 40 percent in size. The SMSA's were also ranked high to low on percent non-white. The category "high" represents roughly the upper half of the distribution. The category "South" consists of the SMSA's in the traditional South and in the Southwest.

ASSESSING THE CONTRIBUTIONS OF FAMILY STRUCTURE, CLASS AND PEER GROUPS TO JUVENILE DELINQUENCY
Lee N. Robbins and Shirley Y. Hill

1 Rumney and Shuman, *A Study of the Social Effects of Public Housing in Newark, New Jersey* (1946).
2 Nye, *Family Relationships and Delinquent Behavior* (1958), p. 47.
3 Powers and Witmer, *Prevention of Delinquency* (1950).
4 Tait and Hodges, *Delinquents, Their Families, and the Community* (1962).
5 Meyer, Borgatta, and Jones, *Girls at Vocational High* (1965).
6 It has been argued that the fact that unofficial as well as official delinquents report that they have delinquent friends tends to support the differential association theory. See Short, "Differential Association and Delinquency," *Social Problems,* 4 (1957), p. 233; and Voss, "Differential Association and Reported Delinquent Behavior," *Social Problems,* 12 (1964), p. 78. However the same problem of proving the friendship with an already delinquent peer preceded the delinquent behavior exists for unofficial as for official delinquency.

7 For a review of the studies related to this issue, see Browning, "Differential Impact of Family Disorganization on Male Adolescents," *Social Problems*, 8 (1960), p. 37.

8 Nye, *op. cit.*, p. 23.

9 The results of these analyses have been somewhat ambiguous. Indices of social class that "wash out" in one city remain statistically significant in another. See Lander, *Towards an Understanding of Juvenile Delinquency* (1954); Bordua, "Juvenile Delinquency and 'Anomie'; An Attempt of Replication," *Social Problems*, 6 (1958–1959), p. 231; Bates, "Social Stratification and Juvenile Delinquency," *Am. Cath. Soc. Rev.*, 21 (1960), p. 221. This summarization of their findings is open to question, however, since the original data from Baltimore and Detroit have been reanalyzed and compared with Indianapolis data by Ronald J. Chilton, "Continuity in Delinquency Area Research: A Comparison of Studies for Baltimore, Detroit, and Indianapolis," *Amer. Soc. Rev.*, 29 (1964), p. 71. Chilton concludes that, once recalculated, the results in Baltimore, Detroit, and Indianapolis are in essential agreement. But inspection of his tables shows the only variable clearly associated with delinquency in all three cities to be percent of houses owner-occupied.

10 In St. Louis, Missouri, a city of about 800,000, for instance, the number of youths 10–16 years of age in 1963 was estimated at 74,000 (9%), and of these youths, less than 3000 became delinquents in that year, or less than .5% of the total population, according to *Youth in Court, A Study of Delinquent Youth Referred to the St. Louis City Juvenile Court in 1963*, Health and Welfare Council of Metropolitan St. Louis and Metropolitan Youth Commission of St. Louis and St. Louis County, 1964 (mimeo.). Obviously, it is risky to assume that the description of the overall population of a census tract applies with any precision either to the .5% who were delinquents on an average, or even to the 8.5% who constitute their non-delinquent age peers. Since high delinquency areas typically contain many single adults, the juvenile population in high delinquency areas is an even smaller proportion of the total population than 9%. And in low delinquency areas, delinquents constitute even less than .5% of the total tract population.

11 S. and E. Glueck, *Unraveling Juvenile Delinquency* (1950), p. 27.

12 When the inference from school records was checked against answers obtained in adult interviews with 70 ex-school boys, it was found to be correct in 84% of cases. The error of inferring the father present when he was actually out of the home during the child's attendance in elementary school was twice as common as the error of assuming him absent when he was in fact present.

13 The criteria used were Negro males with IQ of 85 or more, born in the St. Louis metropolitan area between 1930 and 1934, attending public schools at least 6 years, without thereafter transferring to a

different elementary school system, and guardian's name and occupation recorded. Half were to have guardian's occupations with a
Duncan Socioeconomic Index score of 11 or higher, half were to
have a father in the house, and half were to have significant school
problems. School problems were defined as:

Moderate or serious retardation:
(1) placed in ungraded room; or
(2) no graduation from elementary school and repeated at least
one quarter in Grade 3 or later; or
(3) graduated from elementary school, but repeated at least three
quarters, at least one of which was in Grade 3 or later.

Moderate or serious truancy or behavior problem:
(1) absent at least 11 days (out of 50) in three or more quarters,
one of which was in Grade 3 or later; or
(2) notation of truancy; or
(3) expulsion or transfer to a correctional institution.

URBAN CRIME PATTERNS
Sarah L. Boggs

1 David J. Pittman and William F. Handy, "Uniform Crime Reporting: Suggested Improvements," *Sociology and Social Research, 46*
(1962), pp. 135–143.
2 Merton's is the classic theoretical statement of the anomie theory
of criminality (see Robert K. Merton, *Social Theory and Social
Structure* [rev. ed.], Glencoe, Ill.: The Free Press, 1957, pp. 131–
169). Following from this is Lander's empirical work in which
anomie is used to explain differences between white and non-white
delinquency rates (see Bernard Lander, *Towards an Understanding
of Juvenile Delinquency*, New York: Columbia University Press,
1954). This study stimulated several attempts to replicate the relation between social class, race, and anomie. Among these studies
are David J. Bordua, "Juvenile Delinquency and 'Anomie:' An Attempt at Replication," *Social Problems, 6* (1958–1959), pp. 230–
238; William M. Bates, "The Ecology of Juvenile Delinquency in
St. Louis," unpublished Ph.D. dissertation, Washington University,
St. Louis, Mo., 1959; and Kenneth Polk, "Juvenile Delinquency and
Social Areas," *Social Problems, 5* (1957–1958), pp. 214–217.
3 This is the conclusion reached in the studies of intracity distributions of crime occurrence. The most recent of these is Calvin F.
Schmid, "Urban Crime Areas: Part I," *American Sociological Re-
view, 25* (1960), pp. 527–542, and "Urban Crime Areas: Part II,"
American Sociological Review, 25 (1960), pp. 655–678. Prior to this
are three very early studies: Clyde R. White, "The Relation of
Felonies to Environmental Factors in Indianapolis," *Social Forces,*

10 (1932), pp. 498–509; Calvin F. Schmid, *Social Saga of Two Cities,* Minneapolis: Minneapolis Council of Social Agencies (1937), pp. 334–341; and Stuart Lottier, "Distribution of Criminal Offenses in Metropolitan Regions," *Journal of Criminal Law and Criminology,* 29 (1938), pp. 37–50.

4 See references cited in footnote 2.

5 Although the typology and procedures used in the Uniform Crime classification system are subject to criticism, these data represent the best existing measure of crime. See Marvin E. Wolfgang, "Uniform Crime Reports: A Critical Appraisal," *University of Pennsylvania Law Review,* 111 (1963), pp. 708–738. A special theoretical value of the "official data" has been pointed out by Kitsuse and Cicourel. In response to the argument that "official statistics" are inappropriately organized for sociological research, these authors argue that the "official statistics" are *the* "cultural definitions" of deviance used to differentiate the official offender from the deviant, even though their behavior is the same. See John I. Kitsuse and Aaron V. Cicourel, "A Note on the Uses of Official Statistics," *Social Problems,* 11 (1963), pp. 131–139.

6 These data were compiled and tabulated by the Crime Research Center of the St. Louis Metropolitan Police Department.

7 Kendall's *Tau* was used as the rank order statistic. See Hubert M. Blalock, *Social Statistics,* New York: McGraw-Hill, 1960, pp. 319–324.

8 Eshref Shevky and Wendell Bell, *Social Area Analysis,* Stanford, Cal.: Stanford University Press, 1955.

9 Particularly relevant are the crime studies by Bates and Polk, cited above. Studies using the social area typology to predict phenomena other than crime are: Scott Greer, "Urbanism Reconsidered: A Comparative Study of Local Areas in a Metropolis," *American Sociological Review,* 21 (1956), pp. 19–25; Wendell Bell and Maryanne T. Force, "Urban Neighborhood Types and Participation in Formal Associations," *American Sociological Review,* 21 (1956), pp. 25–34; Walter C. Kaufman and Scott Greer, "Voting in a Metropolitan Community: An Application of Social Area Analysis," *Social Forces,* 38 (1960), pp. 196–204.

10 This change was also made in a test of the generality of the indexes in ten cities. The Negro population consistently occupies a subordinate status, whereas the status of a given foreign-born population is subject to considerable regional variation. See Maurice D. Van Arsdol, Jr., Santo F. Camilleri and Calvin Schmid, "The Generality of Urban Social Area Analysis," *American Sociological Review,* 23 (1958), pp. 277–284.

11 For a fuller discussion of this variable see Scott Greer, "The Social Structure and Political Process of Suburbia," *American Sociological Review,* 25 (1960), pp. 514–526. See also Walter C. Kaufman, "Social Area Analysis: An Explication of Theory, Methodology, and

Techniques," unpublished Ph.D. dissertation, Northwestern University, 1961, pp. 69–73 and 76–79.

12 Greer, *op. cit.*, found less participation in, involvement in, and knowledge about local neighborhood affairs in high as compared with low urban population.

13 A. M. Rosenthal, *Thirty-Eight Witnesses*, New York: McGraw-Hill, 1964.

14 Karl Schuessler, "Components of Variations in City Crime Rates," *Social Problems*, 9 (1962), pp. 314–323.

15 Henry Allen Bullock, "Urban Homicide in Theory and Fact," *Journal of Criminal Law, Criminology and Police Science*, 45 (1955), pp. 565–575.

16 Schuessler, *op. cit.*, pp. 319–321.

17 Schmid, "Urban Crime Areas, Part I," *op. cit.*, p. 538.

ISSUES IN THE ECOLOGICAL STUDY OF DELINQUENCY

Robert A. Gordon

1 Bernard Lander, *Towards an Understanding of Juvenile Delinquency*, New York: Columbia University Press, 1954.

2 David J. Bordua, "Juvenile Delinquency and 'Anomie': An Attempt at Replication," *Social Problems*, 6 (1958–1959), pp. 230–238; Roland J. Chilton, "Continuity in Delinquency Area Research: A Comparison of Studies for Baltimore, Detroit, and Indianapolis," *American Sociological Review*, 29 (1964), pp. 71–83. Somewhat related papers are those by Kenneth Polk, "Juvenile Delinquency and Social Areas," *Social Problems*, 5 (1957–1958), pp. 214–217; Bernard L. Bloom, "A Census Tract Analysis of Socially Deviant Behaviors," *Multivariate Behavioral Research*, 1 (1966), pp. 307–320; and Desmond S. Cartwright and Kenneth I. Howard, "Multivariate Analysis of Gang Delinquency: I. Ecologic Influences," *Multivariate Behavioral Research*, 1 (1966), pp. 321–371.

3 Donald T. Campbell and Donald W. Fiske, "Convergent and Discriminant Validation by the Multitrait-Multimethod Matrix," *Psychological Bulletin*, 56 (1959), pp. 81–105.

4 All three correlation matrices appear in Chilton, *op. cit.*, p. 73.

5 This trend is documented for Harlem in *Youth in the Ghetto, op. cit.*, pp. 168–195, and for the country at large in James S. Coleman *et al.*, *Equality of Educational Opportunity*, Washington: U.S. Government Printing Office, 1966, pp. 220–275.

6 Coleman *et al.*, *op. cit.*, pp. 219–220.

7 Bernard Levenson and Mary S. McDill, "Vocational Graduates in Auto Mechanics: A Follow-up Study of Negro and White Youth," *Phylon*, 27 (1966), pp. 347–357.

8 Otis Dudley Duncan and Beverly Duncan, *The Negro Population*

of Chicago: A Study of Residential Succession, Chicago: University of Chicago Press, 1957, pp. 81–84.

9 Eshref Shevky and Wendell Bell, Social Area Analysis, Stanford, Cal.: Stanford University Press, 1955, pp. 23–24.

SOCIAL DISORGANIZATION AND STAKE IN CONFORMITY: COMPLEMENTARY FACTORS IN THE PREDATORY BEHAVIOR OF HOODLUMS

Jackson Toby

1 It is of course possible to question these statements about the real incidence of stealing behavior. Data exist for arrested persons but not for offenders who eluded the police. Walter Reckless, for example, speaks only of "categoric risks in crime," and thereby avoids the danger of unwarranted inferences. See his text, The Crime Problem, 2nd ed., New York Appleton-Century-Crofts, 1955, pp. 26–42.

2 Even in the worst "delinquent areas," juvenile court cases never constitute more than one-fifth of the juvenile population in a given year. Clifford R. Shaw and Henry D. McKay, Juvenile Delinquency and Urban Areas, Chicago: University of Chicago Press, 1942, p. 154. And, of course, other activities besides authenticated stealing find their way into juvenile courts.

3 It is difficult to secure accurate data on the earnings of hoodlums. However, it is a fact that many indicted offenders languish in detention facilities prior to conviction because they are unable to raise the money for bail. This is one indication of low earnings. J. Edgar Hoover addressed himself to the question of the rewards of crime in a popular article published in Woman's Day in 1950. The title is a clear statement of his point of view: "The Poorest Paying Job in the World—the 'Wages of Crime.'"

THE FUNCTION OF SOCIAL DEFINITIONS IN THE DEVELOPMENT OF DELINQUENT CAREERS

Carl Werthman

1 The concept of a moral career has been defined by Erving Goffman as "the regular sequence of changes that career entails in the person's self and in his framework of imagery for judging himself and others." See Erving Goffman, "The Moral Career of the Mental Patient," in Asylums (New York: Doubleday & Company, Inc., 1961), p. 128.

2 The data on which this study is based consists of taped interviews with fifty-six "core" members of eleven "delinquent" gangs or "jacket clubs," plus observations and more informal conversations involving over one hundred members of these eleven gangs. The boys were drawn from the clientele of a delinquency-prevention

program in San Francisco called Youth for Service, and the research was conducted largely out of their offices for a two-year period. Of the fifty-six boys interviewed on tape, thirty-seven were Negro, eleven were Mexican, and eight were Caucasian. This report is thus based primarily on a sample of Negro gang boys.

3 I am indebted to a recent paper by Goffman for much of the analysis of gang activity that follows. See Erving Goffman, "Where the Action Is: or, Hemingway Revisited," Center for the Study of Law and Society, University of California, Berkeley, 1965.

4 According to Goffman, "action" is located "wherever the individual knowingly takes chances that are defined as voluntary, and whose conduct is perceived as a reflection on character," Goffman, *op. cit.,* p. 48.

5 It was largely on the basis of an argument such as this that Norman Mailer suggested "medieval jousting tournaments in Central Park" and "horse races through the streets of Little Italy" as delinquency prevention programs for the City of New York. See Norman Mailer, *The Presidential Papers* (New York: Bantam Books, 1964), p. 22.

6 See Edwin H. Sutherland, *The Professional Thief* (Chicago: The University of Chicago Press, 1937).

7 Goffman, *op. cit.,* p. 60.

8 *Ibid.,* p. 63.

9 James F. Short, Jr., and Fred L. Strodtbeck, *Group Process and Gang Delinquency* (Chicago: The University of Chicago Press, 1965), pp. 248–264; also J. Short and F. Strodtbeck, "Why Gangs Fight," *Trans-Action,* 1 (1964).

10 I encountered two boys who dropped out of gang activity for this reason. In one case, the boy decided it was time to leave after he was shot at twice in one week from passing automobiles driven by members of different rival gangs.

11 Claude Brown cites an incident such as this as his reason for leaving Harlem. See Claude Brown, *Manchild in the Promised Land* (New York: The Macmillan Co., 1965), p. 171.

12 W. B. Miller, H. Geertz, and S. G. Cutter, "Aggression in a Boy's Street-Corner Group," *Psychiatry* (November, 1961), pp. 283–298.

13 David Matza, *Delinquency and Drift* (New York: John Wiley & Sons, 1964), pp. 42–44.

14 Goffman, *op. cit.,* p. 68.

15 Walter B. Miller, "The Corner Gang Boys Get Married," *Trans-Action,* Vol. 1 (November, 1963), pp. 10–12.

16 Max Weber, *The Theory of Social and Economic Organization,* translated by A. M. Henderson and Talcott Parsons (New York: The Free Press of Glencoe, 1947).

17 It is largely for this reason that vehicles for public transportation such as buses become scenes of mass confusion when children ride them unsupervised to and from school. The bus drivers do not have access to parents and the children know it.

18 Gans notes the tendency among working-class Italians in Boston to treat their children as "little adults." It could well be that the posture of the boys described in this paper is simply an exaggerated version of lower-class socialization generally. See Herbert J. Gans, *The Urban Villagers* (New York: The Free Press of Glencoe, 1962), p. 59.

19 Richard A. Cloward and Lloyd E. Ohlin, *Delinquency and Opportunity* (New York: The Free Press of Glencoe, 1960), p. 102.

20 Albert K. Cohen, *Delinquent Boys* (New York: The Free Press of Glencoe, 1965), p. 116.

21 Walter B. Miller and William C. Kvaraceus, *Delinquent Behavior: Culture and the Individual*, National Education Association of the United States, 1959, p. 44. See also Walter Miller, "Lower Class Culture as a Generating Milieu of Gang Delinquency," *Journal of Social Issues*, Vol. XIV (1958).

22 For the general discussion of the problems created by contingent or purposive infraction of irrelevance rules, see Erving Goffman, *Encounters* (Indianapolis: The Bobbs-Merrill Co., 1961), pp. 17–85.

23 Bertrand de Juvenel, *Sovereignty: An Inquiry Into the Political Good*, translated by J. F. Huntington (Chicago: The University of Chicago Press, 1957), p. 29.

24 See Aaron V. Cicourel, *The Social Organization of Juvenile Justice* (New York: Wiley, 1968). See also John I. Kitsuse and Aaron V. Cicourel, "A Note on the Uses of Official Statistics," *Social Problems*, Vol. II (Fall, 1963), pp. 139–152.

25 Harvey Sacks, "Methods in Use for the Production of a Social Order: A Method for Warrantably Inferring Moral Character," MS., p. 4.

26 David Matza, "The Selection of Deviants," MS., p. 2.

27 These indicators are discussed at length in Carl Werthman and Irving Piliavin, "Gang Members and the Police," in David J. Bordua, ed., *The Police* (New York: John Wiley & Sons, Inc., 1966).

28 Cicourel, *The Social Organization of Juvenile Justice, op. cit.*

29 Irving Piliavin and Scott Briar, "Police Encounters with Juveniles," *American Journal of Sociology*, LXXX (1964).

30 Nathan Goldman, *The Differential Selection of Juvenile Offenders for Court Appearances*, National Council on Crime and Delinquency, 1963, p. 106.

31 Short and Strodtbeck, *Group Process, op. cit.*, pp. 25–46.

32 See James F. Short, Jr., Ramon Rivera, and Ray A. Tennyson, "Opportunities, Gang Membership, and Delinquency," *American Sociological Review* (February, 1965), p. 60; see also Delbert S. Elliott, "Delinquency and Perceived Opportunity," *Sociological Inquiry* (Spring, 1962), pp. 216–228.

33 This process has been described in somewhat different terms by Lemert as a transformation from "primary" to "secondary" deviance. See Edwin M. Lemert, *Social Pathology* (New York: McGraw-Hill Book Co., 1951), p. 75.

34 This view suggests that the various processes discussed by Cloward and Ohlin tend to effect outcomes of the transition between youth and adult status at the end of the delinquent career. See Cloward and Ohlin, *Delinquency and Opportunity, op. cit.*

35 Cohen, *Delinquent Boys, op. cit.*

36 Harold Finestone, "Cats, Kicks, and Colors," *Social Problems,* Vol. 5, (July, 1957), pp. 3–13; G. M. Sykes and David Matza, "Techniques of Neutralization: A Theory of Delinquency," *American Sociological Review,* Vol. 22 (December, 1957), pp. 664–670.

DEVIANT BEHAVIOR AS AN UNANTICIPATED CONSEQUENCE OF PUBLIC HOUSING

Gerald Suttles

1 Robert K. Merton, "Manifest and Latent Functions," *Social Theory and Social Structure,* Glencoe, Ill.: The Free Press, 1957, pp. 19–84.

2 Notice that this does not assume on the part of the poor any *systematic* tendency or interest in offending one another. All that is assumed is that they do occasionally offend one another and that by doing so they do not endanger the peaceful exchange of benefits. This problem has been examined at greater length in another paper, "Social Exchange and Social Control."

3 Incidentally, it is legally impossible for project dwellers to elect a local representative to most public offices. Usually the new found income would force the electee out of the project.

4 For example, see Richard A. Cloward and Lloyd E. Ohlin, *Delinquency and Opportunity,* Glencoe, Ill.: The Free Press, 1960 and R. K. Merton, *op. cit.,* pp. 131–160.

5 In practice this ideal must be balanced against the danger that the elimination of any member of a community will hazard the welfare of another. Thus, such a community must have a certain "redunding" of types so that the demise of one will not hazard the continuity of all the others.

6 The rules that affect project dwellers often strike one as an attempt to impose a certain ideal of asceticism. It is almost as if those governing the projects assumed that the residents would not voluntarily remain sober and frugal people. Also there tends to be an implicit belief that if only the residents would covetously save their funds and resources *rather than exchange them,* they would be less a liability to the wider community. This is a doubtful assumption.

7 Gustavus Myers, *The History of the Great American Fortunes,* New York: Modern Library, 1907.

8 The situation was quite different when an attempt was made to restrict the wine drinking practices of Southern European immigrants by passing the prohibition amendment. Once in effect, this amendment affected everyone as well as those against whom

it was directed. See Joseph R. Gusfield, *Symbolic Crusade*, Urbana, Ill.: University of Illinois Press, 1963.

9 In some instances, project dwellers have retreated to the roofs and "rocked" the police cars below while those on the ground have later overturned these vehicles. It is worth mentioning that one of the most noteworthy areas in Chicago for this sort of collusive reaction to policework is a near North Side project that has earned the name of "The Casbah."

10 Harold Finestone, "Cats, Kicks and Color," *Social Problems*, 5 (July, 1957), pp. 3–13.

11 For example, outsiders often take gang fights and gangland killings as a sign of utter disorder. As Zorbaugh shows, however, these are not indiscriminate acts; they occur almost wholly within a local group. Thus, they are social rituals which reassure an existing order within a local strata, rather than signs of disorder. Harvey Zorbaugh, *The Gold Coast and the Slum*, Chicago: University of Chicago Press, 1929.

STRUCTURAL DEVIANCE AND NORMATIVE CONFORMITY: THE "HUSTLE" AND THE GANG

Michael Lewis

1 Robert Merton, "Social Structure and Anomie," in *Social Theory and Social Structure*, rev. ed., (Glencoe, Ill.: The Free Press, 1957), pp. 131–160.

2 See, for example, the depiction of the "hustler" in *The Autobiography of Malcolm X* (New York: Grove Press, 1964).

3 Merton, *op. cit.*, p. 149.

4 Walter Miller, "Lower Class Culture as a Generating Milieu of Gang Delinquency," *The Journal of Social Issues*, Vol. XIV, No. 3 (1958), 5–19.

5 *Ibid.*, p. 19.

6 *Ibid.*, p. 17.

7 Albert Cohen, *Delinquent Boys: The Culture of the Gang* (Glencoe, Ill.: The Free Press, 1955), p. 122.

8 *Ibid.*, p. 124.

9 For the most cogent statement of this thesis see Cohen, *ibid.*, pp. 129–137.

10 In positing his sub-cultural thesis W. Miller makes esesntially the same criticism. See Miller, *op. cit.*, p. 19.

11 See Cohen, *op. cit.*, pp. 24–32.

12 Note: I am indebted to Mr. Howard Altstein for information on the formal structures of large scale gangs. As a social worker in New York City's Youth House for Boys, Mr. Altstein had the opportunity to collect information on gang organization in New York. He has kindly shared this information with me.

VIOLENCE IN THE CITY
Daniel Glaser

1 Phillip H. Ennis, "Crimes, Victims and The Police," *Trans-Action,* Vol. 4, No. 7 (June, 1967), 36–44; Phillip H. Ennis, *Criminal Victimization in the United States: A Report of a National Survey* (Field Surveys II of the President's Commission on Law Enforcement and the Administration of Justice), Washington, D.C.: U.S. Government Printing Office, 1967; Daniel Glaser, "National Goals and Indicators for the Reduction of Crime and Delinquency," *Annals of the American Academy of Political and Social Science,* 371 (May, 1967), pp. 104–126.

2 Glaser, *op. cit.*

3 Theodore N. Ferdinand, "The Criminal Patterns of Boston Since 1849," *American Journal of Sociology,* Vol. 73, No. 1 (July, 1967), 84–99; Elwin H. Powell, "Crime as a Function of Anomie," *Journal of Criminal Law, Criminology and Police Science,* Vol. 57, No. 2 (June, 1966), 161–171.

4 U.S. Department of Justice, *Uniform Crime Reports for the United States, 1967,* Washington, D.C.: U.S. Government Printing Office, 1968, p. 7.

5 Ennis, *Criminal Victimization in the United States, loc. cit.*

6 Thomas F. Pettigrew and Rosalind B. Spier, "The Ecological Structure of Negro Homicide," *American Journal of Sociology,* 67 (May, 1962), pp. 621–629.

7 Richard Quinney, "Structural Characteristics, Population Areas, and Crime Rates in the United States," *Journal of Criminal Law, Criminology and Police Science,* Vol. 57, No. 1 (March, 1966), 45–52.

8 Lewis Lipsitz, "Working-Class Authoritarianism: A Re-evaluation," *American Sociological Review,* Vol. 30, No. 1 (February, 1965), 103–109.

9 Arthur L. Stinchcombe, *Rebellion in a High School,* Chicago: Quadrangle Books, 1964.

10 *Uniform Crime Reports, 1967, loc. cit.*

11 Herman Goldstein, "Police Discretion: The Ideal Versus the Real," *Public Administration Review,* 23 (September, 1963), pp. 140–148; Wayne R. LaFave, *Arrest: The Decision to Take a Suspect into Custody,* Boston: Little Brown, 1965, chaps 5 and 6; Herman Goldstein, "Administrative Problems in Controling the Exercise of Police Authority," *Journal of Criminal Law, Criminology and Police Science,* Vol. 58, No. 2 (June, 1967), 160–172.

PART IV: URBAN SOCIAL CONTROL

1 See, for example: Elaine Cumming, Ian Cumming and Laura Edell, "Policeman as Philosopher, Guide and Friend," *Social Prob-*

lems, Vol. 12, No. 3 (Winter, 1965), 276–286; James Q. Wilson, *Varieties of Police Behavior,* Cambridge, Mass.: Harvard University Press, 1968.

THE SOCIAL CONTROL ROLE OF THE POLICE IN CHANGING URBAN COMMUNITIES
Robert L. Derbyshire

1 Marvin K. Opler, Ed., *Culture and Mental Health* (New York: Macmillan Co., 1959).
2 David Riesman, *The Lonely Crowd* (New Haven: Yale University Press, 1950), p. 22.

THE JUDGE AS BUREAUCRAT
Abraham Blumberg

1 U.S. Bureau of Census, *Statistical Abstract of the United States, 1963,* Washington, D.C., 1964, p. 158.
2 Some of the outstanding examples are: Albert J. Beveridge, *The Life of John Marshall,* Boston, 1916; Catherine D. Bowen, *Yankee from Olympus,* Boston, 1944; Samuel J. Konefsky, *Chief Justice Stone and the Supreme Court,* New York, 1945; Alpheus T. Mason, *A Free Man's Life,* New York, 1946, and *Harlan Fiske Stone: Pillar of the Law,* New York, 1956; Carl B. Swisher, *Roger B. Taney,* New York, 1935; Merlo J. Pusey, *Charles Evans Hughes,* New York, 1951; Joel F. Paschal, *Mr. Justice Sutherland: A Man Against the State,* Princeton, 1951; Henry F. Pringle, *The Life and Times of William Howard Taft,* New York, 1939; John P. Frank, *Mr. Justice Black: The Man and His Opinions,* New York, 1949. But see also, by way of contrast, Joseph Borkin, *The Corrupt Judge,* New York, 1962.
3 Wallace S. Sayre and Herbert Kaufman, *Governing New York City,* New York, 1960.
4 The law school that has no university affiliation is known as a proprietary law school. These were at one time private, profit-making institutions, although most are now chartered as non-profit educational institutions. Even some university affiliated law schools have a "factory"-like character in the number of students in attendance, the curriculum being geared solely to the state's bar examination. See Lowell S. Nicholson, *The Law Schools of the United States,* Baltimore, 1958.
5 Jerome Frank, *Courts on Trial,* Princeton, 1949, chaps. 11 and 12.
6 Glendon A. Schubert, *Quantitative Analysis of Judicial Behavior,* New York, 1959.
7 See the entire issue entitled "Jurimetrics," *Law and Contemporary Problems,* Vol. XXVIII, No. 1 (Winter 1963), especially Fred Kort,

"Simultaneous Equations and Boulean Algebra in the Analysis of Judicial Decisions," pp. 143–163.

8 Jerome Frank, *Law and the Modern Mind*, Garden City, 1963, p. 112. See also Joseph C. Hutcheson, "The Judgment Intuitive: The Function of the 'Hunch' in Judicial Decisions," *Cornell Law Quarterly*, XIV (1929), 274–278.

SOME NOTES ON THE URBAN JAIL

Daniel Glaser

1 The statistical statements in this paragraph and in that which precedes it are based on a survey of American corrections conducted in 1966 by the National Council on Crime and Delinquency for the President's Commission on Law Enforcement and the Administration of Justice. The survey report is published as Appendix A of the Commission's *Task Force Report: Corrections*, (Washington, D.C.: U.S. Government Printing Office, 1967) and as Volume 13, No. 1 (January 1967) of the Council's journal *Crime and Delinquency*.

2 *Ibid.*

3 See, for example, Alan J. Davis, "Sexual Assaults in the Philadephia Prison System and Sheriff's Vans," *Trans-action*, Vol. 6, No. 2 (December, 1968), 8–16.

4 See Daniel J. Freed and Patricia M. Wald, *Bail in the United States: 1964;* (Washington: U.S. Department of Justice and Vera Foundation, 30 E. 39th St., New York, 1965), reprinted in part in Walter C. Reckless, *The Crime Problem*, 4th ed. (New York: Appleton-Century-Crofts, 1967), pp. 660–663.

THE SHAPE OF THE FUTURE

John C. Bollens and Henry K. Schmandt

1 *The Polity* (Chicago: Rand McNally, 1962), p. 161.

2 *Megalopolis* (New York: Twentieth Century Fund, 1961), pp. 7, 15.

3 "Today's Urban Regions," *National Municipal Review*, XLV (June, 1956), 274–280.

4 Scott Greer, *The Emerging City* (New York: The Free Press, 1962), p. 162.

5 Quoted in Mitchell Gordon, *Sick Cities* (New York: Macmillan, 1963), p. 318.

6 *The Culture of Cities* (New York: Harcourt, Brace & World, 1938), p. 249.

7 "Suburbanization and Surburbia," *American Journal of Public Health*, 45 (January, 1955), 9.

8 *The Withering Away of the City* (University, Ala.: University of Alabama Press, 1963), p. 47.

Index

305

69 70 71 72 73   12 11 10 9 8 7 6 5 4 3 2 1